LOCATION
R Air
AUTHOR
EGLIN
DATE of CATALOGUING
5 JAN 82
HOUSE OF COMMONS LIBRARY

TO BE
DISPOSED
BY
AUTHORITY

Fly Me, I'm Freddie!

Fly Me, I'm Freddie!

Roger Eglin and Berry Ritchie

Weidenfeld and Nicolson
London

Copyright © Times Newspapers Limited 1980

First published in Great Britain by
George Weidenfeld & Nicolson Limited
91 Clapham High Street London SW4 7TA

All rights reserved. No part of this publication may be reproduced, stored in a retrieval system, or transmitted, in any form or by any means, electronic, mechanical, photocopying, recording or otherwise, without the prior permission of the copyright owner.

ISBN 0 297 77746 7

Printed and bound in Great Britain by
Morrison & Gibb Ltd, London and Edinburgh

HOUSE OF COMMONS
LIBRARY
CATALOGUED

To enterprise

Contents

Acknowledgements

Many people in government and the aviation industry have given us much time and help in preparing this book. For this we are very grateful but in particular we would like to thank Bob and Angela Beckman, Ray Colegate, John de la Haye, Sir William Hildred, Adam Thompson, Hugh Welburn and Douglas Whybrow for their help and encouragement. Barry Humphreys was kind enough to loan us his unpublished thesis on the development of British airlines which was most useful. We are particularly indebted to Mrs Patricia White for her efforts in transcribing our notes and typing out the manuscript under great pressure.

We would also like to thank the *Sunday Times* for providing us with the photographs used on the jacket, and the time to write this book.

Illustrations

The authors and publishers would like to thank the following for kind permission to reproduce the photographs: Flight International, 1, 4, 6, 8, 10, 11; Louis Meyer, 2; Camera Press, 3; K. Woolcott, 5; Sport and General, 7; B. Boyd, BUA, 9; *The Sunday Times*, 12, 13; The Press Association, 14; Topix, 15.

Prologue

Mid-morning, 6 June 1979, senior managers at Laker Airways learned that the British Civil Aviation Authority was issuing an order to ground the DC–10 jet.

Twelve days earlier, Flight 191, a DC–10 belonging to American Airlines, had crashed on takeoff at Chicago's O'Hare airport, killing 274 passengers and crew. The pylon holding the left engine to the wing had failed and despite all the pilot's efforts the aircraft had rolled into the ground. It was a horrific crash, the second major disaster involving the DC–10.

It was the sort of crash the airline industry had convinced itself could never happen. Either the pylon's failsafe design should have prevented the accident or the aircraft should have been capable of continuing its takeoff safely on two engines. Airlines operating the DC–10 were appalled and none more so than Laker Airways.

The aircraft that had crashed at O'Hare was identical to the DC–10–10 models that made up Laker's long-haul fleet and was about the same age. Already it was emerging that American Airline's practice of removing engine and pylon from the wing with a forklift truck could have caused the pylon's failure. Although it was still not publicly known, Laker's own DC–10s, his main financial asset, were overhauled in the US by American Airlines.

When the US authorities finally grounded the DC–10 by withdrawing its type certificate, the British Civil Aviation Authority [CAA] had no choice but to follow suit. Grounding Laker's six DC–10s, all his long-haul fleet, threatened to wipe out his airline. Even his fiercest competitors reckoned that after his six-year struggle to launch his revolutionary Skytrain, this would have been a bitterly unfair end to the Freddie Laker story.

But the most immediate problem facing Laker's managers that June morning was whether they should tell him. He had been under exceptional stress. In the first year of operation, Skytrain had made a profit of more than £2 million flying between London and New York. Emboldened by this early success, Laker had extended Skytrain to Los Angeles in September 1978 on the anniversary of the first New York service. In the ten months since then, the Los Angeles leg had come close to wiping out the profits Skytrain had earned across the Atlantic. At the same time, Laker was facing tough competition from major airlines like British Airways, Pan Am and TWA.

Two days before the Chicago crash, Freddie's mother had died at the age of eighty. 'Gran', as she was known to everyone at Laker Airways, was always very important to her son. She had brought him up alone from the age of five when his father had deserted them and more than anyone was the inspiration that had led him to success. They had always been very close.

Later that summer day, immediately after lunch, Laker was due to give evidence at a CAA hearing into his application to run a booking system on Skytrain. Laker's application to the CAA was for the right to match the major airlines' range of bookable and walk-on, cheap stand-by tickets as well as the right to carry cargoes. The hearing was bound to be a searching one. CAA officials, who had given Laker's early efforts to win approval for Skytrain so much support, wanted to know how Freddie proposed to care for his original market, the students, grannies, tourists and working men, all the 'forgotten people' for whom he had launched his cut-price, no-booking transatlantic Skytrain.

Laker's colleagues should have known better than to worry how their boss would withstand the pressure. The final confirmation of the DC–10 groundings came just as the CAA official chairing the hearing, Raymond Colegate, was in the middle of cross-examining Freddie. A CAA secretary slipped quietly in and gave Laker a plain brown envelope. He opened it and glanced swiftly at the contents.

Colegate spoke down the length of the table: 'That looks like a press notice. Do you want to read it out?'

Firmly, Laker read: 'The CAA has decided to suspend for the time being the UK certification of the McDonnell Douglas DC–10...'

He paused and added wryly, 'You have to do everything in these hearings.'

Even under this enormous pressure he could still try to raise a laugh.

In fact ever since he set up in business on his own in 1947 at the age of twenty-five he has shown an ability to pick up the pieces and build again. Sometimes literally. Anyone who has managed to prosper as Laker has done for so long in the harsh, uncertain world of independent aviation is a survivor. In the aftermath of the grounding there were times when even Laker looked unhappy. But within four months he was back on top. Business was picking up. Passenger loads to New York and Los Angeles were better than ever. Skytrain had carried over 600,000 people and was making money. And Freddie was already looking for someone to sue for the £13 million he estimated the DC–10 grounding had cost his airline.

Freddie Laker is an old-fashioned capitalist. His management style is direct, some would say rudimentary, even brutal. He operates from spartan concrete offices clinging to the side of Skytrain's hangar at London's Gatwick airport and the most effective means of communication for his staff is to catch him as he races up and down the stairs.

Freddie makes a point of enjoying his business. He is on first-name terms with his senior staff. But the relaxed appearance is deceptive. As he says, 'Once I have made up my mind I am very unswerving.'

He practises instant management on the working directors of Laker Airways who share the second floor with him and he demands dedicated and unquestioning service from his executives. Freddie Laker tells his men what to do and they go and do it.

He might not get away with it if he did not inspire loyalty. He does not buy it – if anything he has a reputation for paying badly. He earns it through a combination of personal charm and practical ability. He is one of the few airline bosses who can do any job in their business, from figuring the complexities of a multi-million dollar aircraft deal to repairing their own planes.

This depth of experience is the foundation of Freddie's success as an airline entrepreneur. He is not dependent on experts. He has a considerable technical background but his unique talent is to be able to visualize every aspect of aircraft and their operations in money terms.

Trade unions are a blind spot. They do not fit into the Laker scheme at all. Freddie claims he has nothing against trade unions as such and says that if there were none, people would still be working in bad conditions. Where there are bad employers, workers should band together to protect their rights. But Laker thinks he is a good employer. He reckons he knows how to run his business best and he is not prepared to let any outside organization interfere.

Not surprisingly he has earned the enmity of union leaders but they have so far failed to establish a power base in Laker Airways. As late as August 1979 the government-sponsored Arbitration, Conciliation and Advisory Service [ACAS] had to admit itself powerless to force Laker staff or Freddie himself to recognize the country's biggest union, the Transport and General Workers. Freddie would not distribute TGWU membership forms and few of his staff responded even when ACAS appealed to them in newspaper advertisements. However, as Laker Airways grows in size, Freddie's vulnerability to organized labour increases.

He gives the impression of putting customers much higher up his scale of values. When a press officer once referred to passenger handling, Laker told him, 'You don't bloody well handle passengers, you look after them.' But it is doubtful that this reflects more than enlightened self-interest. Enough complaints have been voiced about conditions in Skytrain to make it clear that Laker Airways is no kinder to passengers than most airlines. The cost-conscious simplicity of Skytrain ensures this.

One of Freddie Laker's outstanding talents is as a negotiator. His aeroplane deals are legendary, from his purchases of ex-wartime bombers at scrap prices to his recent acquisitions of American DC–10s and European Airbuses.

The advantage he carries into the negotiating room is his ability to make his own decisions. This is where his practical knowledge of aircraft is invaluable. When Airbus Industrie invited British and American journalists to its Toulouse factory in May 1979 to show off the Airbus, it was Freddie who took them round the production line, discoursing on the technical merits of the planes he was buying.

At the same time he gave an example of typical Laker bargaining cheek, in which he acquired a tiny extra advantage from Airbus Industrie. Asked when he was planning his first commercial passenger flight in his new Airbus, Freddie pondered the question for a moment.

'Let's see,' he said. 'I like to spend Christmas on my yacht in Majorca, so let's say we'll fly down the Saturday before Christmas

1980. We'll take off at half past ten in the morning if that suits my pilot and you're all invited.'

He turned to the senior Airbus management at the press conference which they had organized but he had virtually monopolized.

'Is that all right with you?'

They nodded numbly. To have complained would have seemed churlish. Freddie laughed. 'You may not realize it,' he told the assembled press, 'but they've just committed themselves to delivering my new plane three weeks early.'

Physically, Freddie Laker is big enough to be noticeable, six feet tall and solidly built. His face is pleasant but not handsome, round and slightly heavy, lightly tanned with a halo of receding curly hair. He smiles easily and often, the bright eyes screwing up. In repose Laker's face is unlined and composed, showing few signs of stress. He looks thoughtful and aware, responding alertly to events around him. When he scores a debating point, his lips twitch in a little grin.

It is when he talks that his dominant personality is revealed. He is a great talker, fluent and witty, cajoling, flattering, questioning, commanding. He gravitates automatically and irresistibly to the core of any group, moving confidently into the centre of any space he enters.

Freddie has been married three times. His first wife, Joan, is still the only other shareholder in Laker Airways, although they have been divorced since 1968. One of the most traumatic events in Freddie's life was the death of their son Kevin in 1965. Laker was planning a future which included his only son as his partner and heir in the still to be created Laker Airways. He had already made plans to leave his job as managing director of Britain's biggest independent airline when Kevin was killed in a crash driving the Aston Martin sports car his father had just given him for his seventeenth birthday.

Laker was deeply saddened and perhaps for the only time in his life emptied of purpose. He spent hours sitting in churches, looking for some sign that his son's death was not a pointless waste. Kevin's death adversely affected his relations with his colleagues and his family.

His son's death did not draw Freddie and his wife closer

together; friends saw it as a wedge driving them apart. Throughout his life Freddie, like many dedicated men, has put his business before his family. Although he loves his children, he sees very little of them for long periods of time. His absences also contributed to his estrangements from his first and second wives.

Joan Laker divorced Freddie in 1968. Almost immediately he married Rosemary, a South African he had met in Zambia in 1967. This marriage was short-lived. His third marriage is to a handsome American called Patricia, who has given him another son, Fred Junior, the image of his doting father down to the baby face and the curly hair.

In his late fifties, Freddie has acquired many of the conventional trappings of the rich. He owns a Bentley with a personalized registration – FAL 1 – and an eighty-five-ton motor yacht called *Tutinella*, moored in Palma harbour. He breeds racehorses on a seventy-five acre stud farm at Epsom, home of the English Derby, and owns a farm a few miles west of Gatwick on which he lives. Although he is enthusiastic about his racehorses and his farm, he runs them as businesses. Laker is a shrewd horse trader.

His real love is his yacht. There have been a number over the last twenty-five years, kept in the Mediterranean. Many Friday evenings will find Freddie hopping on to one of his charter flights to Majorca for a weekend aboard *Tutinella*. Once he is there, his cares appear to fall away, even when he is entertaining business acquaintances. It is where he shows himself at his most hospitable, his generosity even extending to providing guests with local currency. On the boat he is a diligent entertainer, indulging in knockabout comedy sketches with his crew. He is a well-known figure in Palma, where he spends freely.

Since Skytrain took off, Freddie has received worldwide public recognition for his achievements. He has become a widely sought-after public speaker and has been deluged with awards and acclaim. Two honours in particular have given him satisfaction. One was the decision by Lord Brabazon's family to present Laker with FLY 1, the car number-plate which belonged to the aviation pioneer, the first man to hold a British pilot's licence.

The other was his knighthood in the Queen's Birthday Honours in 1978. Freddie was overwhelmed by this. It reaffirmed, he said, his faith in Britain, bruised by his treatment at the hands of civil servants and his legal battles with Labour Party politicians.

'Isn't it marvellous?' he said to his friends. 'There is hope for this country yet.'

He has always flaunted his patriotism, occasionally for political or commercial advantage, but it is obviously real.

The impact of Laker Airways, a very small airline by world standards, has been dramatic. Skytrain has alerted the public – and politicians – all round the world to the fact that air fares have often been kept artificially high because there was no genuine competition. The effect is startling. You can now fly half-way round the world to Australia for little more than £300, half the fare five years ago, and not much more than a fortnight's package holiday in Majorca. In Europe, where air fares are twice as expensive as in the United States, the scheduled fare structure is about to crumble. In spite of high fuel prices, flying has become cheaper in real terms.

Until Skytrain took off in September 1977, the major airlines of the world operated a cartel under the rules of the International Air Transport Association [IATA]. Fares had to be agreed by every member of IATA. In practice, this meant they had to be high enough to suit the least efficient operator. The public was paying through the nose.

In its first year, when it carried 250,000 passengers between London and New York, Skytrain proved that cheap, readily available air tickets attracted a new market of travellers. More passengers meant fuller planes. Fuller planes lowered individual seat costs. Airlines made more money and consumers received better value.

Laker was opposed throughout by national airlines who feared the impact of low fares on their business, and by civil servants and politicians. He had to outlast two Presidents of the United States, Richard Nixon and Gerald Ford, and to win a court action against one British Labour Minister, Peter Shore.

Freddie Laker did not set out to be a crusader for the rights of the 'little man'. But the struggle for Skytrain revealed how little attention airlines paid to the interests of the consumer. It also uncovered the extent to which British and American politicians and officials were prepared to act as guardians of vested interests without regard to the consumer. It is hard to find a stronger case to illustrate the need for open government.

The Laker story is not over yet. His 1979 order for more DC-10s and Airbuses was so large it staggered his competitors. Far from content with his present role of gadfly to the airline establishment, Laker is planning to stretch Skytrain to Australia and the Far East as well as into Europe. To succeed, he will have to transform his personally managed airline, which he affectionately still calls Fredair, into a major international organization to rival Pan American and British Airways.

Luckily for the authors, this book is not about the future. It is about Freddie Laker's personal business history and his battle for Skytrain. We hope our account does him justice.

Chapter 1

'Pay me back when you can'

The big break came in 1948. Freddie Laker was sitting in the lounge bar of the Silver Cross public house in Whitehall, London. He had just been bought a drink by a friend called Bobby Sanderson. They were talking about what Laker was going to do next. At twenty-six, Freddie was a big, round-faced, smiling man with the overbearing charm of the ultra-confident young.

Sanderson, much older, Scottish and rich, was drawn to Laker. Shrewdly, he saw past the unsophisticated Kentish accent and the brash ebullience to the qualities that were already marking the young man down as someone who was going to make his way in the world.

They were discussing the sale of a dozen planes by British Overseas Airways Corporation. BOAC was offering twelve Haltons, civilian versions of the wartime Halifax bomber, for sale by tender, along with spares to keep the fleet flying. Sanderson asked Laker why he did not make an offer for the planes himself. Laker laughed enviously. He had only started up his own company a few months earlier to deal in aircraft spares and other surplus materials with a capital of £240. He could raise about £4,000, which was a long way from the £40 gratuity with which he had left the RAF's Air Transport Auxiliary at the end of the war, but nothing like enough. He reckoned he would need to bid £42,000 to buy the Haltons. Half seriously, he told Sanderson he could certainly use £38,000. Sanderson took out his cheque book and wrote Laker a cheque for the amount. 'Pay me back when you can,' he said.

Sanderson had already learned more than a little about Laker's eye for business. He enjoyed his gesture, indulging the rich businessman's liking for backing young talent but he also owed Freddie a debt. Two years earlier, Sanderson and his brother had set up an air charter company called Payloads in association with another company, London Aero Motor Services [LAMS]. Payloads operated out of London's Croydon and Hanworth aerodromes using three light aircraft to carry passengers. In April 1947, however, it had begun buying ex-RAF Halifax bombers with the idea of converting them into civilian freight aircraft. The completed conversions were to go to LAMS to be flown from Stansted airport, north-east of London. The plans did not really work out. The planes that Payloads converted were never flown by LAMS. Instead, two of LAMS's own Halifaxes were transferred to Payloads in the autumn of 1947. In September the company lost one of its light aircraft in an accident at Perpignan in France and at the same time one of the LAMS's Halifaxes was damaged beyond repair at Bovingdon aerodrome in Essex. To the Sandersons, Payloads began to look like a liability. They hired Freddie Laker with the impressive title of chief engineer to see what he could make of it.

Laker was precociously qualified for the job. He combined ten years of training and experience as a practical engineer with a barely tested raw talent as an entrepreneur.

Laker first made up his mind about what he wanted to do when he was fourteen years old and still a pupil at the local school in Canterbury. When he left two years later, he went to the nearest aircraft factory. This belonged to Short Brothers, which built flying boats at Rochester about twenty-five miles from Canterbury.

'My name's Fred,' he said, 'and I want to be in engines.'

At the age of nineteen, two years after the Second World War began, Laker joined the Air Transport Auxiliary as an engineer. The ATA, nicknamed the Ancient and Tattered Aviators, had as its first rule of service rejection by the RAF as unfit to fly. It boasted three one-armed pilots and a number of women, including the great pioneer Amy Johnson. The ATA's job was to ferry planes to the RAF and it rapidly became indispensible, expanding and recruiting engineers and ground staff as well as pilots. To begin with, however, the ATA lacked equipment of any kind and had to compete with the RAF for supplies. What could not be obtained had to be improvised.

An improviser and entrepreneur by nature, Laker fitted in naturally. He seized the opportunity to learn to fly, becoming a flight engineer or 'flying spanner' as the RAF called them. With his buoyant personality and boisterous sense of humour he gravitated naturally to the top of the ATA, ending up as flight engineer to the ATA's chief test pilot, Captain James 'Molotov' Watson.

The ATA's role became increasingly important, until towards the end of the war its members could say truthfully that every aircraft in the sky had been or would be flown by its pilots. It flew everything from Airacobras to Yorks. At its busiest in 1944 it had over 600 pilots operating out of twenty-two airfields, with a ground staff of 2,600, and flew nearly 80,000 planes. Gradually its role expanded to delivering Spitfires to the Free French in the Vosges mountains and warplanes of all kinds to Arnhem, Berlin and beyond. As the invasion of Europe advanced, ATA pilots were doing two round trips a day to Brussels, their aircraft so loaded with supplies they had to climb into the cockpit through the window.

In the closing months of 1944, the ATA imperceptibly began to accept 'charter' work for destinations all over central Europe. When his outbound load had been delivered and a ferry pilot had checked he was not wanted back at White Waltham immediately, he was given permission to take on other work in Europe. By August 1945 the ATA had extended its reach to the ultimate objective – Berlin.

Freddie Laker learned more than how to fly in the ATA. With no time to spare, crews were expected to take over strange aircraft at a moment's notice. Laker soon taught himself to maintain and fly a whole range of planes that after the war were to be converted to civil operations. From his own and other pilots' experiences, he also became familiar with the airfields of the UK and Europe. The ATA's *ad hoc* charters taught him the techniques of cargo carrying.

And he made friends. One was 'Molotov' Watson. Another was Christopher Treen, another ATA pilot. A third was Jim Mollison, Amy Johnson's husband, who was awarded an MBE in 1946 for his war work for the ATA. Mollison was a devil-may-care pilot with a string of record-breaking flights to his name and a determination not to be taken seriously. He often said that in an emergency he would rather jettison his navigational instruments than his bottle of brandy. Freddie Laker had to learn to handle a plane in any conditions as Mollison's flight engineer.

By the end of the war, Freddie was married. Joan was six years older than her new husband who had fibbed about his age when they met. When they married in 1942 he was still only nineteen. By the end of the war they had a newly born daughter called Elaine and their son Kevin was born in 1948. To begin with they lived in a flat in the south London suburb of Streatham and immediately after the war Freddie went to work.

He qualified for a civil flying licence and for three months worked for British European Airways. Then he joined London Aero Motor Services. When he wasn't working for them he worked for himself on the side. He bought government war surplus trucks, painted over the camouflage and sold them. He gambled on buying the crop of a cherry orchard when it was still in blossom. He and his wife picked the fruit when it ripened and sold it. He sold seedlings to housewives from the back of a van and because he knew next to nothing about plants he stuck a leaf from each variety on the inside of the back door with a label to identify it. He bought aircraft radio and electrical surplus at government sales and resold them to British South American Airways.

By the middle of 1947 he was ready to start up on his own. Ready is not the right word. He needed to. All his energies were pushing him into doing it for himself. His own business was modest. He sold spares out of the boot of a succession of second-hand cars he owned. The back seat was his office where he tapped out the rudimentary paperwork on a typewriter so old that it had an inkpad instead of a ribbon. But he had already developed a taste for running his own show.

Freddie left LAMS and set up his own company in October 1947. He called it Aviation Traders. He got off to a poor start. His capital went in three weeks and he had to borrow to keep going. Laker was disappointed but not too surprised. In any case, his new company was largely created to formalize his personal trading. He was used to having more than one iron in the fire and he was happy to take on an extra job as chief engineer for Payloads.

He was not the only employee of LAMS to be looking for work. A bricklayer turned aviation engineer called Bob Batt was also out of a job and he went to see Laker in the Payloads offices opposite the Whitehall Theatre. Laker had a board covered with details of Payloads' planes in various places and he was looking for qualified engineers to maintain them. Batt asked for £12 a week and Laker told him it was more than he was getting himself.

Laker looked more closely at the company he was working for

and realized that Payloads had little future. Its associate LAMS was teetering on the brink of bankruptcy. LAMS was actually wound up in July 1948, but five months earlier most of the planes were idle for lack of work and the staff was leaving. Freddie told his boss Sanderson that his best bet would be to get his money out as fast as he could. Laker found a buyer for Payloads' last Halifaxes and worked himself out of a job.

This was the favour that Sanderson wanted to repay. When they drank together in the Silver Cross, Freddie Laker was a young man with a long way to go. Although by then he had recovered from his false start with his infant company, his assets were only a little over £4,000 and his horizons were limited. The older man's act of confidence was to prove a vital piece of good fortune.

Among the engineers and pilots thrown out of work by the collapse of LAMS were a small group which had gone out to man its abortive Australian venture. Stranded in Sydney were three in particular, Ricky Brown, Dave Rosser and Jack Wiseman, who was there with his wife. Brown and Rosser hitch-hiked their way back to Britain on a Silver City twin-engined Bristol freighter. Wiseman and his wife came home by boat. When Jack arrived in England it was the beginning of August. He was contacted by Brown who told him that Freddie had given him and Rosser jobs and wanted to offer Wiseman one as well.

Wiseman had a good idea of his own value, as he was one of the few engineers with an unrestricted A and C licence, which meant he could certify any plane as fit to fly. When he went to see Laker at his office in Buckingham Gate, Wiseman knew he had the choice of going to work for Eagle Aviation, which had been founded by Harold Bamberg, another young entrepreneur.

Freddie told Wiseman that he wanted him to look after the engineering side of his company. 'I've got all these Haltons from BOAC,' he said. 'I'm having to send them out for maintenance and I want someone to make sure I'm not being taken to the cleaners.'

Wiseman was in his thirties, several years older than Laker and more experienced. But he came from the same kind of down-to-earth, unpretentious background and he responded to Freddie's openness. He was interested.

'I don't know what I can pay you,' said Freddie. 'Whatever we've got in the kitty we'll share among the four of us.'

Chapter 2

'Work for Fred and burn your bed!'

On 24 June 1948, the Russians imposed a total blockade on all traffic into Berlin. It was the culmination of months of increasingly bellicose behaviour by the Russians, who were determined to prevent the western Allies from rehabilitating post-war Germany. The Russians blamed 'technical difficulties' for their dramatic move. In reality, this final provocation was intended to undermine the Americans' insistence on including West Berlin in their plans for reconstructing West Germany's shattered currency.

The blockade was the beginning of a calculated attempt to force the Allies to withdraw from Berlin and surrender it to the eastern bloc. Its implications were only too clear. Either the Allies gave in, or Berlin would be starved into submission.

It was the first real confrontation between the erstwhile Allies. Along the borders of the two blocs, Soviet armies deployed threateningly. In America and Britain, the politicians shifted uncertainly, faced with the threat of a new war. In West Germany and Berlin, the commanders of the allied forces discovered with dismay that they had no bilateral agreements with the Russians on road or rail access to the beleaguered city.

On the evening of 24 June, General Lucius Clay, military governor and commander-in-chief of US forces in Europe, told newsmen at Tempelhof air base in Berlin that the Russians were putting on the final pressure but it would take a war to drive the Allies out. Clay planned to call the Russians' bluff. He was convinced that they were not prepared to go to war and he decided on an armed convoy of two hundred trucks, escorted by troops and an engineer battalion, to bulldoze its way along the *autobahn* between Helmsted and Berlin. It would carry bridging and repair equipment in case the Russians blew up the road.

Before he could put it into effect the commander of the British forces, General Sir Brian Robertson, hurried to Clay's headquarters. 'If you do that, it will be war – it is as simple as that,' he told him. He added, 'In such an event I'm afraid my government could offer you no support.'

Robertson, however, put up an alternative. Air Commodore Reginald Waite had suggested an all-out effort by British transport aircraft to supply Berlin with its basic needs. Robertson had already put the British side of Waite's plan into operation, eight planes from Cambridge were to fly over the next day, and the British general was sure his American opposite number would agree. Clay stalled, but the next day he was telling Ernst Reuter, the elected but Russian-opposed Mayor of Berlin, that he planned to try to feed Berlin by air.

To begin with very few people believed that the airlift would last more than a few days. Labour Government Minister Ernest Bevin in London, giving his backing to the decision to outface the Russians, insisted it would not work in the long term. 'You could never feed two and a half million people by air,' he said. Quick estimates showed Berlin needed 5,000 tons of food and fuel daily to survive. The RAF thought it could contribute perhaps 750 tons of this and throughout the airlift, the main burden fell on the American Air Force.

To Bevin, it was Dunkirk all over again. After a month he realized that the airlift was not a nine-days' wonder and he urged Arthur Henderson, Secretary of State for Air: 'Fill the sky with our planes.'

Henderson could do nothing to increase the RAF contribution, and he decided that the only solution was the sky tramps, Britain's motley collection of charter airlines. The British Government made an offer of £45 per flying hour, roughly £8 more than the current commercial freight rate, with a higher rate of £98 an hour for diesel fuel.

In Berlin, Edwin Whitfield, manager of British European Airways, was given the job of coordinating the civil lift and the planes began arriving. In just over a year from 4 August 1948, 104 planes from 25 companies flew nearly 60,000 hours and carried 146,000 tons of cargo into Berlin. Compared with the total of 2.3 million tons, the civil airlift's contribution was small. But it came in the early stages of the blockade, when Berlin was under its greatest threat.

One of the first private companies to fly into Berlin from Wunstorf aerodrome in West Germany was Bond Air Services. Bond had been taken over in October 1947 by Robert Treen, brother of Christopher Treen, Freddie's friend in the ATA, who became the company's chief pilot. In the first half of 1948 Bond had flown cheese and fruit in from the Continent, but when the Berlin airlift started it had just lost one of its two Halifaxes in a crash at Bovingdon in Essex.

Treen did a deal with Freddie Laker. Laker's company, Aviation Traders, provided Bond with six planes and contracted to service them from its vast stock of spares. In return, Freddie was to get half the freight fees as payment.

Suddenly Aviation Traders was no longer a four-man band sharing what was in the kitty. It was only for a couple of months that they operated on such a hand-to-mouth basis. After that there was a considerable cash flow and they were all drawing regular wages.

The planes were the ones that Freddie had bought from BOAC. They called them the Kennel Club, because the penultimate registration letter on all of them was D for dog. The BOAC Halifaxes had been modified, with the gun turrets removed and cargo panniers fitted underneath. By the standards of many of the planes that arrived in West Germany to take part in the civil airlift, Freddie's planes were in good condition.

The Berlin airlift was the making of British independent airlines. The roll call of the companies which took part included many of the names which were to become well known in the next twenty years and many more that died early deaths: Eagle Aviation, Silver City Airways, BOAC, BEA, British South American Airways, Lancashire Aircraft Corporation, Airwork, Air Flight, Aquila Airways, Flight Refuelling, Scottish Airlines, right down to Ciro's Aviation, which had been formed to provide luxury passenger transport for the members of Ciro's Club late in 1946 and put its two Dakotas on the airlift.

The generous charter rate and the huge number of hours flown produced enough cash flow for the independents to set up complete organizations, with flying crews, ground staff, UK bases, plant and equipment. And the unrelenting tempo of the airlift, with month after month of round-the-clock flights, taught the independents a lot about how to run a continuous air operation.

There has never been an air operation like the Berlin airlift. Modern jumbo jets could haul in the tonnage shifted by the 692 assorted aircraft that laboured for over a year supplying Berlin with ease. But to shift 2.3 million tons with planes like the Halifaxes, which only carry one twenty-fifth of a Boeing 747's cargo load, was a miracle of ruthless timing and unrelenting work.

Keeping the primitive post-war propeller-driven planes in the air was a never-ending battle. The US Army Air Force and the RAF had their own engineers, but the independents were expected to fend for themselves. All the RAF provided them in West Germany were hastily prepared airfields. The exhausted flying crews and mechanics made do as best they could labouring to keep their planes in the air.

Freddie Laker was in his element. One of his first moves was to find a proper base for major maintenance in the UK. The hangar at Bovingdon in Essex, full of Halifax spares, was off the aerodrome, so no maintenance work could be done from it, forcing Laker to contract the work out. He and Jack Wiseman toured round Essex and found a hangar available at Southend airport, half full of Ministry of Supply grain. With the airlift to give him priority, Freddie leaned on the Ministry to get the grain out quickly. Within a few days of extracting authority to use the hastily emptied hangar, Aviation Traders moved in and Wiseman began to build up an engineering operation. He found lodgings for his wife and himself in Southend but Ricky Brown and Dave Rosser slept in a disused corrugated-iron Nissen hut on the airfield.

As the airlift gathered momentum, Aviation Traders mushroomed. When it was at its busiest, Freddie was overhauling twelve planes for Bond Air Services and acting as spares supplier and servicer to many of the other ninety-odd planes on the civil airlift. He had nearly four hundred men working for him at Southend and more than thirty in Hamburg, where they carried out the day-to-day servicing and repair of the planes.

'Work for Fred and burn your bed' was one slogan scrawled on the operations notice board at Hamburg. Every four hours, night and day, the heavily loaded Halifaxes, stripped of every non-essential piece of equipment in order to increase their payloads, would lumber off in waves, one and a half minutes separating each aircraft. Hamburg had about forty minutes to get its wave off and if any pilots were not on time they did not go. If they did not go Freddie wanted to know how the lost revenue was going to be recouped.

Jack Wiseman travelled up and down the line to see how the operation was going. Like all the others involved, he was caught up in the irresistible momentum of the airlift. It generated a spirit of teamwork that welded the entrepreneurial, freebooting sky tramps into teams as closely knit as the RAF and USAAF regulars.

Freddie ran his company autocratically, making instant decisions and backing them up unfailingly. He won a reputation for being as good as his word. He expected anyone he dealt with to be the same.

Under the pressure of continuous flying, the old planes gradually fell to pieces. One of Eagle's captains felt his plane shaking as though alive. When he landed in Berlin, the entire skin had to be rerivetted.

In March 1949, Bond pilot Joseph Viatkin was taking off from Berlin's Gatow airport after delivering a load of dehydrated potatoes. When an engine failed at 1,000 feet, he shrugged, flew on on three and the engineers promptly slotted in another engine. Six weeks later the same plane ran into a construction trench while taxiing at Tegel airport in the French sector and was promptly bulldozed out of the way to make room for the never-ending flow of planes taking off. Laker's men cut the Halifax up for scrap at the side of the runway.

The money was good. Freddie Laker's planes, under the operation of Bond, flew 2,577 round trips into Berlin and carried 17,131 tons of supplies. That was 11.6 per cent of the total tonnage shifted by the civil airlines and made Laker one of the biggest operators on the civil lift. His company was one of the few that worked throughout the airlift. The Russians had admitted defeat, lifting their blockade in May 1949, but the Allies were taking no chances and went on supplying Berlin by air until in August they had created a stockpile that made a repeat impossible. If the Russians were to try again it would have to be with different tactics.

It was a very profitable airlift for Laker. Bond itself was paid about £300,000 in charter rates, of which half went to Freddie, but this was bread and butter money. Most of that went in paying the pilots, who earned £65 a month plus 30 shillings for every round trip, which meant many of them were earning over £200 a month, and the maintenance staff, who were also being paid overtime and bonuses. What was left over was used by Freddie to pay off the planes themselves.

Freddie even then was working on the basis that he has always used since. He covered his overheads with his contract work which meant that any other income was almost all profit. The jam on the Berlin airlift was the servicing and spares he supplied to other companies. His hangar, full of ex-BOAC spares, was worth its weight in gold. To operators on the Berlin airlift, the value of any spares that kept their battered and overstressed planes flying was measured in terms of flying hours lost. A carburettor was worth as much as an engine.

Laker bought more Halifaxes for the lift, including a couple used by the RAF for target towing which he converted. In March 1949 he came into possession of a Halifax he had chartered nearly a year earlier to Alpha Airways. Within a fortnight he had that one on the airlift. It was the one that Joe Viatkin had to nurse home and was written off three months later.

That particular aircraft had a history as colourful as any. At Alpha Airways it had been used for a wide range of charter work between the Mediterranean and South Africa before Alpha ran into trouble early in 1949. One of the crew of this Laker plane was Bob Batt, who had gone to work for Alpha as a flight engineer after turning down Freddie's job offer at Payloads.

Batt and his crew arrived in Johannesburg in January 1949 and found themselves still there with no work to do a month later. One morning a man from Alpha's Johannesburg office called round to Batt's hotel and asked for the plane's log book and registration papers. Batt advised his captain not to hand them over. They cabled Freddie: 'Might be in danger of losing aeroplane. Send carnet for fuel and will deliver Halifax Southend.'

Laker sent the carnet without comment. The Halifax picked up nine British coloured merchant seamen who had been wowing the locals with their London-made zoot suits. They had been stuck there, unable to get a flight back to the UK on South Africa's white airline. They took off on 4 March and arrived at Bovingdon three days later. The crew called *en masse* on the UK director of Alpha, put the revenue they had collected from their various charters on his table, took out their wages and expenses and left him with a profit of £100. The next day they flew the plane to Southend and handed it over to Freddie.

Once again Laker offered a job to Batt, with his precious licence to approve complete overhauls on Halifaxes as distinct from normal servicing. Batt accepted £8 a week as chief inspector, moved into the Nissen hut at Southend along with the other men and went to work.

Chapter 3

'Take your bloody elbow out of your managing director's face'

At the end of the Berlin airlift, Laker looked a made man. The Halifaxes from BOAC were paid for and written out of his books. He drove a large Austin Princess. His growing family had moved from the Streatham flat into a spacious detached house in genteel Carshalton on the southern outskirts of London. The new house had five bedrooms, a built-in garage and a double driveway filling the whole of the front garden behind a wall topped with scalloped brickwork. Laker had arrived.

Aviation Traders had a workforce of nearly four hundred and was the biggest operator at Southend airport. Thanks to his instinctive care with money, Freddie had a very handsome bank balance and no liabilities. At least, that is what it looked like. The trouble was that when the airlift ended, all the embryonic airlines which had sprung up found themselves unemployed. Many of them collapsed almost overnight. Bond Air Services was one of the first to go.

Freddie took a calculated decision to get out of flying, realizing that the market would be awash with too many planes chasing hardly any business. But although he was not an airline operator, he still had a big workforce which the slump in the air left desperately short of work. He did not want to let it disintegrate. It was a concentration of skilled workers which he would find it hard to replace and he had a strong sense of responsibility to his employees. He let the dross slip away, the men he did not like or felt were not worth their keep, but he refused to sack most of them.

Instead he went out and found work for them – any work. The only work for a company called Aviation Traders was scrapping planes. Laker went to government surplus sales and bought everything and anything. He bought aircraft in batches of fifty and sixty and engines by the hundreds. At one sale he bought ninety-nine Halifaxes and six thousand engines. He paid prices of as low as £50 per plane. He bought armoured trucks, radios, US war surplus planes, weapons, ammunition, crates of equipment that had never been opened, job lots that could contain anything. The government departments hardly knew and cared less what they were getting rid of as long as they could sweep their vast stockpiles clean. Freddie was prepared to buy anything provided it was cheap enough.

Cheap enough meant that he could guarantee to make a profit just from melting down the metal of which the planes were made, mostly aluminium.

Laker organized his men into teams. After he had bought a job lot of war surplus planes they flew up to the aerodromes where the auctions had been held and cut the planes to pieces on the spot with hacksaws and oxyacetylene cutters. The teams built brick melting pots, big tanks with oil-injected heating like glorified blowlamps. Then they threw the bits of fuselage and wings into the pot and tapped off the molten metal into aluminium bricks. They took samples to check on the specifications and adjusted the quality by adding pieces of other metals.

Freddie copied the idea from a company called John Dale, which was supplying aluminium ingots to saucepan manufacturers desperate for raw materials to enable them to start production again. Dale's gangs were mainly Irishmen. Laker was buying planes to fly back to Southend to recondition and resell. The airfields at the War Office auctions were covered with rows of Halifaxes and when Laker looked at them he found that some of the planes John Dale's Irishmen were about to cut up were in better condition than those he had bought to fly. They were quite happy to swap parts or even whole planes. It was not long before Freddie had a deal with John Dale to supply aluminium. Apart from the temporary furnaces, Aviation Traders had its own permanent melting pot on Southend airport.

Not all the planes and war surplus materials were scrapped. One of Freddie's first deals after the airlift had ended was a contract to supply the Egyptian Air Force with a dozen Mark 9 Halifaxes, converted by Aviation Traders to carry paratroops. Bob Batt was in charge of this operation and equipped the planes with .5 calibre machine guns. At various times Laker had fairly large supplies of weapons and ammunition, which he treated with a casual disregard for red tape. In the case of the Halifax machine guns and ammunition, they were stacked in an old air-raid shelter on the edge of Southend airport.

One evening Bob Batt was sitting on the other side of the airport in the little wooden hut Aviation Traders used as an office when a policeman knocked on the door and asked him if he had any firearms. He explained he was just checking on the company's firearm licence to see if they were being held correctly.

'Oh, sure,' said Batt, and led him over to the shelter. He opened the door on the stacks of .5 and .303 machine guns and the cases of bullets. The policeman was aghast.

'I was talking about two Very pistols,' he said.

Laker also sold the Egyptians some Staghound armoured cars, which Aviation Traders overhauled first. When the Korean war started, Freddie suddenly had a market for a vast stockpile of Mustang fighter spares which he had bought on spec. Another purchase turned out to be hundreds of tons of snow chains, which he was able to sell at a handsome profit to the Canadian army, which also wanted them for Korea.

When they had nothing else to do Laker's men broke up aero engines, salvaging the brass and copper scrap. Freddie paid them five shillings an hour.

All this time, however, he was aware that he was only making ends meet and he was searching for a new outlet for his company.

In September 1949 he started a new venture with Robert Treen of Bond Air Services which briefly looked as though it might lead to bigger things. Billy Butlin was another of Britain's post-war entrepreneurs with his new holiday camps and he was finding himself unpopular with local traders because they were not sharing in the cash that Butlins holidaymakers were spending. Butlin disarmed these criticisms by offering franchises for restaurants, shops and entertainments at his camps. Where there was a local airfield, he advertised for people to run joy flights.

Freddie and Treen took up a Butlin concession at Skegness on Britain's east coast. They formed a company called Skegness (Airport) Ltd and began operating charter and pleasure flights from Ingoldmells aerodrome. The company bought four light aircraft, still in their Butlins colours of blue and primrose, one of which

Freddie flew down to Southend and treated as a private plane. He and Bob Batt used it to collect Halifaxes, although it sometimes went back to Skegness when trade was brisk, which was not all that often. After a time the Skegness operation became Batt's responsibility as Freddie decided the franchise was not sufficiently promising to occupy his time. After two seasons Freddie and Robert Treen folded the company and sold the planes.

Aviation Traders was also making a name for itself as an engineering organization under the control of Jack Wiseman. In 1949 Freddie bought three Vikings which had previously belonged to British European Airways. Wiseman renovated them so well that Laker sold all three to British Overseas Airways Corporation at a profit. Early the next year he bought a selection of Yorks and Lancasters damaged in accidents and cannibalized them to make three airworthy Yorks. One of the planes butchered to make these three good was Churchill's personal Skymaster, which brought back a wartime memory. Late in 1945 Freddie had been flight engineer to Captain Watson when the ATA sent them to collect Churchill's plane. The ATA had a Hudson specially equipped for aerial photography, and Watson and Laker flew Churchill's plane for the Ministry of Supply, which wanted propaganda pictures.

Freddie did not sell two of these rebuilt Yorks. He was ready to branch out on a far more ambitious scale on his own. The days of keeping the pot boiling on hand-to-mouth scrap dealing were coming to an end.

At the beginning of 1951 Freddie Laker was only twenty-eight and still looking it, in spite of the moustache he had grown to make himself look as old as the small group of business intimates who had become his lieutenants, chief among them Wiseman, Batt and Norman Jennings, Laker's chief pilot. But the big man with the neat hands and feet had already established himself as one of the leading figures in the thrusting independent aviation industry. Now he was poised to soar into an extraordinary period of expansion, in which he was to exhibit a remarkable range of abilities and ambitions.

For someone who had shown so little promise at school, Laker's achievements in the next seven years were phenomenal. Not all of them were successful, but all were innovative. They were based on an intensely personal management style. Freddie had no organization as such. He operated through a few people he trusted. They were all similar to him in being practical engineers or aviators, their qualifications gained through apprenticeships and experience rather than university degrees and their social backgrounds unpretentious. They tended to be quiet, unflappable men, foils to Freddie's own ebullience. He inspired them with his enthusiasm and convinced them with his own practical ability, so that they undertook projects with breathtaking implications.

Big as Aviation Traders had grown to be, it was still directly under Freddie's supervision. He spent a great deal of time at Southend, commuting between his London office down the arterial road link to the Thames estuary town, arriving and departing at all hours of the day or night as part of his hyperactive business life. Some mornings he arrived very early and would sit in the cockpit of a plane parked in the hangar watching his employees clocking in. If he saw one try to cover up for a late companion Freddie leaped out.

'Have you got two clock cards, then?'

'No, Mr Laker.'

'You're wasting your time. I know all the fiddles there are.'

He had charm and he gave the impression of knowing every detail that happened. He was in fact a very good engineer with an exceptional memory and he could do just about everybody's job as well as they could themselves.

When his business began to expand he was forced to delegate, although he found it difficult. When he had a new idea, he discussed it with three or four of the people he wanted to involve and then he said, 'Okay, this is what we'll have a go at.' In theory he then left it entirely to them to get on with the job, taking decisions on their own. In practice, though, he was always at their shoulder, advising, criticizing, encouraging and interfering. He was the boss and no one else. What enabled him to get away with his behaviour was that when they succeeded, Freddie patted them on the back.

The first of Freddie's new ventures was started early in 1951. One day he called his lieutenants into his office and told them he was going to become an airline operator. They were stunned. Laker had always insisted he was never going to fly planes, just service them and sell them. Their protestations were swept aside. As usual, Freddie had already made up his mind.

He had been planning his new operation ever since he had turned the motley collection of damaged aircraft into three serviceable Yorks and kept two. Laker had been watching the few companies, like Silver City and in particular Harold Bamberg's Eagle Aviation, which had succeeded in continuing flying after the airlift. He had seen them pick up charter work, especially for the Government, flying supplies and troops to and from the Continent and the outposts of Empire. He decided that there was going to be a growing market for air traffic and that there was room for him.

In February 1951 Laker bought up a bankrupt company called Surrey Flying Services. In May it was back in business with a single plane. Later in the same year he bought Air Charter, another nearly moribund company with a single plane and some useful tax losses. One of the constant problems of the aviation entrepreneurs was dealing with the Inland Revenue. Bankrupt companies with losses were a convenient way of writing off earnings from scrap and other dealings that would otherwise have suffered penal tax. Finally, in November Freddie took over a company called Fairflight, which had two assets, a plane called a Tudor and a contract to carry freight between Berlin and Hamburg.

When he bought Fairflight late in November 1951 it was primarily for the contract to and from Berlin. It is almost unbelievable now, so quickly does today's crisis become yesterday's history, but in 1951 Stalin was still alive and the Iron Curtain countries were going through a series of vicious internal purges while the West was on the verge of its economic miracle. It did not yet show in Britain, where the meat ration was reduced to eightpence a week, but this country was within a year of exploding its first atomic bomb and the US had already perfected the far more powerful hydrogen bomb, although it was still secret. Stalin reacted savagely to Tito's independent attitude – which by 1951 had led to Yugoslavia winning assurances of support from the western powers and actual shipments of arms from the US – by ruthlessly suppressing Communist heresy internally and intensifying confrontation with the West. In the case of Berlin, Communist anger was roused by the admission of West Germany to the Council of Europe and the official ending of the state of war between that country and the US, France and the UK.

The little Berlin airlift began early in 1951. This time the Russians tried a more subtle approach. They attempted to throttle

West Berlin's emerging industry, mostly electrical components and other products of skilled labour which gave vital work to Berliners and even more vital revenue to the city. The Russians began impounding manufactured goods moving out of Berlin along the road and rail links, as well as blocking supplies of raw materials, such as copper, coming in from the West.

Another Berlin problem was creating work for charter planes under the control of BEA. This was the growing flood of refugees, who were still able to cross into the western zones of the city. The infamous wall was ten years away. The Russians then saw these dissidents as an extra burden to the Berlin authorities, whose only solution was to ship them on to the West.

The economic blockade merely added another dimension to the problem of Berlin, but it was naturally attractive to Freddie and the other independents who had taken part in the first major airlift. Like the first, the little airlift was very lucrative. Within a year of taking over Fairflight's contract, Freddie was running seventy flights a week between Berlin and Hamburg or Hannover. He put all his flying operations together under the name of Air Charter in July 1952 and Bob Batt designed a neat logo, with the A and the C curving together rather like the AC car logo, but with a wing flaring out behind.

Gradually Air Charter became the dominant independent airline on the Berlin run. Soon it expanded to service and organize the operations of other companies involved in the carriage of materials like metal ingots and graphite to Berlin and the subsequent freighting of finished products or refugees out of the city.

Before this happened, however, Freddie came within an inch of his life. Soon after lunch on 11 March 1952 he boarded one of his Yorks which was flying back to Hamburg after servicing at Southend. The plane was being piloted by Norman Jennings, with Joe Viatkin as his co-pilot and Jack Wiseman as the other passenger. Viatkin had been hired by Laker soon after he bought Fairflight specially to work on the Berlin run, which the pilot knew like the back of his hand from the first airlift.

As they came in to Hamburg shortly before 5pm, both Wiseman and Laker had come forward into the cockpit to watch the landing, with Jack sitting behind Viatkin and Freddie standing between the two pilots, performing his old job of flight engineer. Suddenly, at

600 feet, with the flaps and landing gear down, both port engines stopped and the plane shot seventy degrees off course to the left. As Norman Jennings tried to correct the wild swerve, both the starboard engines also cut out, leaving the powerless plane heading at right angles for a large cemetery. A major fuel leak was the only cause a startled crew could imagine.

Freddie reached up and retracted the undercarriage, to reduce drag and give the York more flying time. He also raised the wing flaps, in a last-ditch effort to reduce the angle of descent and get the plane over the cemetery's big crematorium directly in front. This slowed the plane and the pilots both kicked hard on the rudder to prevent it rolling over.

As the two pilots struggled with the controls, Freddie ran a lightning mental check of the fuel system. He remembered that there was an accelerator pump between the throttles and the carburettors which might have a little petrol left in it. He started to push the throttle levers to and fro and pumped a tiny spurt of fuel through into the engines which burst into a few seconds of life. Freddie pumped again and there was another brief burst of power. The York skimmed over the crematorium, tore through some power lines, glided over terrified children in a school playground, ripped the roof off a small house with its tail and buried its nose five feet into the soft earth of an allotment. Jack Wiseman had broken his nose, Norman Jennings had badly bruised his face and they were all shaken, but that was all.

Freddie was the first to speak. 'Will you take your bloody elbow out of your managing director's face?' he said to Viatkin.

Chapter 4

'A mind like a cash register'

By the end of 1952 Freddie Laker's various enterprises were flourishing. Aviation Traders had grown under Jack Wiseman's management into a large organization and had developed a manufacturing side. The previous year it had won a contract to make wing centre sections for Bristol freighters and between the beginning of 1952 and the end of 1955 Aviation Traders Engineering built fifty wing sections for Bristol Siddeley. Apart from the Berlin contract, Freddie had landed some trooping contracts from the Government to the Middle East. This was partly due to Harold Bamberg, who had sold all his ten Yorks as a protest against the BEA and BOAC monopoly of scheduled flights. Freddie had snapped up four of Bamberg's Yorks and promptly put them to work trooping to the Suez Canal Zone, flying from Lyneham, Abingdon and other RAF Transport Command bases.

This was *ad hoc* flying for the War Office and Freddie was very keen to win some long-term trooping contracts. He was a relative latecomer to a business which had grown since 1950 into one of the most important markets for the independents but was largely in the hands of Skyways, Airwork, Hunting and Eagle.

The idea of flying troops instead of shipping them had first been proposed by Airwork, through the medium of Colonel 'Boy' Wilson, whose adventurous war record meant he was well known at the War Office. Airwork was virtually the 'chosen instrument' for the first trooping by air, but unfortunately its Hermes aircraft suffered from engine faults and often crash landed. While Airwork grappled with this problem, others moved in to fill the breach and its monopoly was lost. But the War Office had become convinced that air transport was cheaper as well as much quicker. In 1952 it calculated it was saving £4 a head on transport to the Middle East.

The Government also promoted the idea that using independent airlines helped maintain a flying potential which at any time could be called on to augment the RAF's resources. This concept conveniently married with the less palatable truth that Transport Command had lost out to Bomber and Fighter Commands in the battle for defence budgets.

Trooping business for the independents exploded. All the independents in the business had their political lobbyists like Wilson, but their flying operations were not impressive. Their flights suffered from chronic unreliability. Three- or four-day delays were quite common. Almost all the flying was in ex-wartime bombers, mostly Yorks, which were uncomfortable as well as unreliable. For the troops the only advantage was that days of uncomfortable flying were better than weeks in austere trooping ships. The comments that officers in charge of flights made in their voyage reports, on the seating, the food and the journey, were frequently scathing. One said pungently, 'The flight was quite comfortable until we crashed at Malta.'

Freddie's opportunity came when Skyways lost a York carrying women and children over the Caribbean. Up till then, although the army had inspected the independents' planes before awarding them contracts, it had always favoured the company quoting the lowest price. However, the Skyways crash, apart from losing the firm its contract, changed the Government's attitudes towards standards.

Laker was fighting to win a share of the market. Unlike the other companies, he had no political lobbyist and had made his own approach to the War Office, where he met Major Douglas Whybrow.

Whybrow went down to Southend and inspected the planes that Air Charter proposed to use for trooping. He met Jack Wiseman, who showed him over one of their Yorks. It was the best trooping aircraft that Whybrow had ever seen. It offered a measure of comfort that soldiers had never had before. The seats faced backwards for safety and had headrests. Until Laker installed headrests, troops had always flown long distances in uncomfortable seats that only came up to the middle of their backs. Apart from the obvious quality of the plane, Laker also proposed placing spare parts along the routes. This was something the other companies had not done, although it rapidly became standard practice.

Putting spares down the line was not expensive, but Laker shone against a dull background. The other independents were, however, lobbying hard for the next contract which was a series of flights to Singapore and then on to Fiji. Whybrow was summoned to the Under-Secretary of State at the War Office, Sir James Hutchison, to brief him on which tender to accept. Whybrow, slightly overawed, told him he felt the new contract should be given on merit and made no secret of his partiality for Air Charter. Laker was awarded the contract.

He had won it on price as well as standards. The rate was about £90 per flying hour, which made trooping in the cheap planes that were being used very profitable. Amortizing the cost of a York bought for something like £5,000 was relatively easy, especially when, like Aviation Traders, the company already had its own massive stockpile of spare engines and parts bought at rock-bottom prices in government surplus sales.

Part of the credit for the contract went to Laker's new commercial manager, George Forster, another ex-ATA pilot who had joined him in August 1952. Forster had been Freddie's captain late in 1945 flying to Brussels and they had delivered a Stirling aeroplane to Northern Ireland together as late as January 1946. They had met again when the company Forster joined after the war, Lep Air Services, had chartered a Halifax from LAMS to fly textiles to Milan for Dormeuil Frères. Five years later Freddie rang Forster and offered him the job of commercial manager of Air Charter. Laker also hired Forster's wife as the office factotum but within three days of starting work she was acting as hostess on the Fairflight Tudor to a passenger load of workers and immigrants being flown to South Africa by Norman Jennings.

Forster's first fortnight was spent tying up the trooping contract which was twenty-five round trips to Singapore and on to Fiji. Laker and Forster went to a conference with Whybrow to discover details of the service Air Charter was going to provide. Laker wanted to know what the load would be to Singapore and then back from Fiji to Singapore. Out to Singapore the load was light because there were a number of women and children. Passengers on the flight from Fiji, however, were all Fijian soldiers who were being used to garrison Singapore. One of the army contingent at the conference was a Guards colonel. When Freddie asked about the payload from Fiji, the colonel, who had a reputation as a bit of a know-all, said: 'They're all little fellows, just dwarfs, y'know.'

Freddie told Forster to organize the flight planning. Methods were primitive. Forster went out and bought an edition of the six-volume *Times World Atlas* and worked out a route to Singapore and Fiji with Norman Jennings. They measured the distance with a ruler and calculated the flight times by rule of thumb. On the long leg from Fiji, the weight of the passenger load was crucial. When they arrived at the end of their first proving flight they found that far from being dwarfs, the Fijians were enormous, throwing out all the careful calculations.

Forster also brought Freddie a line in charter work from Lep Air Services. There was a demand for transport of all kinds of livestock to the Continent: racehorses, sheep, pigs and cattle. Air Charter installed horseboxes and cattle stalls in its Bristol freighters and began doing a considerable amount of work. It carried showjumping teams to Copenhagen and Hamburg and racehorses to Paris and the Curragh in Ireland.

When the Mau Mau troubles were flaring in Kenya, Air Charter flew pedigree cattle to replace livestock that had been hamstrung and killed. One of the flights to Kenya on which Forster went was with a cargo of calves in a converted Dakota. The animals were between four and ten weeks old and Forster had to find water tanks for the journey, which took three days, with stops at Malta and Wadi Halfa. With classic sky-tramping ingenuity he got in touch with the Express Dairy Company and bought some of its old-style milk churns, which were being replaced by modern equipment.

On a stopover in Lagos, Freddie found he could not buy any ice cream or fresh meat. When he came back to England he bought some pre-war bicycles with Wall's ice-cream boxes on the front, shipped them out to Nigeria and recruited local boys to sell ice cream from a cold store he financed which also supplied meat and other perishable goods. For a brief time he saw himself as the Wall's of West Africa.

Until Air Charter began to be really profitable, Laker was often under financial pressure, especially when he was buying Yorks and other planes to build up his fleet. His senior employees knew, but although they offered to help he always refused. Tight though the money situation was, Freddie always managed to produce what was needed for wages and the expansion he wanted.

Jack Wiseman said that Freddie had a mind like a cash register. He would do sums on the back of envelopes, but he got the answers right. He saw planes in money terms. Pounds of pressure, revolutions per minute, all the details that other engineers saw as technicalities, Freddie appreciated but also looked at as pounds, shillings and pence.

His rival was Harold Bamberg. Bamberg had the grandest vision of any of the independent operators in the early fifties. No sooner had he sold out his fleet of Yorks for £160,000 than he began to buy Vikings to replace them, some of them from BEA, as well as operating Dakotas. Eagle began to take on a growing amount of passenger work, including aerial cruises around the Mediterranean in the summer of 1953 and in June started a scheduled weekly service between Blackbushe and Belgrade.

Freddie was very conscious of Bamberg. When Bamberg appeared in a new Bentley with a stainless-steel body Laker looked it over thoughtfully and then gazed disparagingly at his own Austin Princess. Shortly after Laker bought his first Rolls-Royce. It was not so much that he was jealous of Bamberg, but the Bentley was a bit too much to swallow.

In February 1953 Air Charter's fleet was seven Yorks, one certificated Tudor, a Dakota and a new forty-eight-seat Mk 31E Bristol 170 freighter. Freddie also owned three more Tudors, two unregistered and one in Canada leased to Lome Airways, which it had planned using to carry passengers to the mining provinces.

It was a very good year for Air Charter. During 1953, the new airline carried nearly 28 million pounds of cargo, which put it second in the freight league to Silver City, and nearly 10,000 passengers. Freddie's planes flew 750,000 paying miles. Once again he had plenty of cash.

He spent some of it buying more Tudors.

Chapter 5

'Keep her going Mac!'

Freddie's fertile brain had been putting together a complex jigsaw puzzle. He knew that when he started up as an operator, he would need work and he would need planes. The work was mainly trooping contracts for the War Office and these were won by competitive tender. Most independent operators were prepared to cut their margins to the bone in order to get these contracts and Laker saw that in order to make money he needed a plane with low operating costs. The planes currently competitive were Avro Yorks, with Harold Bamberg emerging as the front runner in the race to win government contracts. In August 1951 Bamberg began the first regular contract flights – between Britain and Singapore – instead of one-off contracts.

Ever since the Berlin airlift, Freddie had been watching another plane made by A.V. Roe called the Tudor. It had a bad reputation and an unfortunate history but it was potentially more economic than the York, with its longer range and greater passenger capacity. The Government had planned that BOAC would use the Avro Tudor, which received its airworthiness certificate in November 1946, as a passenger plane across the Atlantic. BOAC had, however, already insisted on 357 modifications to the prototype before committing itself to buying Tudors and within six months the state airline had rejected the new plane as unsuitable for a transatlantic carrier. Irrespective of possible improvements in performance and capacity, BOAC did not want the Tudor, although it was forced to buy some.

Avro did everything it could to modify the Tudor, strengthening the undercarriage, moving the hydraulics, improving the de-icing and redesigning the wings and tail. It found a new customer, British South American Airways, which had the legendary Air Vice-

Marshal Donald 'Pathfinder' Bennett as its new managing director. Only thirty-five, Bennett held the world long-distance seaplane record from Dundee in Scotland to Alexandra Bay in South Africa and his textbook, *The Complete Air Navigator*, was regarded as a standard work. In the war he had led the Pathfinder forces which pinpointed targets in Germany for the bombers following behind. After the war Bennett had been made managing director and chief executive of BSAA, which had been nationalized but was still independent from BOAC.

Bennett thought the Tudor was a good plane and insisted that BSAA buy it. However, even before the airline began using the Tudors purchased for its south Atlantic routes, the prototype Tudor 2 crashed in August 1947, killing the designer Roy Chadwick as well as test pilot 'Bill' Thorn. A mechanic had fitted the aileron circuit back to front, so it worked in reverse, causing the plane to crash on takeoff.

In January 1948, BSAA's own Tudor, *Star Tiger*, took off from the Azores with a crew of six and twenty-five passengers *en route* for Bermuda and was never seen again. The mysterious disappearance was one of the first aerial disasters in the area that has become known as the Bermuda Triangle and one of the few that still cannot be explained.

Bennett was sacked. But he refused to admit that the Tudor was a bad plane. With his golden handshake of £4,500 he bought two Tudors from the Government, formed a company called Air Flight and promptly used them as diesel carriers in the Berlin airlift.

After the airlift, Bennett converted his Tudors back into freighters and put up plans to Avro and the Air Registration Board for modifying the design to make them acceptable as passenger planes. These included changes to the suspect hydraulic and air-circulation systems. In the meantime, Bennett began hauling fruit from the Continent, although not without effort. The Tudor had a tiny door, which made it a poor aircraft for bulky loads. It took two hours to unload.

At the end of August, Bennett's Tudor 2 was given a passenger certificate and he formed a new company called Fairflight to start charter work. Throughout the winter the Tudors flew long-distance charter flights, making Fairflight one of the pioneers of passenger charter work.

On 12 March 1950, disaster struck. Fairflight's crew of five and seventy-five Welsh rugby supporters were killed as a Tudor tried to land at Llandow in South Wales on the return flight from Dublin after the Wales–Ireland match. Just before touchdown, the Tudor was seen to climb rapidly on full power and then crash. All the committee of inquiry could establish was that the plane had been loaded so that its centre of gravity was between seven and thirteen inches too far back, but this did not explain the tragedy. Perhaps the pilot's seat had slipped, or the approach airspeed had been too low, suggested the inquiry.

Although profoundly shocked, Bennett continued to fly his other Tudor on general charter work up to August 1951, when he once again returned to Berlin, using the Tudor and his other plane, a Lincoln, on the little airlift. In the next three and a half months Fairflight carried over 2,500 tons from Berlin to Hamburg and back.

Freddie had not missed any of this. Like all the other civil operators, he had watched the Tudors' uncanny reliability and performance on the Berlin airlift. He had seen British South American Airways bring its own Tudors to the airlift as well, after withdrawing them from all passenger work following a second mysterious crash over the south Atlantic almost exactly a year after the first.

Laker had paid attention as BOAC withdrew the last of its Tudors from passenger service late in 1950, keeping ten as freighters, and had read in March 1951 of Lord Pakenham's (later Lord Longford) decision as Minister of Civil Aviation not to grant any more passenger-carrying certificates to Tudors.

What really interested Freddie was that they were going cheap. The Yorks he was using on the trooping contracts he had won for Surrey Flying Services were running out of time. The obvious replacement, the American DC-4, cost about £250,000 even with 12–15,000 hours flying time to their name. Freddie was not that rich. Even if he had been, exchange control restrictions would have made it very difficult to find the dollars to buy US aircraft. The Tudor, after all had been planned to provide a source of British-built passenger aircraft.

Laker could not see what was wrong with the Tudor. To his practical engineer's eye it looked right. He did not believe there was anything that could not be solved. With the exception of the two disappearances on the South American routes, all the accidents had been human error. The fact that the Tudor looked a bargain worked like yeast in his brain.

Suddenly his opportunity seemed to have arrived. The previous December, Alan Lennox-Boyd cancelled the order made by his predecessor as Minister of Transport, Lord Pakenham, that Tudors were only to carry cargo.

Pakenham's refusal to grant passenger licences was making it impossible for the Government to sell off eleven Tudors it had put on the market a few months earlier. Freddie had bought one – which he had leased to Lome Airways – but the others were a drag on the market. All the Government was asking was £10,000 each, against their £100,000 cost new. But they needed overhauling to get airworthiness certificates and most had been stripped for cargo carrying. Without passenger licences they were not economic.

Freddie went into long negotiations with the Ministry. He met the designers from the Air Registration Board with his own engineers and they worked out exactly what would be needed to make the Tudors serviceable. Eventually they agreed a whole range of modifications. They tried them out on a Tudor 1 which had first been used as a test plane in 1946 to win the new design its first airworthiness certificate. Aviation Traders dealt with the suspect pressurization system by taking it out. This cut the Tudor's operational ceiling to 10,000 feet, but for the kind of business Freddie had in mind that did not matter.

The original heating system, which was suspected, although without proof, of blowing up the two Tudors unaccounted for over the Atlantic was also removed and an electric heating system took its place. The de-icing was improved, the hydraulics moved, the wiring, pneumatics and radio systems revamped, and small changes made to the designs of the wings and tail.

Then Freddie's engineers gutted the interior of nearly a ton of brackets and fittings to 'add lightness'. By the time they had finished, they had a passenger plane capable of carrying forty-two passengers on non-stop flights of 3,250 miles.

Next Freddie's test pilots, along with a pilot from the Air Registration Board, flew a series of long-distance proving flights from Stansted to Fayid in Egypt and Nairobi in Kenya, distances of over two thousand miles. It was no coincidence that these were normal stopping-off airports for British troops.

After more than two hundred flying hours, the ARB pronounced itself happy. The Tudor was up to 1951 certification standards and the test plane was granted a full certificate. That was September 1953. Freddie finally bought the rest of the Ministry's fleet of Tudors.

He got what looked like an amazing bargain. Apart from the test plane, he acquired two brand new Tudor 1s and one with less than five hundred hours flying time, two new Tudor 3s, the VIP version, and four new Tudor 4Bs. As with the Halifaxes he bought from BOAC, Freddie also acquired the planes' extensive spares stocks, including eighty-eight unused Rolls-Royce Merlin engines.

The Merlins alone underwrote the deal. They were engines which could be modified to fit into other planes being flown in Britain, like the Canadian-built DC–4s being used by BOAC. Even if the Tudors came to nothing, Freddie would be able to cover his costs. He was suddenly in control of a monopoly of Tudors. He had picked up five more from BOAC which had been standing in the open for several years. Laker only wanted these for spares, but it meant he owned every Tudor on the British register.

The next job was to get them in the air. Laker told the ARB and the Ministry that it would cost him about £30,000 to make each plane airworthy. This put a potential figure of £400,000 on his investment. As always, he was full of confidence that his gamble would pay off a hundred times over.

He started by flying a party of journalists to Hamburg and back. They were suitably impressed by the improved Tudor, although one or two complained about the noisy Merlin engines. But they were only armchair critics. Pilots found the Tudor a pig to fly.

It was a bastard design in every sense of the word. Its original designers were instructed to base as much of the Tudor as possible on the wartime Lincoln in order to cut production costs. The wing and tailplane, as well as the undercarriage, were derived from the Lincoln and Rolls-Royce Merlin engines were standard.

The aircraft was very difficult to handle on the ground, due to the combination of its rear wheel and its long nose, plus its primitive pneumatic brakes. The pilot could not see where he was in relation to the ground and taxiing was hazardous. The rear wheel under the tail made cross-wind landing a wavering matter of pilot judgement. Takeoff was even hairier. The inbuilt swing to the left from the torque of the four Merlin engines, a feature shared by Yorks and Lancasters, was even more extreme in Tudors. Pilots kept a thumb firmly on the button for the left-hand engine to keep it at full throttle to counteract this swing. The aircraft surged down the runway like a chariot with four unbalanced horses.

The War Office, unfortunately, was unenthusiastic about the revamped Tudors. Though they had a full airworthiness certificate and complied with 1951 civil airworthiness requirements, the army would not use them for trooping.

This came as a blow to Freddie. He had every reason to expect the services to be satisfied with the aircraft. In the middle of 1953, when he had been negotiating with the Ministry, the old Fairflight Tudor 2, hired for thirteen trooping flights to the Canal Zone and Nairobi for the War Office and the Air Ministry, had carried 760 passengers and covered 80,000 miles without any snags or delays. He had also carried out simulated trooping test flights with his 'new' Tudor.

The objections were more subjective than real. The Tudors' reputation as unlucky planes was all that was needed to put the armed forces off although they usually justified their aversion with unanswerable complaints about insufficient flying experience.

Freddie was undaunted. On St Valentine's Day 1954 the first of his uprated Tudor 4s had started flying between Stansted and Hamburg on the little Berlin airlift and in March was joined by another. The original converted Tudor with its forty-two seats was used for general charter work, including flying refugees out of Berlin under contract to BEA and on a colonial coach-class passenger service from Stansted to Idris and Lagos in Wext Africa. The War Office also used this plane and the Fairflight Tudor 2 for trooping. But it never quite got over its prejudice.

In the main, Laker was forced to use his Tudors as freighters. With typical inventiveness he proceeded to make the best of the situation. As cargo carriers, their great disadvantage was their small passenger doors, which had made Bennett's fruit-carrying such a laborious exercise. Freddie cut this gordian knot by carving larger cargo doors into the sides of his Tudor 4s. This modification was straightforward. The fuselage was strengthened around the cut-out and the floor stiffened. Double doors opened outwards to give an opening 6 feet 10 inches wide and 5 feet 5 inches high. But the ARB was so impressed that it gave the Tudor the accolade of a new name, the 'Supertrader'. Freddie's influence can be seen in the choice.

He did not design the modifications himself. Practical engineer that he was, he did not pretend to this kind of expertise and he was far too busy running his growing corporation. Moreover he already had a design team of his own at Southend, where it had just moved from Stansted. It was headed by a remarkable and innovative designer called Toby Heal, who had left the Hunting group a year earlier to work for Freddie. Heal was in the process of building up a staff and a little job like sticking new doors into an aeroplane was child's play. He was planning something far more grandiose, but in the meantime the concentration of design talent he was assembling had time to spare for improving existing planes.

In spite of setbacks, Laker managed to make his new fleet of Tudors pay its way. For three years most of the Tudors were kept busy on the Berlin run. A large part of their payload was not freight, but refugees. BEA was responsible for this human freight, which poured drearily and continuously across from the East, but subcontracted much of their transport out to the West to Air Charter. Unlike the War Office, the refugees were not fussy about the Tudors, just grateful that there were any seats at all.

When the little Berlin airlift came to an end in 1957, Laker found new business for his converted Tudors with the Supertrader soubriquet, flying Black Knight and Blue Streak rockets to the Woomera rocket-testing range in Australia for the British Government. The Tudor was particularly suitable for this run, as it was one of the few 'old' planes big enough to carry such bulky freight.

Between 1953 and 1959 Freddie's fleet of Tudors flew 46,000 profitable hours. Of the total of seventeen planes he bought, eleven were made airworthy and kept flying on the backs of the cannibalized carcases of the remainder. Memorable long-distance flights were made by some of them. In September 1956 one flew round the world via Christmas Island; in August 1958 another Tudor flew to Christchurch in New Zealand to collect spares for a Bristol freighter.

There were two fatal crashes in 1959, however, which hastened their final retirement. The second, over Turkey towards the end of April, was a particular blow to Laker, who up to then had been able to boast an almost miraculously good record for safety. Freddie and his old lieutenants were equally affected. The crews they had lost were all close personal friends and their death had been particularly unpleasant. Within the next six months Freddie retired the last two Tudors, which in any case were suffering from wing-spar fatigue.

During their six years in operation, the Tudors had more than paid for themselves. With their initial cost rapidly written off and with Freddie's flair for finding new business keeping them working, they had produced a cash flow of something like £1 million a year between 1954 and 1958. Laker had had no trouble in spending this revenue. As usual, it went on more planes.

He acquired his first brand new plane in February 1953. It was a Bristol freighter, irreverently called the Gold Brick, which went straight onto the Berlin freight run. A year later Air Charter bought a second Bristol for use as a trooping plane and in the next three years Laker added another seven. Most of them were used on the Channel Air Bridge, which Laker began on an experimental basis in 1954 and expanded into a regular scheduled car and passenger service in April 1955 with four Bristols shuttling seven times a day between Southend and Calais. This built up to twenty-four round trips daily to Calais and then expanded to include Ostend and Rotterdam in partnership with Sabena, the Belgian airline.

The Channel Air Bridge was not a Laker invention. Silver City Airways had been operating a car ferry service between Lydd and Le Touquet since 1948. Using a hired Bristol freighter, an ungainly looking aircraft with doors in the nose, the twenty-five-minute flight cost £27 each way for a medium-sized car and four passengers.

The flights were more expensive than ferries, but the boats were heavily booked and notorious for their poor standard of service. In 1949, the first real summer of car flights, Silver City's traffic was 2,600 cars and 7,900 passengers. Repeated price cuts stimulated traffic until in 1955 Silver City carried nearly 50,000 cars on seven routes to Europe and two to Northern Ireland, leading the airline to claim that it was the non-Communist world's largest air cargo carrier.

Laker's entry into competition was a business venture. Three years after his first Bristol freighter flight in 1954, airlifting three cars at a time between Southend and Calais, Air Charter's subsidiary Channel Air Bridge was carrying nearly 15,000 cars a year.

Freddie tempted his War Office contact Douglas Whybrow to apply for a 'golden bowler', the contemporary term for early retirement from the armed forces, and join him to manage the Channel Air Bridge. Based north of the Thames, the Channel Air Bridge siphoned off a considerable proportion of Silver City's traffic from the Midlands and shattered its monopoly. Silver City had accumulated losses of over £110,000 in its start-up years. The last thing it needed was a rival.

The Bristol freighters not on the Channel Air Bridge joined in Air Charter's bread-and-butter business. With their large carrying capacity, they handled all kinds of cargoes. One was a partly dismantled helicopter from Croydon to a survey camp at Mesters Vig in Greenland, via Stornoway and Keflavik, for a Danish mining company. With spares and personnel, the entire load weighed around three tons. Another load, twice as heavy, was a Bedford lorry loaded with Howard Rotovators from Southend to Calais.

The Bristol freighters also provided Laker with charter work in Africa. West African Airways, which operated a fleet of five Bristol freighters, lost one in the jungle during a storm and promptly grounded the rest. This created a twofold vacuum. One side of the airline's business was ferrying British troops and personnel to and from West Africa and the other was internal scheduled services in Nigeria – from Lagos to Kaduna and Kano in the up-country tin-mining region – and in Ghana and Sierra Leone. West African Airways' refusal to fly was a crisis. The British Government asked Freddie to send an engineer to inspect two Bristols at Accra in Ghana to see if they were airworthy. He sent Batt, who reported they were all right to fly provided they were looked after. Laker set up a small maintenance base at Accra, the only airport he could find in West Africa with a hangar big enough to carry out servicing. A small team of Aviation Traders' engineers stayed in West Africa keeping the planes in the air until Nigeria was granted its independence in 1960.

At the beginning of 1955 Freddie bought his first DC-4. This was the Douglas Corporation's successor to the ubiquitous DC-3.

The DC–4 was a much larger aeroplane. With the confusing nomenclature beloved of the aircraft industry, Laker's first DC–4 was the US military version, the C54B Skymaster.

Unlike the Gold Brick, this plane, with the registration number G–ANYB, 'Yankee Bravo' for short, was not new. Freddie bought it from an American called Ed Daley, who owned an airline modestly called World Airways.

Laker flew across the Atlantic with P.A. 'Mac' Mackenzie, a former RAF Pathfinder pilot with a distinguished war record, who had been one of Freddie's first pilots at Air Charter. They travelled on an overnight flight in a Stratocruiser equipped with bunks. When Mackenzie woke, he found Laker in the rather elegant washroom. Laker was stropping the blade out of his safety razor up and down on the mirror over the washbasin. 'Have you ever done this?' he asked Mac. 'The blade lasts four times as long.'

When they arrived in America, they were met by one of Daley's managers who welcomed them by saying, 'I understand you limeys haven't had a real meal since pre-war days,' and took them out for the toughest steaks they had ever eaten. In the afternoon they went over to Daley's stores to look at the spares they were going to take with the plane. Freddie had been told one of the engines was using a lot of oil and he did not want to be sold any other doubtful equipment. He poked about among the spares and focused on an exhaust manifold.

'Look here, cock,' he said. 'This has got a crack in it.'

Mackenzie had never seen anyone as impressed as Daley's engineer. 'This guy's just spotted a crack with his bare eyes,' he said admiringly to his colleagues.

On the flight back to England, it was soon only too obvious to Mackenzie that one of the DC–4's engines was indeed an oil-burner, a real smokey joe. But the first trouble came on the final approach to their refuelling stop at Gander. At about 5,000 feet the plane flew into cloud and began icing up faster and more heavily than Mackenzie ever remembered an aircraft doing. In a matter of minutes, the DC–4 was covered in a thick layer of ice and Mackenzie was struggling to keep it under control.

Just then he felt a blast of freezing air. He looked up to find that Freddie had opened the direct vision window and was hanging out of it, hacking ice off with a fireman's axe. 'Keep her going Mac, we've got to get this stuff off somehow,' he shouted cheerily.

With the smokey joe playing up as well, Mackenzie decided to overshoot Gander. Slowly, sluggishly, the overweight plane climbed clear of the cloud into a full moon and flew on to land at Sydney in Nova Scotia.

The next morning the ice was still there and Laker was supervising its removal. When it came to paying for the extra labour as well as the airport fees, Freddie said to the manager, 'Tell you what, I'll toss you double or quits.' Freddie won, leaving the poor manager wondering just how he had got himself in the position of losing $80 of his employer's money.

The DC–4 went on the Berlin run, mainly to carry passengers, and Freddie soon bought two more.

In 1958 Freddie ordered two new Britannias from Bristol Aircraft to replace his ageing Tudors on the long-distance charter work to Australia for the Government. The first was delivered on 12 September and on 1 October made a trooping flight from Stansted to Christmas Island with 124 passengers.

Trooping was still a vital part of the business of the independents, although competition was forcing profit margins down. The flights that Freddie's new Britannia was undertaking so frequently were not, however, directly on contract from the War Office. Two years earlier the Government had called for tenders for trooping to Europe and the Far East, giving the option of buying three new Britannias tied to five-year contracts. An alternative option was three-year contracts and the lease of the new planes, which had been bought by the Government in order to replace the battered Hermes used for most trooping at the time.

Unfortunately for the Government, several independents had already managed to buy their own new equipment. Transair bid successfully for the European business with its new Viscounts, while Air Charter vied with Hunting Clan and Airwork for the Far Eastern contract. Hunting won, but at a price so low it left no room for any depreciation on its two new Britannias. The Government calculated that it would save £1.75 million a year on the Far Eastern route compared to the cost of using Hermes.

Hunting, the aviation offshoot of the Clan Line shipping interests, famous for its 'Safari' economy-class service to British colonies on the West Coast of Africa, was almost immediately in trouble meeting the War Office's requirements and was soon subcontracting to Air Charter, making a loss in the process.

When Laker eventually discovered the terms, he put together a new deal for sharing the business which effectively transferred its management to Air Charter.

Chapter 6

'I've just resigned for all of you'

While Freddie's mainstream operations with Air Charter and Aviation Traders were gradually developing into substantial and increasingly recognized commercial enterprises, he managed to find time for a couple of follies. There is no doubting that Laker has a brilliant mind. But in spite of his apprenticeship at Short's and his qualifications as an engineer and a pilot, Freddie lacked formal academic training. When it came to aircraft design and performance, his approach was that of an inspired handyman.

But Laker is a radical thinker when it comes to aircraft and their use. In the 1950s this irrepressible urge to find breakthrough solutions to all and any problems showed itself in do-it-yourself answers like the Tudor.

He tried another short-cut with the Hunting-Percival Prentice. In 1956, this bulky three-seat RAF training plane became obsolete. The Prentices were big, slow, safe, single-engined trainers, with large, greenhouse-like glass canopies and odd little tilted tips at the end of their generous wings. They took off and climbed at 70 miles per hour with a top speed only twice as fast.

Since the war the RAF had taken delivery of over 350 Prentices and ten years later there were still 252 left. In the air they gave a feeling of rock-like security and solidity. Indeed, as a trainer the RAF had found the Prentices almost too stable. The upturned wingtips were added to diminish stability when the planes were upside down. Before that they were quite difficult to roll back the right way up.

Freddie bought the lot, all 252. He paid scrap prices for them and promptly looted most of them of their RAF radio equipment. His hope, though, was to convert them into civil light aircraft. The market for private planes was growing. At first glance the Prentice seemed ideal, roomy and safe. What could be better?

The first problem proved to be collecting them. The job fell to Bob Batt, who was Aviation Traders' acknowledged light-aircraft enthusiast. Over a period of eighteen months Batt ferried Prentices from all over the country. He used some fifty pilots, taking them up to RAF aerodromes and then giving them an instant training circuit to make sure they could fly the Prentices back to Stansted or Southend. It said a great deal for the ease of handling of the Prentices that they were all ferried in without an accident, although most of the pilots were amateurs, some with as little as forty hours' experience. Refinements like airscrew pitch controls were completely new to them.

The second problem was what to do with the planes when they arrived. They were parked all over Southend and Stansted airports in droves, while Aviation Traders grappled with the third problem. This was getting them a civil aviation airworthiness certificate. Unlike with the Tudor, this was not a major difficulty. Most of the 120 hours of test flying was concerned with finding out how to provide a civil pilot with advance warning of a stall.

Laker painted the Prentices silver grey and upholstered them in grey vinyl and red trimmings with a bench seat for three behind the pair of pilots' seats. At £1,500 including a four-channel radio they should have been remarkable value.

The civil Prentice was a total flop. Whether it was its sheer size – over 31 feet long with a wing span of 46 feet and a total height of 10 feet – or the bulbous spats over the wheels to increase aerodynamic efficiency, or its well-deserved reputation for guzzling fuel, Aviation Traders sold less than twenty. It cost £10,000 to win a civil licence for the Prentice and £75 a plane to put in the American safe flight indicator unit which was the final answer to the stall warning problem. In addition Batt had half a dozen men working on the planes and a full-time secretary to organize flying permits for the ferry pilots and to handle the registration application.

What was probably the real reason for Freddie's failure to sell the Prentices was a relaxation of import controls on light aircraft. Smaller, more modern planes like the Cessna or Piper were coincidentally available and much more attractive.

For once Freddie failed to think of a way to turn the situation to his advantage and most of the Prentices were broken up for scrap.

Perhaps it is unfair to call their purchase a folly. In a way it marked the end of an era. It was the last big scrap deal that Laker ever did and the last time he bought any plane that dated from the war.

His real folly was the Accountant.

At the beginning of the 1950s it became obvious that the indefatigable and invaluable Dakota needed replacing. The market for the successor was worldwide and the British Government was keen that a British replacement should be manufactured. Big aircraft manufacturing corporations like Handley Page and Hawker Siddeley were the natural organizations to try to fill the coming gap, but against all the odds Freddie decided to have a go.

He had met the brilliant but unorthodox Toby Heal when the latter was assistant chief designer at the Hunting aircraft group. Heal was one of several eminent aircraft experts at Hunting who were running out of work. He had become enamoured of a manufacturing process he referred to as tension-skin construction. It was a development of the discovery that if you take a piece of metal and bend it in two directions at once it becomes rigid. In theory, this means that much thinner metal fuselages can be used to build aeroplanes, making them lighter but at the same time stronger. Short's had used the method successfully on its flying boats which it built at Rochester when Freddie was an apprentice and Lockheed adopted it for their Constellation airliners after the war.

Heal wanted to try out the theory on an eight- to nine-seat replacement for the little Avro Anson. He was immensely enthusiastic and he captivated Freddie, whose penchant for radical solutions was seduced by the concept of tension skin. Lighter and stronger! The economic implications of that were dazzling.

Heal had put his idea up to Hunting only to have it rejected. He left in disgust and Freddie put him on Aviation Traders' payroll and installed him in a small office at Stansted, where he began to build up a small design team. Before very long Freddie was talking about a Dakota replacement. Instead of a nine-seater, the plane was going to be a twenty-eight-seater, 60 feet long and over 82 feet in wing span, capable of flying over 1,500 miles at a speed of 250 miles an hour and a height of 25,000 feet.

As well as using the 'Heal' method, the plane had features that were ahead of its time. It was the first twin turbo-prop. The fuel tanks were built in as an integral part of the wing and both wings and fuselage were failsafe in design, with alternative load paths so that if one part cracked, another section would take the strain. For the first year the design team operated out of a small office at Stansted, but in 1953 Heal and his assistants moved to Southend.

Freddie raided Hunting for a project manager. He hooked another senior man called 'Johnny' Johnson, who arrived at Southend unaware that the plane he was going to build incorporated Heal's tension skin.

The irony of this was not lost on him. He had been the man who had turned down the concept for Hunting.

Johnson had to start from scratch at Southend. When he arrived at the airport, he found a wooden hut and a staff of one or two ex-milkmen. When Aviation Traders finished building the prototype, they had to take the shed apart to get it out onto the runway.

Johnson began by hiring and training labour. There was no aircraft industry worth the name in Essex and he found his best source of workers were ex-carpenters. Freddie made skilful use of government training schemes, but the rest of the expertise had to be created by the company. To begin with Johnson recruited a workforce of about a hundred, but by the time the Accountant project was in full swing he was employing closer to a thousand men at Southend.

Apart from the training schemes, Laker received no help from the Government, but he managed to enlist a great deal of aid from the aviation industry. Dowty provided an undercarriage and Rotol instrumentation, while Rolls-Royce loaned the Accountant a pair of Dart turbo-prop jet engines. Rolls-Royce did not actually mean them to be a free loan at first, but even a man as forceful as Lord Hives, Rolls's chairman, was no match for Freddie.

Over the years Freddie had built up a close relationship with Rolls-Royce due to his large stocks of Merlin engines, in which he had been a major scrap dealer since his first coup in 1948, when he had acquired so many with his BOAC Halifax fleet. With his purchase of the Tudor fleet his business with Rolls grew even more. He had been useful to Rolls as a supplier of spare parts as well. When Aviation Traders dismantled Rolls-Royce engines it kept crank cases, gears, cylinder blocks and camshafts on one side. When Rolls wanted replacement parts for its overhaul line it would have been bad for its image to be seen buying second hand from dealers. Instead it was able to ring up Laker, who discreetly sent up several from which Rolls chose.

Freddie was able to boast that he had never paid for an engine overhaul at Rolls. He operated a contra-arrangement, setting off what each owed the other. The whole arrangement ran, like most of Freddie's deals, on trust. Throughout the aircraft industry Laker was known as a man who always fulfilled his side of any bargain. It was a fetish with him. In return, he demanded an equally high standard from anyone who dealt with him or worked with him.

Lord Hives, unfortunately, was not *au fait* with this aspect of Freddie's dealings with his company. Faced with a request for an indefinite loan of two new Dart turbo-prop engines, he let it be known that Laker would find it easier to get the shirt off his back. Freddie, Jack Wiseman and Bob Batt were invited up to Derby to visit Rolls and Laker was entertained to dinner by Hives. When Freddie mentioned that he wanted the Darts he was told he really could not expect to get them for nothing in view of the fact that he owed Rolls money, some tens of thousands, which, moreover, appeared to have been outstanding for some considerable time. 'Oh,' said Freddie blandly, 'I didn't think you were worried about sums like that. I never usually bother. As a matter of fact you owe me considerably more.'

The two Darts were on the next train to Southend.

Help from the major aircraft manufacturers was less satisfactory. Freddie realized that he could not contemplate manufacturing the Accountant himself. Once the prototype was flying successfully, he hoped with his perennial enthusiasm to sell it to one of the major manufacturers and sit back and collect a percentage on sales. Well, not sit back. He would have been the salesman.

First to come down to look at the plans for the new plane was Hunting. This company sent down a survey team which pored over the project and then spent months deciding not to help. Next Freddie went to the Gloucester Aircraft Company, which was part of the Hawker Siddeley group. Gloucester had already helped with resonance and flutter tests and proved to be enthusiastic to build the Accountant.

Laker let the Gloucester representatives see all the designs and flight information and told them he had already done a deal with the

Indian Government to make the Accountant under licence at Hindustan Aeronautics's factory. Gloucester Aircraft was extremely interested. It was getting towards the end of its Javelin fighter production programme and it needed more work. Unfortunately Gloucester Aircraft was not represented on the main Hawker Siddeley board of directors and when its proposal to manufacture the Accountant was put forward it was turned down.

In the meantime Freddie was going ahead with his pet project, paying for it out of Air Charter's cash flow. Early on in the development it became obvious that Heal's tension skin was not going to be simple to use. None of Freddie's lieutenants liked it.

People like Wiseman and Batt could not imagine what would happen to the carefully stressed fuselage if anything punched a hole in it. They thought the idea was too clever by half. More seriously, although Freddie was constantly jeering at conventional planes as nothing more than 'aloominum toobs', they had one overriding advantage compared to tension skin. The Heal method meant that the fuselage had to come to a point at the back in order to maintain the two-way twist on the metal skin which gave the stressed strength. And this meant the back sections of the fuselage were far too narrow to be of any use, so the Accountant's capacity was severely limited.

Eventually, Heal's tension skin was dropped. When it came to the crunch, Freddie's enchantment with theory was no match for his practical commercial genius. By the time the prototype was ready to fly in 1957, its production plans were for a straightforward unstressed body – one of the aluminium tubes at which Laker had at first scoffed. The original Accountant, however, was still largely built to Heal's design, the fuselage the shape of an elongated water drop with the flight cabin stuck on the front. In practice it looked elegant and graceful, but the narrowness of the after-section was only too obvious. It had also become obvious to Laker that it would be impossible to 'stretch' the plane without having several entirely different fuselages.

Aside from Heal's tension skin, the Accountant incorporated a number of developments which have since become standard aircraft practice. The fuselage was flush-riveted and designed to meet the American safety standard on structural strength. A lot of attention had been paid to making the aeroplane easy to service and safe to fly. The prototype was fitted out as a conventional twenty-eight seater, but the four-abreast seating arrangement could be replaced by an executive layout with a couple of three-seater settees and eight single seats. A later version stretched to carry forty passengers on short-haul flights was also envisaged. The two Dart engines, similar to those used in the Vickers Viscounts, gave plenty of power with their square-tipped Rotol propellers.

As soon as the prototype was completed early in 1957, Freddie began pestering Johnson for a date for the first flight. Johnson found this difficult as he still had lots of trials to complete – taxiing, high-speed runs, complete inspections after each trial – but eventually he gave Laker a specific date.

Freddie turned up at Southend with the press, photographers and everyone he wanted to impress by seeing his pet project leap into the air. Johnson's mechanics were busy putting inspection panels back into the Accountant after checking the electrical circuitry on the crash system. There were crash pads built into the underside of the wings and fuselage which automatically let off foam fire extinguishers in the engines. When checking the electrics, the mechanics took out the fuses and put in a bell circuit instead. The idea was that someone would hit the pads with a mallet and the bell would ring, proving that the system worked. In all the excitement of Freddie's arrival, one of the mechanics took out the bell and put the fuses back in before the test. When the mallet hit the pads, both fire extinguishers went off. It took a week to dry the engines out and Freddie fired Johnson and everyone working on the plane on the spot.

He often used to sack people. If things went wrong he lost his temper and fired the culprit out of hand. But he only meant it if he found people cheating him. He told Johnson, whom he used to sack frequently, that people could make mistakes costing thousands and he would forgive them – the first time anyway. But if he found someone stealing a small piece of metal worth two shillings he was out for good.

The Monday after the debacle Freddie telephoned Southend to make sure everyone had reported for work.

In September the Accountant flew at the Farnborough air show and Laker did his best to find both customers and a major manufacturer. For once Freddie's salesmanship was not enough.

His efforts to persuade larger manufacturers to build the Accountant under licence were unsuccessful, partly because the whole industry was passing through a difficult time. Test flying went on until January, but then Freddie threw in the towel. He telephoned Southend and told his disappointed employees to take out the two Dart engines and scrap the plane. Most of the workforce was laid off, including the bulk of the design team, and the Accountant died.

Or nearly died. The Gloucester Aircraft Corporation disappeared, closed down by Hawker Siddeley after its work on the Javelin ran out, but in due course the parent company produced a plane which it called the HS–748. It had a suspicious resemblance to the Accountant minus the influences of Heal. Hawker even collected the Hindustan contract. It was built by A.V. Roe, another part of the Hawker group, and Laker always called it bitterly the Avro Accountant. For a time he contemplated suing Hawker, even taking legal advice, but in the end he let it die. From that day forward however, he never dealt with Hawker again. The reverse side of his fetish for keeping his own word is that he bears an undying grudge against anyone he feels has cheated him.

There was another factor influencing his decision not to fight Hawker Siddeley. The Accountant cost Freddie Laker £650,000. This money came out of the cash flow of Air Charter and Aviation Traders, but it had put a heavy strain on their resources. When Freddie ordered the prototype's destruction it was because he had realized that unless he called a halt he would go on pouring money into it endlessly. He had been able to afford to finance it so far because Air Charter was awash with cash and like many entrepreneurs Freddie preferred to back a gamble than tamely hand over a large slice of his profits in tax.

Fundamentally the Accountant was a brilliant piece of foresight. The 'twin Dart' formula was absolutely right and aircraft like the HS–748, the Fokker F–27 and the Japanese Y5–11 employing it sold by the hundred. But Freddie knew that he did not have the resources to manufacture the plane on his own. He was deeply disappointed that none of the major manufacturers had backed him and suddenly disillusioned with the struggle to do everything on his own. He had also become aware that the tide was running in favour of big corporations in the aviation industry.

Whether the Accountant would have been as good a plane as the HS–748 eventually became it is impossible to assess. Apart from the industry's reservations about the Heal tension-skin construction technique, the Accountant's first test flight had shown that the centre of gravity was too far forward. So far forward in fact, that the co-pilot had to leave his seat and shift some of the plane's ballast into the tail before the Accountant could be landed. Not that this proves much. All prototypes have their idiosyncrasies which test-flying programmes are designed to uncover. The real problem was that Laker did not have the capital to finance the proving and manufacture of the new plane himself.

Getting as far as he did was a minor miracle. The gutted ghost of the Accountant stood forlornly on the edge of Southend airport for four years before it was finally dismantled for scrap but there was never any suggestion of reviving it. Its fate was finally sealed by another event which brought an end to this chapter in Freddie's life.

One day in 1958 Jack Wiseman was called up to Freddie Laker's office in Cumberland Place. He found four others there apart from Laker: Bob Batt, who had become chief inspector, Norman Jennings, the chief pilot and operations manager, Douglas Whybrow, who was in charge of the Channel Air Bridge, and Alan Nicholls, the chief accountant. They were Laker's inner circle, men who had been with him for a long time and who had won his deepest trust.

'I've just resigned for all of you,' Freddie said. He looked at their stunned expressions and grinned broadly.

'I'm selling out to Airwork. I've told them they can take my companies with no encumbrances at all. If they want you, they'll ask for you.'

Freddie had sold Air Charter and Aviation Traders for £600,000 cash, plus another £200,000 subject to valuation of stock. He had decided that if he could not beat the big companies, the time had come to join one of them.

As a thank-you to his loyal lieutenants, he gave them cash bonuses. They started at figures like £250 to George Forster, Air Charter's commercial manager, and ran up to five figures for men like Wiseman.

When Freddie Laker sold his personal empire to Airwork, he was not quite thirty-six. It was the climax of ten years' non-stop driving, wheeling and dealing, seizing opportunities as they came along, inspiring others towards barely defined goals, turning failure into success or at least something passably like it, capitalizing on profits and ruthlessly cutting losses.

Throughout it all Freddie had been tireless, working all hours, commuting between Stansted and Southend and his London headquarters, dreaming up new ideas and opportunities while his sharp eyes probed into the corners of his growing companies to prevent waste, stamp on corruption and inspire further efforts. Still with the little dark moustache and addicted to a shapeless panama hat, his youthful appearance was increased by the plumpness that had crept on his six foot frame. Throughout this decade Freddie had eaten and drunk as he wished, ever ready for a party, a laugh, a bit of fun.

Now, in early middle age, he had made it. He was the best kind of millionaire – a cash one. He had moved his growing family from the house in Carshalton to a modern £20,000 luxury home at Epsom with a loggia looking over the Royal Automobile Club's golf course and the club's swimming pool handy for the children. Freddie called the house Charters, built in a private bar and hung the walls with pictures by his daughter. Elaine was fourteen and Kevin ten.

Freddie had begun indulging one of his greatest hobbies, racehorse ownership, a year or so earlier, and he was just about to sell the farm he had bought with some earlier profits at Ashford in Kent and buy a seventy-five acre stud farm near his new home.

The battle to the top had put strains on his family life. His wife Joan complained it had meant a lot of very hard work, long hours at nights and at weekends for Freddie and a lot of loneliness for her. Much as he loved his children, they did not see much of him. When he sold out to Airwork, his wife hoped that he would stop. She did not have much hope. Freddie's idea of a relaxing day at home was nine holes of golf in the morning, lunch at the RAC clubhouse, another eighteen holes and then back home in the evening with half a dozen cronies to play poker into the small hours. He was a walk-round golfer but a brilliant poker player.

Chapter 7

'I'm not your bum boy'

The man who called on Freddie Laker to buy his business at the end of 1958 was in his late forties, slim and brown-haired with a humorous, sun-tanned face and the casual good manners of an ex-RAF pilot. His name was Gerald Freeman and he was well known to Laker. They were not socially close, but they had met as members of the British Independent Air Transport Association (BIATA) and had both been subcontractors to BEA on the little Berlin airlift. Freddie, in fact, had helped Freeman to win his share, which was mostly freighting refugees to the West.

Gerry Freeman found that Freddie was keen to sell. The Accountant had drained Laker of cash, the Hunting-Percival Prentices were still hanging round his neck, the Channel Air Bridge was a *succès d'estime* but was not earning much profit, the Tudors were dying; the Berlin traffic had dried up and the outlook was, well, uncertain.

Freeman's problem was that it was difficult to value Freddie's two businesses, Air Charter and Aviation Traders. He started easily enough by listing Freddie's planes, eighteen 'big ones' and fifty-odd Prentices which Freeman agreed generously were worth £40,000, about half the price Laker was asking for them as converted civilian light aircraft although everyone knew he had bought them for scrap prices. With the two Britannias, four DC-4s, seven Bristol freighters and a number of Tudors, plus their operating spares, Freeman put a value on the Air Charter fleet of £600,000.

When it came to the rest of Freddie's assets, it was not so simple. Laker had kept no stock lists of his still mountainous collection of miscellaneous spares and equipment, compiled over the years and never properly sorted through. Freddie said it was worth at least £200,000.

Freeman looked him in the eye. It was not so much that he wanted to argue, but that he could not be answerable for a pig in a poke. He suggested a compromise. His chief engineer Bill Richardson should join with Jack Wiseman in a joint valuation of the remaining assets. What they settled on should be paid. Freddie agreed and his wife Joan threw her arms round Freeman's neck. A short time afterwards, when the Lakers went to dinner with Freeman and his wife in Surrey they took with them a large urn-shaped silver wine cooler as a house-warming gift. It is still sitting on Gerry Freeman's sideboard.

Freeman was not very impressed with what he had seen of Laker's business. He thought the Southend operation looked messy and Freddie's neglect of formal accounting records meant that much of what he said his businesses were worth had to be taken on trust. It says something for his reputation as well as his personality that Gerry was largely prepared to do just that.

What also influenced the sale, though, was that Freeman was keen to buy. He had a clear mandate from the board he represented – Airwork – to acquire Air Charter and money was not the only criterion.

Freeman himself was a new member of the Airwork board, as his own company, Transair, had been taken over by Airwork only a year or so earlier. What was happening was the creation of a major independent airline consortium under the impetus of a political strategy dreamed up by the Conservative Party.

Two years previously, Freeman had been chairman of BIATA when he had been told by the then Air Minister, Harold Watkinson, that the Government planned to give the independent airlines a slice of the civil aviation cake. It would not, however, be a very big slice. At the time there were only fourteen independent airlines of any size, but if the slice was cut up among even that few it would mean they only got crumbs each.

Freeman was not the only independent to be given the nod. Another was Airwork, which had by far the best political and financial connections of any of the independents, apart from being the oldest. It had grown from a desire to provide technical services and training to private fliers by Sir Nigel Norman, who had in 1928 built Heston aerodrome just north of where Heathrow is today. (His younger son went on to preserve the family interest in aviation by founding Britten-Norman, the builder of the Islander light aircraft.)

Airwork expanded into flying in the 1930s, especially overseas, with two of its ventures metamorphosing from feeder routes into Indian Airlines and United Arab Airlines, although another venture, an airline in Iraq serving oil companies, was less successful. In the Second World War Airwork trained RAF pilots, supplied technical assistance and became a major aircraft construction subcontractor.

After the war, using a fleet of new Vikings, which were similar to the legendary Dakota, Airwork built up a respectable charter business, much of it for governments. Between 1947 and 1950, for example, it flew 10,000 passengers, including 394 babies, on a twice-a-week service between London and Wadi Halfa and Khartoum for the Sudanese Government. It operated an inclusive-tour business for the Civil Service, as well as getting in on the intermittent business of flying Muslim pilgrims to Mecca for the Hadj religious festivals and becoming the first trooping airline.

In the middle of 1952 Airwork had begun a new scheduled business between London and Nairobi in partnership with the Hunting group. Twin-engined twenty-seven-seat Vikings left London once a week, taking three days compared with twenty-four hours on some regular BOAC flights. But at £98 single the fares were £42 cheaper. Operators on routes like this to a country's colonies escaped minimum fare control under the already byzantine rules of IATA. When Airwork and Hunting introduced their 'colonial coach service' they were fully booked five months ahead only a fortnight after starting flights. Their plans to convert their East African service into a more normal third-class service, sharing the traffic with BOAC on a 30–70 per cent split, caused a major political row.

Airwork had also suffered a major financial setback with the collapse of an ambitious transatlantic freight service after only nine months for a loss of £650,000. This was an attempt by the airline to grasp a share of the booming business with North America, but when it began its service it found that the British Government was not even prepared to give Airwork a share of its mail, refusing either to allow the Post Office to use it or to negotiate on Airwork's behalf with the US for the right to fly passengers on charter. When it came to the crunch, the financial health of the national airline was more important than enlarging opportunities for predatory private airlines.

Myles Wyatt, chairman and managing director of Airwork, remarked ruefully that, 'We discovered that playing in the first league was a very different affair to schoolboy football.'

For Myles Wyatt, though, it was a crisis that established him in effective control of the company. He had been a sceptic from the start about the scheme. Airwork lacked the lesser routes to feed cargo to the main Atlantic run and the competition was formidable. Wyatt made his own reputation by selling three Viscounts and Airwork's place in the queue for two DC-6s. The planes were no longer needed and the demand for new aircraft was so great that Wyatt made back enough to recoup Airwork's losses with a handsome capital profit.

Although Myles Wyatt was a personal winner from the affair, the major shareholders in Airwork were not very happy with their investment. They were very substantial men: Lord Cowdray, the polo-playing peer who was reckoned to be the richest man in the UK; Blue Star Shipping, owned by the Vesteys who rivalled Cowdray for wealth; Furness Withy, another shipping barony; and Thomas Loel Evelyn Bulkeley Guinness, once MP for Bath, a member of White's, Buck's, the Turf, the Beefsteak and the Royal Yacht Squadron. He had a personal fortune inherited from his father Benjamin, who had lost one in the San Francisco earthquake and made another in New York, put at £30 million.

The big British shipping groups had diversified into aviation as a defensive reflex. They had enough imagination to see that this new-fangled means of transport might become a threat to sea traffic. The big shipping lines all ran virtual monopolies. Cunard dominated the North Atlantic sea lanes. P&O had the Far East buttoned up. Blue Star ruled the waves to South America. Their managements thought vaguely that air traffic must be the same. All they had to do, they reasoned, was get big enough to exert muscle. So when the Government started talking about slices of cake, their reaction was simple – buy.

The first purchase was a good one. It was Gerry Freeman's Transair. Freeman had begun as an air-taxi operator at Croydon airport in 1947 and after a shaky start gone on to create a very profitable airline. He had made a speciality out of distributing newspapers, by 1952 running over three thousand newspaper flights a year and setting standards of performance the envy of many larger airlines. His annual dinners for Fleet Street newspaper circulation managers were riotously successful.

In 1953 Transair started flying holidaymakers for Vladimir Raitz's Horizon Holidays. Gerry Freeman's planes were a fleet of ten Dakotas, of which over ten thousand had been built in the war. Transair's aircraft were immaculately maintained.

Towards the end of 1956 Freeman was planning to move from Croydon to Gatwick and to swap some of his ageing Dakotas for three new Viscounts from Vickers. He had £500,000 in retained profits, but he needed another £1 million to pay for the new planes and build a £300,000 hangar at Gatwick. At that time aircraft were considered doubtful security and Freeman was searching for finance. When Airwork offered to buy him out, leave him in control of his own airline and make him an executive director of the holding company, he agreed.

He was already part of Airwork when its board held a meeting at the Savoy at which it decided to buy up more independents. Present were Gerry Freeman and Myles Wyatt, Cowdray's man, Lord Poole, Loel Guinness and Geoffrey Murrant, deputy chairman of Furness Withy of which his father was chairman. The choice in front of them was limited. Apart from Laker, the obvious targets were Eagle Aviation, Morton Air Services, Bristow Helicopters, Silver City and Hunting.

Freeman was delegated to look at them all. First he called on Harold Bamberg at Eagle Aviation. Bamberg was interested enough to let Freeman look at his books. Freeman did not much care for what he saw and began looking elsewhere.

Morton Air Services were more modest. Captain 'Sammy' Morton, who had flown scheduled services to Paris with Amy Johnson in the 1930s, was another ex-RAF pilot like Freeman. He had built up a fleet of Dove aircraft on charter work, much of it to racecourse meetings on such a regular basis that it almost amounted to a scheduled service. Morton had also won the right to scheduled flights from Croydon to the Channel Islands, Deauville, Le Touquet and Rotterdam. Morton succumbed to Airwork's offer.

A substantial stake in Bristow Helicopters was bought a little later. Freddie was already part of Airwork and holidaying triumphantly in the Caribbean where he met Alan Bristow, a fierce, unrelenting operator who was a genius with helicopters.

Laker told Bristow, 'I've just sold out to Airwork. Why don't you?'

What made Bristow particularly attractive to the growing group was that Airwork had a loss-making helicopter subsidiary, half owned by Fisons, involved in crop spraying. Freddie was authorized to deal with Bristow, which he did with his normal hard-bargaining enthusiasm.

Hunting was a different kettle of fish altogether. It was in many ways another Airwork. The original Hunting interests had split in two, with one side an aircraft manufacturer and the other, Hunting Air Transport, becoming the subsidiary of Clan Line, another shipping group, although some of the Hunting family still sat on the board. Hunting Clan were partners with Airwork in the colonial coach services into Africa and shared the 30 per cent slice of freight and tourist business that they finally won from BOAC in the middle of 1957 thanks to Harold Watkinson.

Hunting Clan in turn was part of the giant British and Commonwealth Shipping group, controlled by the Cayzer family headed by Sir Nicholas Cayzer. The Cayzers, like Airwork shareholders, were steeped in shipping and saw aviation as a threatening competitor in which it would be wise to have a stake. Moreover, their own airline, Hunting Clan, had also suddenly run into some nasty problems with one of the biggest sides of its flying: trooping. After underquoting for the latest contract Hunting was losing money, while at the same time Freddie was picking up its operational pieces by subcontracting his own Britannias to Hunting Clan.

Trooping was still vitally important to the independents, but over the years the Government had squeezed prices until the profit margins had become almost invisible. In 1957 a committee of inquiry headed by Sir Miles Thomas reported that, 'So meagre is the return from the principal source of the independents' revenue that the committee finds it difficult to believe that the majority of these companies can continue to operate indefinitely on their present basis of earnings.'

Ironically, the Tories' initiative in creating a second-force airline embodying most of the independents had the effect of bringing the War Office's 'divide and rule' method of allocating trooping contracts to an end by reducing the number of competitors.

Prime Minister Harold Macmillan brought Duncan Sandys into the Ministry of Supply in autumn 1959 with the express intention of having him break it up and create a separate Ministry of Aviation that could concentrate on the aircraft manufacturers' problems.

Sandys was at first reluctant to take on what was an obviously difficult job. The various aircraft companies were strong-minded and independent. They were taking ever-increasing sums of public money – more than £4 million for the Comet's development, about £5 million for the Viscounts and nearly £6 million for the Britannia – and quite clearly not all of them could expect to survive, as aircraft projects became fewer yet ever more expensive and riskier to launch.

Under Sandys's tough rule as Minister of Aviation, the pace of the mergers accelerated. Bristol was added to the TSR2 partnership of Vickers and English Electric to make a more permanent one in the form of the British Aircraft Corporation. Hawker Siddeley swallowed de Havilland, Blackburn and Folland to become the industry's other pillar.

Sandys made it clear that he intended to apply much the same merger prescription to the independent airlines in the run-up to the Civil Aviation Licensing Act of 1960. 'I have been encouraging the independent airlines to get together and form stronger units and I am glad to say that good progress is being made,' he told the Commons during a debate on the new Act. To underline his message, he called the chairmen of the airlines in one by one to explain his new policy to them.

When he also made it clear that the Act's creation, the Air Transport Licensing Board, would have the power to demand that applicants for routes demonstrate the strength of their financial resources and engineering capability as well as operating standards, this was no time to hesitate. Within a year or so at least six airlines merged.

While the lesser airlines were chasing each other around the pond, within Airwork it was widely believed that Sandys had put it directly to Wyatt that his airline should take the lead in rationalizing the industry. With its powerful and ambitious shareholders, Airwork certainly lacked neither will nor resources. Nor did Wyatt need any encouragement.

The Cayzers were not, however, interested in a quick sale. They wanted far more than that. If there was going to be a major new airline they were not going to let it belong to their shipping rivals. This was no takeover: this was going to be a full-scale merger.

By March 1960 the two airlines had confirmed the merger. Some 72 per cent of the shares in the new group were held by shipping companies: Blue Star, Furness Withy and British and Commonwealth. The Hunting Group owned 8 per cent, Loel Guinness and Whitehall Securities, the Cowdray company, 10 per cent each. The balance of power had shifted, with the Cayzers becoming the dominant shareholder.

One of the main problems was the name. The Cayzers were certainly not going to let Hunting Clan operate under the name Airwork. Gerry Freeman solved this. He asked Duncan Sandys to use his influence with the Board of Trade to allow the group to be called British United Airways on the understanding that it would not contract the name to BUA and cause confusion with BEA.

By the beginning of 1960, nearly all the pieces of BUA had been brought together. On the main board were Sir Nicholas Cayzer and his nephew the Hon. Anthony, plus Clive Hunting, a jovial, helpful businessman with no interest in becoming involved in day-to-day management at BUA. Neither had the major Airwork shareholders.

But if the shareholders wanted to sit back and collect their dividends, the same was not true of the freewheeling, hard-driving entrepreneurs that had just been bought up. In the big arena of BUA there were a pack of hard-bitten free-enterprise gladiators, all survivors of the fifteen-year elimination contest of independent aviation. Newly rich, they were no longer working just for money. Freddie, for example, did not need his salary of £5,000 a year. What they were used to, though, was power.

BUA was a group in name only. Each of the executive directors ran his own company as an independent fief, jealous of his authority and resentful of any interference from the main board. If any of Freddie's employees wanted to do anything, they went to him. He raised it at board meetings and then went back with the decision. When he could, he gave his approval first and then presented the board with a *fait accompli*. It was obvious that someone had to have overall authority if BUA was to make any progress. Although no one said so, the answer was trial by combat.

The contenders had to have an excuse for fighting, but it did not take long before the battleground emerged. Effectively it was a matter of patronage. Each of the independent companies had brought in its own chief accountant, chief engineer, general manager, chief pilot and sales manager. Their quality varied considerably, reflecting the calibre of their chief.

Freddie had Jack Wiseman, Alan Nicholls, Norman Jennings, Bob Batt and Dougie Whybrow as his front-line team. Gerry Freeman's top-line man was his chief engineer, Bill Richardson, and his general manager was Cliff Nunn.

Hunting effectively had no chief executive – one of the reasons why the merger was important to it. Airwork was run by Myles Wyatt, with a modest Scotsman called Bob Cumming as accountant, and a former night-fighter pilot, Wing Commander the Honourable Kensington Davison, DFC, DSO, brother of Lord Broughshane and now fund-raiser for Covent Garden Opera House, as general manager. And there was a quiet but effective engineer/accountant called George Carroll.

It was clear from the start that only Wyatt, Freeman and Laker were serious contenders for the job of running BUA.

On paper, Gerry Freeman had the best claim. In 1959 Transair had made a profit of £400,000 making it the most profitable part of Airwork. Freeman's business was run with a smooth efficiency that reflected good systems and a rigid attention to detail. As a person he was easy-talking, enthusiastic and knowledgeable.

Freddie, twelve years younger at thirty-seven, was overweight and ebullient, bursting with ideas and enthusiasm and contemptuous of red tape and paperwork.

Overshadowing them both was Myles Wyatt. Wyatt was huge, well over six foot and exceptionally heavily-built – eighteen stone of solid muscle and fat. He was twenty years older than Freddie and a powerful member of the establishment and Admiral of the Royal Ocean Racing Club to which he had recently presented what was to become known as the Admiral's Cup.

Wyatt dressed in the peculiarly dated style of the pre-war gentleman that has been perpetuated by London's most expensive tailors as long as possible. He wore thick woollen pin-striped suits, the voluminous trousers held at chest height by wide red felt braces, and tiny, pebble-lensed round glasses. He ran Airwork the way he sailed his yacht *Bloodhound* – autocratically. His position was very strong. With none of the BUA shareholders in control of a majority of the equity, Wyatt could divide and rule as he wished.

Very often the Airwork staff would see Wyatt leaving their West End offices at about 4pm, an old brown trilby on his head, on his way to the City for a private chat with one or other of the shareholders. They had established their own committee which took key decisions. As the only link between the committee and the airline's board, Wyatt's position was very strong. Board meetings themselves never lasted more than twenty minutes when he was in the chair. All the decisions had been made beforehand with Wyatt, if necessary, playing shareholders and directors off against each other.

Wyatt had joined Airwork in 1934 and was a past master at corporate politics. It was the first time Freddie had come up against someone who was his match. Wyatt was older, bigger, tougher, better educated, better connected, better bred and something of a bully. Not that that stopped Freddie, but for once he was up against the head of the herd. To begin with, though, neither he nor Freeman realized quite what a barrier Wyatt was.

The three met in Freeman's Eaton Square flat to thrash out the problem. Freeman, it was decided, should be in charge of all the group's short-haul operations in the UK and Europe. Transair was the obvious vehicle in which to concentrate all BUA's local activities. Laker was to take charge of the long-haul business, the trooping flights and long-distance charter.

Then the question of subordinate roles came up. Freeman wanted Bill Richardson as group chief engineer and Kensington Davison, he stated categorically, was not quite the man to be general manager.

Wyatt told them he could not continue in an executive role if he was seen to have failed to support his own men. Surprising the other two, he suggested that the simple solution was for him to give up his job as chief executive and take a back seat, leaving the other two to dispose of the top jobs and him free to disclaim any responsibility.

It was a tactical withdrawal in the face of the other two's united front. Laker told him, 'I'm not going to be your bum boy, Myles.'

Wyatt, however, had no intention of resigning his position. For one thing he was entitled to a percentage of the profits of BUA. When the new group was formed, City accountants Deloitte, Plender and Griffiths had advised the BUA board that its best tactic would be not to create a new company but change the name from Airwork in order to retain the losses made on the ill-fated freight operation for tax purposes. These were still in the books because the firm had equally subtly persuaded the Inland Revenue that the profit made by Wyatt on selling the rights to the DC–6s was a capital gain because, 'Airwork did not trade in aeroplanes'. So Airwork became BUA and Myles Wyatt stayed in the same job.

Another factor was that the chairmanship almost certainly meant a knighthood. Not that this was a deciding factor, although Wyatt did have a brother who had collected a KBE in 1949 as a vice-admiral and Hydrographer of the Navy. But the power, that was something else.

Wyatt retreated from the meeting leaving Freeman convinced that he had made his point. He couldn't have been more wrong. Wyatt met Freddie alone and did another deal. This made Laker managing director and left Wyatt in control as executive chairman. Freddie had written to Wyatt saying that he was more than capable of running all BUA. Wyatt told Freeman that he had settled Freddie's outstanding claim for £200,000 for Aviation Traders' stockpile of spares.

Gerry Freeman resigned and left BUA entirely. There was a bitter exchange of letters which he still keeps, but he says now that he thinks it was probably for the best. He would still be there today otherwise.

Ostensibly, Laker was a victor in the skirmishing for power in BUA, but he still had a lot to learn from Myles Wyatt. It was the first time that Freddie had been involved in really big business. It was a basic teaching period regarding the way the City worked, how to float companies, how to borrow really substantial sums. He learned at lightning speed.

At first the invisible puppet strings that Myles Wyatt had tied to Laker did not affect him and he was unconscious of them. He found he had George Carroll as his personal assistant, but they formed an immediate bond of friendship. Carroll had come from a grammar school background and never been at ease in the upper-class manners of Airwork where small charters were designated FJ for fiddly jobs. He felt relaxed with Laker as well as full of admiration at his drive and ideas.

Although Freddie was outweighed by Wyatt, he had some attributes which his new chairman could not match. He was far more knowledgeable about aeroplanes, for a start. His relationship with the group's pilots and engineers was on a basis of practical equality which coupled with his charismatic personality made him instantly acceptable. Everywhere he went in BUA he won personal adherents who were only too delighted to find someone to whom to give their allegiance.

On top of that he was intuitively perceptive about what was needed in the future. The fundamental difference between Laker and Wyatt was that the former was intensely interested in planes and what they could do. BUA's chairman was more in love with yachts than planes. In the long run, Freddie's innovations were to prove far more important to both BUA and British aviation as a whole than Myles Wyatt's power politics.

Chapter 8

'I'll take ten if it will do what you say'

The new airline's most immediate objective was to seize the opportunity offered by the Civil Aviation Act introduced in February 1960. The Act confirmed licences for the route networks airlines were currently operating. More importantly, however, the state corporations' monopoly of scheduled service operations was repealed. In future any airline seeking a route was at liberty to apply to a new body, the Air Transport Licensing Board.

Freddie Laker reacted swiftly. Most people in the industry had assumed that the new Act would, at least at first, lead to a few exploratory applications for routes, but by the start of 1961 Laker was making it clear that BUA was going for bigger things. MPs were circulated with a report from the airline saying that it planned to buy up to £20 million worth of British jets and spare parts if it got the routes it was applying for – over twenty of them.

At BUA, Airwork's Ken Sangster had been given the task of drawing up the applications to present to the ATLB. They had to be accompanied by detailed economic and factual arguments in support of the applicant's case. It was a wholly new task and no one seemed to have much idea of how to go about it.

In desperation, Laker placed a phone call to Alastair Pugh, a de Havilland-trained aeronautical engineer and then a senior journalist on *Flight* magazine, who was his newest recruit. Pugh was meant to join the cross-channel car ferry company, Channel Air Bridge, but Laker's message was terse: don't go there, come to BUA first. At BUA, with only ten days to go to the critical hearing before the ATLB in June 1961, Pugh discovered that the strain was driving poor Sangster round the bend. Most of the material prepared made little sense. It was almost gibberish.

BEA set the pattern for future years by opposing the upstart

BUA's application as vigorously as it knew how. Wyatt had initially tried to defuse the confrontation by seeking a meeting with BEA's chairman, Lord Douglas of Kirtleside. Blunt, forceful Kirtleside, who had sworn to see the independents damned before he gave way, told Wyatt that he could see nothing useful to be achieved from a meeting. 'This is in fact a head-on clash of interests . . . I can see no common ground between us,' he wrote.

At the hearings, held in the ATLB's offices in a new block in the City of London, Henry Marking, then BEA's lawyer and company secretary, led the airline's team. Marking, later to become the airline's chief executive – just as Pugh was eventually to become managing director of another of its rivals, British Caledonian – put a cracking good case forward. Pugh, watching him duelling with BUA's QC, Gerald (now Lord) Gardiner, who posed the question whether, after fifteen years of state monopoly, BEA could stand a reasonable amount of competition, was aware that the days of amicable amateurism were over.

The hearing was crucial. It represented a chance to break away from the catch-as-catch-can business of charters and the military contracts that could as easily be lost as won. With the heavy metal on BUA's board, raising finance ought to present no problems.

The ATLB's verdict was important to Freddie. BUA's brash, thrusting young managing director had already taken the boldest decision of his career to date, one which many in business thought a staggering gamble. He had been as good as his word to the MPs. A month before the hearing, Laker startled an industry more used to wondering where the cash was coming from to buy clapped-out piston-engined aircraft by ordering, not one, but two fleets of jets: ten BAC 1–11s and four VC–10s, costing together nearly £20 million.

This was a bid for the big league with a vengeance and a measure of Laker's aggressive self-confidence. Even today airlines view introducing a new aircraft type into their fleet with some trepidation. Laker seemed to be preparing a plunge straight from the high board into the deep end. BUA had never operated jets. The VC–10s were large, complicated four-engined transports but they were at least flying. The 1–11s were still only on the drawing board. 'When I decided that BUA should put two new jets into operation in the same year, a lot of people said I was mad to do so,' Laker said afterwards. 'Well, partly I was working on a hunch. But the hunch was based on a lot of technical knowledge.'

One big advantage to the gamble was the identity of interest and ambition between airline and manufacturers. Laker and BUA wanted to make their mark in the big league. At the equally new British Aircraft Corporation, formed from a merger of Vickers's aviation business with Bristol Aircraft, Laker's friend, and its marketing director, Geoffrey Knight, was just as keen to see BAC prosper. Freddie had a potentially important role to play in this goal. BEA, normally the obvious target for launching any new British short-haul aircraft, had opted for the Trident, built by BAC's rival, Hawker Siddeley. Laker and BUA were the only major alternative British customer for BAC.

The friendship between Knight and Laker dated back to the Air Charter days when Knight, then with Bristol, had regular contacts over sales of Bristol Britannias and Freighters. By the early 1960s, they were rarely out of each other's pockets.

Before the merger that created BAC, Vickers at Weybridge had begun studying the Vanjet, a Vanguard-style fuselage but with jet engines. They had burned their fingers badly with the original turbo-prop Vanguard, a larger replacement for the Viscount. When the Vanguard was launched, the Vickers team knew that jets were coming but reasoned that the airlines would prefer the turbo-prop's lower operating costs. This proved not to be the case.

BOAC's decision in May 1957 to open negotiations for thirty-five VC-10s had pushed the Vanjet to one side. But in 1960, the Vickers designers were keen to revive a similar project. Knight, from the Bristol team that had gone into the BAC melting pot, was equally determined to stop another 'bus' like the Vanguard being resuscitated as the 130-seat VC-11. What chances he had of diverting BAC's plans rested with the Hunting 107 – a paper project that came to BAC when it acquired the aircraft manufacturing side of Hunting.

During 1960 salesmen had been given the job of sounding out world airlines about a new aircraft based on the 107. Visits were made to over seventy airlines. There was a lot of enthusiasm for a new twin jet, particularly one offering better costs and more space than the French Caravelle. As all this market information flowed back, Weybridge's chief designer was analysing and refining the project. The 107 was getting bigger and the fuselage wider. But by the time the aircraft had grown to a sixty-seater with the range pushing towards six hundred miles, the engines were at full stretch with little more power to be won from them.

Sir George Edwards, who had been concentrating on the VC–11, began to take a greater interest in the 107. His suggestion that the designers take the basic airframe they had developed but re-engine it with the more powerful Rolls-Royce Spey that was being used in the Trident gave the project new impetus. Almost overnight the dainty 107 had become a much bigger aircraft – upwards of seventy seats with a thousand-mile range.

Laker was seeking a new aircraft for BUA as a Viscount replacement but there was nothing suitable on offer outside America. His preference was to buy British and what was to become the 1–11 emerged at a lunch Knight arranged between Laker and Edwards. Knight sat and watched as they thrashed out the key features of the aircraft with Laker insisting on even more performance than BAC were offering.

By the coffee stage, the deal was done. Freddie simply said: 'I'll take ten if it will do what you say it will.'

Back at the office, Freddie told his executive assistant, Mick Sidebotham, 'We've got an *aeroplane*.' Taken aback, Sidebotham asked what sort of aircraft they had got. Surely Freddie hadn't committed them to the 107, which was much too small? No, it wasn't that, Laker said, but Sidebotham had better get down to BAC at Weybridge the next morning and start thrashing out the details. All Sidebotham had to go on was a quarto sheet of paper with a dozen or so features of the aircraft on it. Even so it was clear what Laker wanted and Sidebotham added in his own target: the new aircraft had to improve on BUA's Viscounts, the latest models of which could carry sixty-four package-tour passengers non-stop from London to Gibraltar. Laker's enthusiastic support was vital but not sufficient in itself. The BAC sales engineers led by Derek Lambert took the latest version of the 1–11 to show to US airlines, Braniff and Continental especially among the larger airlines and Mohawk and North Central among the regional carriers.

Braniff, with a high proportion of short-haul routes in its system, was keen to get into detailed specification talks. By now it was clear to BAC that to have worldwide appeal, the aircraft would have to be closely tailored to the US market. Would BUA give up some of its own ideas and preferences to widen the 1–11's sales appeal? The answer was yes and the final detailed negotiations were left to Sidebotham and John Prothero Thomas, BAC's airline development engineer. (Today both men are directors of British Caledonian.)

BAC's goal was to produce an aircraft that had as much as possible in common with the Boeing 720 that looked like dominating the US market for medium-range jets. To encourage airlines to run the 1–11 as a junior team-mate to the 720, BAC gave it the same sort of generators, air-conditioning units and instruments among other items of equipment. Even the seat-track widths were the same.

Sidebotham's worry was that the changes would add to the aircraft's weight and eat into its payload. He discussed this with Laker and told him they would need to keep weight strictly under control. 'Fine,' said Laker. 'I will carry that message to BAC and lay it on with a trowel.' Sidebotham had already come to recognize Freddie as one of the finest exponents of negotiating histrionics he had met and knew that his idea of a trowel was more like a rogue elephant battering through the jungle. When Freddie said Sidebotham should not be surprised if there was a reaction, his assistant was more than amused.

'Blue-eyed, prick-eared bums' was one of the milder epithets Freddie hurled at the luckless BAC negotiators. Launching a strenuous verbal assault on their specification, he claimed that they had ruined the aircraft. It was too heavy. It was a bureaucratic bit of nonsense, he said, accusing them of that worst of all sins.

Taking over the talks, Laker spent the next few days ruthlessly trying to get the best possible deal for BUA. He knew he had the edge over BAC. British European Airways had expressed total lack of interest in the 1–11 and Laker's willingness to compromise over the US specification had strengthened his hand still further.

Thomas, a comparatively junior manager at BAC, found himself facing a man whom many aircraft salesmen acknowledge as the toughest, hardest negotiator they have ever come up against. He has great charm but he also uses blustering, bullying techniques to keep his opponent off balance. He goes at his foe, left and right, all the time, leaving no breathing space. Thomas was no exception. Laker took every possible advantage of his lack of seniority. 'I'm going to have that for free,' Laker said, citing one item in the specification.

When Thomas demurred, pointing out the cost, Laker rounded on him, 'Who are you to say I can't have it? I had dinner last night with Sir George and he promised it to me.' Thomas had no idea whether this was simply Freddie trying to outwit him in the negotiations but recognized he was capitalizing on the situation and fought back as best he could.

In sharp contrast to the bruising negotiations with Thomas, fixing the price and credit arrangements for the purchase of the 1–11 seemed agreeably casual. In early 1961, Knight wanted to pin down the price ready for the spring board meeting. He had been talking the matter back and forth with Laker on the telephone when Laker said: 'Hell, there's not much point in this.' So off he and Knight went to the races at Sandown where the price was fixed in the paddock during the third and fourth races. Freddie wasn't being quite as casual as he appeared. He had kept in close touch with the detailed specification talks, and had told Sidebotham to say nothing about money. They would wait until all the parts of the jigsaw fell into place and then Freddie would 'round up' the price. The final sum added up to £740,000 per aircraft. BAC got their launching airline but Laker got his jets at a very keen price.

Edwards, the driving force behind Concorde and executive director of aircraft at BAC, is blunt at the best of times and never one to tolerate fools. Laker clearly made a very deep impression on him. Some years after the launch of the 1–11, he told the Royal Aeronautical Society that Laker was a man of character, substance and guts. He was the sort of man, he said, that this country had bred in the past. 'A few hundred years ago he would have had brass ear-rings, a beard, a bit longer hair and a cutlass.' For good measure Edwards added, 'there are few people in this world who can give you a kick and you are happy as Larry when you have had it. Mr Laker is one of the few on my list.'[6]

The launch became a gentleman's agreement between Edwards and Laker. Laker had already won Edwards's trust. With anyone else, it would have been regarded as risky in the extreme to have an independent launching a new aircraft. BAC had been talking about the 'little jet' at Weybridge since 1956 but it was launched on the back of Laker's order. A message went to Knight from Edwards saying, 'We're going to build it. We'll call it the 1–11 – that's symbolic for BAC and Vickers.'

On 9 May 1961, BUA became the first airline in the world to order the new short-haul jet with a commitment to take ten of them worth £8 million. In the event Laker was a better customer for the 1–11. If BEA had selected it, becoming the new jet's launching airline, Knight and his colleagues feel it would have been harder to sell it in other countries, especially America. Any aircraft for BEA had to be tailored for its European network and its short but busy routes. Laker's insistence on the 1–11 being able to carry a full load of passengers to further-flung Mediterranean destinations like Malta and Gibraltar bred a longer-range aircraft.

It was not easy for BAC's designers to respond to Laker's pressure for a better payload-range curve but the end product proved ideal for the longer 'short-haul' routes in the valuable US market. Five months after Laker's bold order, the 1–11 made its breakthrough into the US market when Braniff ordered six with options on six more. Within the next three years, two more US airlines, Mohawk and American joined Braniff in placing a succession of orders for the 1–11. Kuwait, Central African Airways and Aer Lingus became customers as well, turning the 1–11 into one of Britain's rare aerospace successes.

With the 1–11, Laker was a one-man computer. Before the apparently casual fixing of prices at the races, Laker did his own detailed evaluations, studying payload-range curves for months beforehand, evaluating the aircraft's economics and seat-mile costs.

When the 1–11 was being built, Freddie poked about the BAC works. Anyone except Laker would have been evicted from the plant in exasperation for the constant intervention, interest and attention to detail he showed, but so much of it was done with high good humour. Norman Barfield, a BAC engineer, was invited to BUA's London headquarters at Portland House, near Victoria, to give a talk about the aircraft's interior and operational factors. At the end, Laker pounced on him with what he said was 'a new bit of 1–11 promotion'. The problem, however, was how to distribute a new toy, an ash tray with a swept fin in the middle. 'Let's go to the pub,' said Laker. 'We'll stick them on the bar. They are bound to get nicked that way.'

Chapter 9

'A complete rebuild'

While Laker was still closely involved in the final details of the 1–11's design and the early build-up of production, BUA took yet another major leap upwards in size with the announcement in January 1962 of the acquisition of one of the largest independents left, British Air Services. Three months earlier in November 1961, BUA had paved the way for this acquisition, making it clear that Wyatt's plan to create a private sector giant was not yet complete, when Air Holdings was created for 'the purpose of amalgamation'. Once this had been formed secret merger talks began with British Air Services with the deal being concluded by Air Holdings buying the shares of both airlines.

Buying BAS was a major coup, making BUA almost half the size of BEA and more than half the capacity of the independent sector. With total assets of about £20 million and more than 4,000 employees, the new combine was probably the largest private airline outside the US at that time.

The acquisition was a take-over, if not quite a rape, rather than a merger. British Air Services, owned by yet another shipping company, this time P&O which had 70 per cent, Eagle Star (20 per cent) and Cable & Wireless, the state-owned international communications company (10 per cent), had been piling up heavy losses. Its biggest component was Silver City Airways.

Once the merger had been agreed in principle between Wyatt and P&O chairman Sir Donald Anderson, Laker dominated the detailed talks, making it clear from the outset who was going to be master. Silver City's management, led by Eoin Meckie, a lawyer from Glasgow, had made careful preparations at their headquarters for the first meeting with chairs and nameplates distributed round the table, splitting Laker's team up. Laker strolled in, took in the arrangements at a glance and ostentatiously settled himself on a sofa under the window, gesturing to Carroll, Richardson and Atkinson to make themselves comfortable where they liked. The talks stretched on through the afternoon and into the evening as Laker, uncharacteristically, sat virtually silent, conceding nothing.

Laker's men were contemptuous of the Silver City management, which they felt had got out of its depth in an effort to diversify into trooping flights with a fleet of Hermes. Meckie and his colleagues responded churlishly by not offering Laker and his men so much as a cup of tea. After nearly six hours the meeting had made little progress and broke up. Laker simply went off and settled the details without further consultation with Silver City's management. As a final snub, BAS men got only two seats on the board of the joint company and Meckie got nothing.

The merger between Silver City and BUA wiped out car-ferry competition at a stroke. Since Silver City's first car flight from Lydd to Le Touquet, the Channel ferry business had grown apace. But Laker's own ferry airline, Channel Air Bridge, had intensified competition. By the time of the merger of BUA and BAS, Channel Air Bridge had become a large business, accounting for a quarter of BUA's one million passengers. The addition of its rival's 650,000 ferry passengers pushed the combined total close to one million.

Whether even Channel Air Bridge was making money out of it is questionable. Although Silver City did better in 1960 and 1961, it had heavy accumulated losses to wipe off. Even without competition, carrying cars by air was never a very easy business. Between 1950 and 1959, the average length of British cars rose ten inches, an embarrassment for the bulbous Bristol freighters whose fuselages had only been long enough to carry three average cars originally. If a booked car failed to turn up, it was a disaster. The one-third cut in payload automatically turned the flight into a loss-maker. The extreme weekend peaks and the British custom of packing summer holidays into the weeks from the end of July to the start of September made for poor utilization of aircraft in the off-peak period.

When the traffic was there, the aircraft had to be worked flat out to make money. Turn-round had to be completed in twenty minutes and even this represented a substantial portion of the thirty minutes' flying time on the short routes. Repeated landings and short flights in turbulent air at lower altitudes also took their toll of the Bristols. They were prone to structural fatigue problems and the airworthiness authorities laid down rigorous and costly modification programmes.

Quite clearly the rapidly ageing Bristols could not go on for much longer. But without them, or at least a suitable replacement, there would be no business. What was needed was a quieter, faster aircraft capable of carrying twenty-five passengers and five British-sized cars, with a purchase price of around £200,000. Several aircraft manufacturers proposed replacements, all of them too costly to be practical.

Such a problem defeated conventional airline thinking. But for Laker, one of the industry's most inventive minds and most consistent of lateral thinkers, with a canny knack of turning to his own purpose other people's aircraft rejects, there had to be some less costly solution. The answer came to him in the bath and he scrambled, wet and dripping, for the telephone to call Jack Wiseman, chief engineer down at Aviation Traders in Southend.

'Jack, go down to the airport and measure the DC-4 at certain points in the fuselage,' he said.

'What the hell do you want that for?' Wiseman asked.

Laker told him he wanted to convert the DC-4 to carry cars. Wiseman did the measuring on the DC-4, and Freddie rushed down into his garage and measured his car. By evening he'd made a cardboard model DC-4 with doors in the nose and the cockpit perched on top.

When Wiseman and the rest of the Aviation Traders team, still largely untouched by their absorption into the BUA group, still very much Laker's men, came to examine the idea in detail, the DC-4 proved ideal. With the advent of the new jets, the Boeing 707 and the Douglas DC-8, there were plenty of surplus DC-4s around on the market for as little as £50,000, which could be converted for about £80,000. Its payload was right, its width slightly more than the Bristols and if the flight deck was raised its hold was just five cars long. The low-altitude cross-Channel flights did not go high enough to need a pressurized cabin and the DC-4's lack of pressurization, while out-of-date for longer flights, made the structural conversion straightforward.

A hundred hours of wind-tunnel tests soon established the best shape for the new aircraft, christened the ATL98 Carvair. 'It was a complete rebuild,' says Laker. 'We kept the wings and the wheels and the tail section of the DC–4 and built a new nose on it and put the crew above the fuselage.' Rerouting the controls, nearly all of them mechanical, from the cockpit, proved one of the trickiest jobs. In the end, with the use of nearly six hundred additional pulleys, many hundreds of cast brackets and over six changes of direction, the work was completed.

Chief test pilot Don Cartlidge was sceptical at flying this curious hybrid but after practising on an RAF Beverley, where the pilot's eye level, as in the Carvair, was twenty-five feet above the ground, he found little problem. Apart from increasing the cargo space, the conversion had surprisingly little impact on the original DC–4's performance. Cruise speed fell by only four knots compared to the wind-tunnel test's predicted eight to ten and with disc brakes the landing distance was slightly less than before.

The Carvair was granted a full certificate of airworthiness at the same time as the BUA-Silver City merger. With it, British United Air Ferries, as it became known a year later, was able to extend its range of flight further into Europe, the 'deep' routes as they were called, where the Carvair's better range and economics supposedly came into their own. In 1960 licences had been granted for services to Lyons, Strasbourg, Dusseldorf and Bremen. By 1962 flights were going as far as Basle and Geneva.

Apart from the ten Carvairs that went to BUA and Channel Air Bridge, six other airlines, among them Aer Lingus, Aviaco in Spain and Ansett in Australia, bought eleven aircraft between them for freight operations.

As a car carrier, the Carvair was not quite up to expectations. Operating an aircraft that was much larger, more complex and inevitably more expensive to maintain than the Bristol proved difficult on the short routes which had relied for their appeal on frequencies of as much as sixty flights a day. The aircraft themselves were getting long in the tooth. There were few DC–4s in service with less than 30,000 hours and the first to undergo Carvair surgery was the original Yankee Bravo Freddie had bought from Ed Daley with 37,000 hours on its log. Nor with newer aircraft in the group fleet did the engineering staff have time for the luxury of cosseting the venerable DC–4s.

Though the Carvair failed to live up to its promise, the intense pressure to maintain the profitability of the air ferries meant that the management were always on the lookout for some new transport technology. The hovercraft looked a likely possibility. SRN1 made the first cross-channel trip in July 1959, and later the same year Whybrow suggested these might be a possibility for carrying cars. Even so the idea hung fire until, just after Christmas 1961, Myles Wyatt began to take a serious interest in the hovercraft's possibilities.

Months of study followed and a whole series of meetings in Laker's Wigmore Street office between Channel Air Bridge management, Hovercraft Developments Ltd, the craft's inventor, Christopher (now Sir Christopher) Cockerell, and Laker. Finally by May 1961, however, they had begun to talk about a first possible trial route across the Bristol Channel from Cardiff to Weston-super-Mare using the SRN2.

As the talks went on into the early hours of the morning, Whybrow came up with a counter-proposal. His family home was in the Flintshire hills in North Wales and he knew the area well. Why not run the service across the sands of the River Dee's five-mile-wide estuary, so linking Merseyside and North Wales?

Hovercraft Developments still favoured the Cardiff route but the decision was tipped in favour of the Dee when Alastair Pugh, then Channel Air Bridge's project and development manager, was able to make a reconnaissance flight in *Flight International*'s Miles Gemini. What he saw looking down from the Gemini helped convince BUA. The access roads were poor, the terminal sites unpromising and the Weston beach especially exposed.

After learning that the SRN2 would be tied up on naval trials and would not be available, BUA opened talks with Vickers which was working on hovercraft development. Vickers made it clear that the company was keen on running a joint service. Its hovercraft team was worried that Britain's lead in this exciting new technology might soon be frittered away for lack of some bold or imaginative approach to operations. And BUA seemed to offer just what was needed.

The project was nearly swamped with enthusiasm. BUA's shipping shareholders, Furness Withy and British and Commonwealth, offered the services of young masters as trainee hovercraft pilots. The Mersey Docks and Harbour Board promised its facilities and the Dee and Clwyd River Board unveiled a large-scale model of the estuary. And well before the start of the world's first scheduled hovercraft service on 20 July 1962, the bookings were already flowing into BUA's office in Piccadilly.

Carrying some 20,000 passengers in a brief summer season, the novel twenty-five-minute service demonstrated its public appeal. But the technology was still at a primitive stage.

The engines, Dart turbines normally used on Viscounts, were not adapted to the harsh marine environment and had to be returned to Rolls-Royce frequently to have the salt washed out with distilled water.

BUA did not lose by running the hovercraft service. The basic formula meant Vickers paying most of the costs and BUA taking the revenue. Certainly there never seems to have been any danger of the exciting new technology overwhelming the financial nous of Laker's team.

There was also a rich publicity harvest. BUA's press officer, Elizabeth de Stroumillo, felt that Laker mainly saw the service as yet one more opportunity to put BUA on the map. The specially printed souvenir tickets claimed eight firsts for BUA, ranging from having the first aircraft company to spray crops from the air to being the first airline to order the 1–11.

Massive press coverage of the service was organized. Rides on the hovercraft were programmed according to journalists' deadlines. BUA-Bristow helicopters took photographers out. Elizabeth de Stroumillo organized three days of special flights for daily, evening, magazine, and finally trade and technical journalists. She had a terrible time coping with frustrated press men and the continual breakdowns. Frequently one of Bristow's helicopters would fly out to see where the hovercraft was and signal back that it had broken down half-way across. The service's first and only season ended with a near disaster when the local lifeboat had to retrieve the hovercraft which had broken adrift from its moorings in a gale.

Laker came away with at least one funny story as well. He and George Carroll had been up there to check how things were going and were having a game of snooker in a Rhyl hotel with two visitors. 'Bloody hovercraft,' said one of them.

'What do you mean?' queried Laker.

'I've just paid £50 a week for a beach bungalow and there are two thousand bloody people standing outside it in the queue,' complained his opponent.

With no more than a handful of civil hovercraft operations in the world today – and many of these still struggling to make a profit – Laker scarcely missed a bonanza.

The days of the car-ferry business were numbered. Traffic peaked in 1962 at 137,000 cars and was down to 101,000 within three years.

In spite of the start of a new service to Liège in 1964, the decline was irrevocable. As business began to drop away, BUA began a steady policy of retrenchment. The deep routes were closed in 1967 and within a year its share of the cross-channel traffic was down to 5 per cent from 27 per cent at its peak.

Chapter 10

'You cannot have two crashes!'

The £4 million or so BUA earned from trooping each year at the start of the 1960s – just over half its revenue – emphasized the importance of this business for the airline. Buying Silver City cut back the competition for these service flights to just Eagle and in October 1961 BUA had little difficulty picking up an important contract to carry 11,000 forces personnel a month between Britain and Germany.

Wyatt and Laker knew this business was vulnerable. The RAF, which had begun to build up its transport capability in the late 1950s, was already taking a growing percentage of the business and would carry more. The unstable nature of trooping and the beginnings of the decline in the car-ferry business underlined the importance of building a scheduled route network.

Amateurish though that early application to the Air Transport Licensing Board for licences had been, BUA was awarded a series of European scheduled route licences in November 1961, a few weeks after the start of a Viscount service from Gatwick to Tenerife in the Canaries. A trading profit of over £2 million had just been announced as well. Prospects looked good for BUA.

True to its chairman's warning that he saw BUA's bids for scheduled routes as a head-on clash of interests, BEA was still fighting the rising independent at every turn. The two airlines had fallen out in summer 1961 when BUA tried to lease some of BEA's unused land at Gatwick for its base. Now in the autumn, BUA was disappointed to discover that while it could operate to Paris, Genoa, Amsterdam, Milan, Zurich, Madeira, Basle, Athens, Barcelona, Tarbes, Palma and Malaga, it would have to wait seventeen months until April 1963 to allow BEA to adjust. In addition BEA appealed against the route award. Disappointed that the ATLB had awarded it fewer routes than hoped for, BUA, with a large new jet fleet on order, commented that 'even taking the most optimistic view, it is certain that the board have left us no margin'.

Aviation Minister Julian Amery squashed BEA's appeal in September 1962 but if BUA thought this was the end of its troubles, there was worse to come. As Wyatt wryly remarked: 'A stranger to this strange industry might suppose that once a licence has been confirmed by the Minister, the coast would be clear for the licensee to start operations without further ado.' Despite the fact that the original application and the appeal had cost thousands of pounds, Wyatt and Laker now faced even greater problems getting foreign governments to approve the new BUA services.

The Greeks were the first to underline how difficult this would be by ruling against the BUA service to Athens in December 1962. Rights to Paris were to meet rock-solid resistance (they were only to be won ten years later) as well as those to Milan. Nor were the ones to Switzerland obtained.

By late spring 1963 BUA had only been able to start flights to Tarbes, Barcelona, Palma and Genoa – all highly seasonal and difficult to operate profitably. The Genoa run had involved yet another row with BEA. Laker accused the state airline of 'machinations' when it attempted to get BUA's licence to Genoa revoked.

The start of the new scheduled services proved a disappointment. By August, Laker had become uncharacteristically despondent, warning that, 'BUA would be lucky to make an overall profit this year'. The late starts meant, Laker said, that they had missed most of the holiday bookings for that year. 'Commercially we should not have operated these services with our bookings for this season but politically we had to use them.'

The first year after the merger with Silver City, 1963, had begun with Laker in high, effervescent good form. In February, he had bombarded the public with a £30,000 advertising campaign persuading them to fly British. He was becoming increasingly well known. 'Driving force behind BUA', 'dynamic', 'intensely patriotic' were just some of the eulogistic descriptions in the press, especially the right-wing Beaverbrook newspapers, whose affection for one of free enterprise's blunter spokesmen grew steadily.

With the start of the scheduled routes in the spring, Laker was anticipating plenty of growth at BUA and a big increase in the number of passengers for the airline. BUA already had ninety-four aircraft carrying 1.8 million passengers, 130,000 cars and nearly 90,000 tons of freight a year. The future looked buoyant.

In mid-summer Freddie had another clash with the state airlines when he said BUA had been 'sacked' from the air transport industry's joint negotiating body with the unions. Six other independents were forced out at the same time. It was no surprise that Laker had become their spokesman. He almost seemed to relish receiving his marching orders, emphasizing his lifelong contempt for 'associations' (in the following year he took BUA out of BIATA), or indeed anything that got in the way of swift, direct individualism. As he told the press, there was no question of the independents giving up their negotiating rights.

Two months after this the other key element of his long-term strategy, basing BUA's operations on a fleet of modern jets, took a nasty blow. Just over a year before the first deliveries to the airline were due, the prototype 1–11, G–ASHG, crashed during a test flight over Wiltshire, killing the test pilot, former world air-speed record holder, Mike Lithgow, his co-pilot Richard Rymer, an experienced pilot with nearly 10,000 hours of flying to his credit, three flight test observers, and two of BAC's most senior designers.

Until the aircraft took off on a fine October morning, the flight test programme had been going extremely well. Only a few days earlier, serious stall trials had started exploring how the aircraft handled during the critical manoeuvre of letting speed decay until, in effect, the aircraft ceased to fly and started to fall from the sky.

The 1–11's handling had been innocuous. Even when the aircraft's nose had been allowed to rise twenty-one degrees above the horizontal, stall recovery presented no problems. On Lithgow's flight, the aircraft was loaded to bring its centre of gravity as far back as the designers thought safe, to make the test even more searching.

Lithgow wasted no time. Only eighteen minutes after the 10.17am takeoff his co-pilot Rymer told the ground control that they were at 17,000 feet and had already completed four stall tests. A minute later he asked for a navigational fix. It was the crew's last message to the ground.

Even today what happened next is still used as a warning to 1–11 crews in training to guard against complacency. As the aircraft moved into the stall, it banked twice to the right and once to the left, dropping its wing in an attempt to recover. On each occasion Lithgow countered this.

On earlier flights he had come across the same phenomenon and had told the post-flight debriefing meeting that 'it should be perfectly possible to fight one's way through the wing drop'.

Suddenly the plane was out of control. The nose rose and the flight recorder showed the aircraft reached an incidence of forty degrees.

Lithgow tried everything. But the elevators simply floated upwards despite his efforts to push them down with the control column. Even opening the engines to full power did nothing to jolt the aircraft out of its 'super-stall'. By this time, G–ASHG was descending at a rate of 10,000 feet per minute and ninety seconds after entering the stall hit the ground in a flat attitude, killing all on board. The stall was so complete that the aircraft was scarcely moving forward when it hit the ground.

The real puzzle was why Lithgow had not realized that the 1–11 was in danger until far too late. It took some time to work out that it was a new characteristic of jets with swept back wings and T-shaped tailplanes. Below a certain speed they literally began to fall out of the sky. This ultra-fast descent – G-break as it is called – meant that although they had already stalled, their angle to the ground was not so acute as planes of the previous generation with conventional tails. What Lithgow thought was a safe angle was a false and deceptive reading once he had forced the 1–11 too far.

It took a long time to work out, however, and in the meantime the whole future of the new jet hung in the balance. In the weeks following the crash, BAC-Weybridge was in a state of shock. The aerodynamic problems the crash seemed to pose were immense. Airline customers, among them BUA, were demanding to know what was being done and whether or when they would get their aircraft.

Throughout this, Laker, while concerned, remained a pillar of support, and particularly so when Knight was called in to try and save the day. That is something of an understatement. Knight was a Bristol man and it was a measure of how bad things had become that the Vickers men at Weybridge had to swallow their pride and give Knight *carte blanche*.

For six months he kept Weybridge totally isolated from the power struggles within BAC – even its chief designer, George Edwards, was not allowed down there and had to make do with telephone calls from London to find out what was happening.

Before the trials were resumed, a number of modifications were made to the test aircraft, including a new wing leading edge and power controls for the elevators which Lithgow had been unable to shift manually. The rules about when to start stall recovery were tightened up. And as a final safety measure, the aircraft was equipped with engine modifications to help stall recovery and a tail parachute. The idea was that if the aircraft did stall again, this chute could be deployed as a last desperate measure, 'jerking' the aircraft back into flight.

None of these changes, nor the tremendous efforts Knight was putting in, averted a second crash, a year after the first one. This time the aircraft was already registered in BUA's name and painted in its colours. The aircraft was soon to be cleared of any blame for this crash. The cause this time was the pressure the test pilots had been under. But when it happened, it was a shock.

Freddie was in Elba. He had taken his yacht over from Genoa, where he normally kept it under the eye of the BUA station engineer there, to the splendid harbour of Portoferraio to meet Geoffrey Knight on holiday. Laker threw a birthday party and a memorable evening developed 'with Freddie buying champagne like it was going out of fashion' but in the evening Knight was called out to take a telephone call from England.

There had been a second 1–11 test crash, he was told, after a stall just like Lithgow's, only this time the crew had not been killed. Seconds before their aircraft had crash-landed on Salisbury Plain, they had managed to get off two messages: 'Mayday', and 'Mayday stable stall condition'. Knight went back into the restaurant and told Laker. For a moment even Freddie was silenced. Then he said, 'You cannot have two crashes.' For a moment, it looked like the end of the 1–11.

Knight returned to England and the post mortem began. Soon it emerged that there had been nothing wrong with the aircraft which the pilot had landed, wheels up, not far from Boscombe Down test-flying airfield which had been trying to direct it in for an emergency landing. The test pilot in command, Peter Baker, had misinterpreted the aircraft's behaviour and believed his plane was in an uncontrollable stall.

During recovery from a stall, he had decided that the elevator response was not normal and ordered the emergency tail parachute streamed as the aircraft entered what he thought was the same trap that had caught Lithgow. With the parachute out, Baker tried various manoeuvres which only reinforced his conviction that the aircraft was stalled. Late in its downward plunge, he discovered that applying full flap and full power reduced the rate of descent sufficiently to make an emergency landing.

The investigation concluded that there had been nothing wrong and that if the parachute had been jettisoned, the aircraft could have been flown normally. Baker, said the report, had suffered an 'oculographic illusion' in which the lower cockpit coaming frame would appear to tilt upwards giving the sensation that the pitch response of the aircraft was not normal.

The investigators also thought Baker could have been influenced by an occurrence called 'set'. On a previous occasion, testing a Handley Page Victor bomber, Baker had had to use the anti-spin parachute after the V-bomber suddenly pitched up uncontrollably. Under the stress of a similar incident, 'set' would subconsciously make him revert to the circumstances of the first one. However blameless Baker was, it was a spectacularly costly false alarm – which among other things may have influenced Alitalia to turn to the American DC-9.

Chapter 11

'Good God, he's brought Blue Streak!'

From the outset of his career with BUA, Laker concentrated much of his energies on developing its substantial African interests, making them his own. Business had grown steadily ever since the early days of the Viking-operated colonial coach air services. Growing connections with Africa had led to a series of plans to operate domestic services there in partnership with particular countries like Sierra Leone, Uganda and The Gambia.

The order for four VC–10 aircraft in June 1961, costing £2.8 million apiece, was placed with the African business very much in mind. Compared to the 200mph Vikings bought at around £37,500 each, which had pioneered the African coach flights, the VC–10s were a signal advance. In buying them BUA was taking a decision comparable with an airline buying 747s today.

Purchasing jets for what was still very much an economy service was typical of Laker's refusal to accept the *status quo*. Even if the terms of the licence precluded BUA from carrying first-class passengers, Laker was still determined to use modern aircraft with all their passenger appeal.

With BUA denied first-class passengers, the VC–10 was larger than the traffic justified. Freddie came up with the idea of putting a large cargo door in the port side of the aircraft and filling the front of the VC–10 with freight. The freight-door idea was copied widely by other civil VC–10 customers and RAF Air Transport Command.

For BAC, costing what was a major modification was a headache. How many could they expect to sell? In the end, Knight and Laker retired from what was then Laker's office in Piccadilly, strolled round the corner to Martinez, a Spanish restaurant in Swallow Street, and clinched the price over a drink at the bar.

That drink proved to be one of those rare occasions when Laker was outwitted in an aircraft deal. Knight's Weybridge estimators wanted £50,000 for installing a freight door. He reasoned that if he went to meet Laker and told him this, he would be lucky to get away with £20,000 – so Knight started with a figure of £100,000. He nibbled and haggled and finally settled at £50,000. Freddie suddenly realized he was delighted and said, 'You bastard, that's what you had in mind all the time.'

By late summer 1964, the first of BUA's VC–10s was complete and ready for a route-proving visit to Africa. John Loader, BUA's press and publicity officer, was asked by Laker to draw up a schedule for the tour. As most of the BUA long-haul pilots were familiar with the airports at the African destinations, the plan was to make the trip a combined route-proving and promotional visit.

Loader's plan was a workmanlike one. A number of journalists, travel agents and business travel managers would fly out with Laker. At each destination, local VIPs, businessmen, and in fact anyone who it was thought could influence travel plans, were to be taken up for a demonstration flight.

Freddie accepted Loader's plan with little comment but in the next couple of days proceeded to turn it into something much more exciting.

His first suggestion was that the trip should capitalize on the big cargo door and show people just what it could do. Loader, he said, should go along to Rolls-Royce and ask to borrow their Silver Cloud demonstrator. They could take that to Africa aboard the plane. Rolls-Royce was only too delighted to take the chance to promote the car in Africa.

The problem of getting the car on and off the plane was soon solved. Laker said that the engineers at Aviation Traders, who were actually building the cargo door and frame for the British Aircraft Corporation to install, should design a hoist.

Aviation Traders had already designed and built a scissors' lift for loading cars into British United Air Ferries' Carvairs but the VC–10 hoist was more difficult. The loading crew had to be able to dismantle it in a few minutes, pack it into the VC–10 and have it ready in twenty minutes or so for use at destination. The end product looked like a giant four-poster bed but it worked.

The idea of flying the Rolls-Royce to Africa and using it as Laker's personal transport there was bound to attract lots of publicity, advertising the forthcoming improvement in the service with the inauguration of the VC–10. But this was not enough.

What, Freddie asked Loader, goes with sleek jet aircraft and Rolls-Royce cars? The answer was pretty girls. So Loader was dispatched to Courtaulds to ask if they wanted to combine with BUA in an aerial fashion tour of Africa.

Freddie added one more spectacular showman twist. The British Aircraft Corporation, he said, was bound to want to show a VC–10, the industry's biggest and newest project, at that September's Farnborough Air Show. Loader should make sure that BAC used the BUA aircraft.

Came the big day at the show and the VC–10, complete with Laker, guests, car and four fashion models roared down the runway 'Africa bound' in front of TV, radio, press and 100,000 spectators.

In the end Laker had had to cheat just one little bit. Farnborough had no customs and there was no way of surmounting that piece of red tape. The VC–10 made a quick detour into Gatwick airport to complete the formalities before resuming its flight to Africa.

Even then, Freddie was not finished. *En route*, he came down the aircraft towards Loader, clutching a long, brown paper parcel. Unwrapping it, Freddie revealed a set of registration plates and set to changing the Rolls-Royce demonstrator's traditional number of 100 LG for RR 1. The switch caused no end of problems and paperwork in Africa. But RR 1 it had to be, said Freddie.

On arriving at Entebbe, Laker was invited to pay a formal visit to the President of Uganda. He was told that a presidential aide would meet them at the airport in a green Peugeot and they should follow it to the palace. RR 1 was hoisted out and the Laker party spotted the Peugeot and set off.

Gradually the roads got worse and the journey seemed to have taken much longer than expected. Then the Peugeot stopped. A family got out and began setting up their roadside picnic in the bush. It was not until later that Laker could laugh about it. He was deeply upset at keeping the President waiting. The dash back to the airport in search of the right car is one of the few times Loader saw him look seriously perturbed.

The tour's high point was a seven-hour cocktail party in Bulawayo, Rhodesia BUA's Britannia flights had been serving Entebbe, Nairobi, Ndola, Lusaka and Salisbury. Bulawayo was not on the network, but, via Salisbury, it generated a lot of traffic for London.

During the Salisbury stopover, Freddie planned a quick flight to Bulawayo where local businessmen and dignitaries would be given a short flight out over Victoria Falls. Laker, being Laker, was determined not to waste a minute of it. So the aircraft set off with a group of Salisbury VIPs. They would be entertained on the ground while the Bulawayo group had their joy ride.

During the approach to Bulawayo, the captain called Laker over the public address system to come up to the cockpit. Far from there being anything wrong with the aircraft, the captain wanted Laker to look at the scene below. Thousands of local inhabitants were determined to inspect what was probably the first jet, and certainly the first large jet transport, to land at the African town. From the cockpit Laker and the flight crew could see traffic jams on every road to the airfield, running back for miles.

After fighting their way through the jams, the new group of passengers was finally boarded and strapped in. Then trouble struck. The first of the VC–10's Conway jets ran up and then wound down. Laker and Loader exchanged anxious glances. They became even more worried when the engine refused to start again. They knew they were stuck. The VC–10's engines started with compressed air and the aircraft itself had enough air bottles for one start. Bulawayo with no jet services lacked air starting equipment.

Mercifully one of the guests was the local British Oxygen manager. He could produce cylinders of compressed air. So he set off, fighting his way through the jungle of traffic. Eventually he returned with a truck and some enormous missile-sized cylinders.

'Good God, he's brought Blue Streak,' exclaimed Freddie as he set about devising connectors.

While all this was going on, both groups of passengers were being entertained to an impromptu party in the hangar. Bulawayo's facilities were limited and the BUA stewardess and Robin Flood, BUA's assistant press officer, were kept busy washing glasses, serving drinks and, as the day merged into evening, cooking bacon and eggs.

By the time the aircraft was ready to start, darkness had fallen. But Laker was undeterred. Even if it had to be Victoria Falls by night, the Bulawayo people had been promised a flight and he was going to keep his word. Late that night, a tired, content, and in some cases thoroughly tight party flew home to Salisbury.

What was great fun for most of the people involved was also good promotional business. Laker had managed to write the VC-10 and the name of BUA into local legend. The new jet services were a tremendous success and generated more traffic and cargo than ever before.

Freddie's final comment on the whole tour was devastatingly in character. One observer remarked how excellently the VC-10 had performed on the rugged proving flight. 'Fantastic. You just pour kerosene in at one end and champagne at the other,' was Laker's reply.

Chapter 12

'Rolling down to Rio'

Freddie flew back from Africa to what was certainly the biggest single development of his career at BUA.

During the tour, his colleagues had noticed he was keeping in constant touch with his office back in London. While he normally liked to know what was going on while away, this time the number of messages seemed exceptional. On the flight back, however, most people were too tired to notice anything. Laker himself was tucked quietly in a seat, writing away. Moving up to have a word with him, Loader discovered that Freddie was writing thank-you letters to all the staff who had helped with the tour. Exhausted himself, he was staggered to discover that Laker was not simply producing a standard letter but individual ones to pilots, engineering crew and staff.

In conversation with Loader, Laker could no longer keep his news secret. Behind the flow of messages to and from London was the likelihood of a completely new opportunity for BUA, one of enormous importance. 'I think we are going to have a go at getting the service to South America,' said Laker.

Freddie knew that the future of the services being operated to South America by BOAC was already in the balance. The state airline was losing money on the route and there were no signs of an improvement. Earlier in the summer, BOAC had sought a £1,250,000-a-year government subsidy guaranteed for at least four years to cover its losses on the route. Aviation Minister Julian Amery, a Tory right-winger, was not interested in hand-outs to state industries. When BOAC then decided to give up the route, he made it clear that he was willing to back a bold offer from BUA to take on the service without any state subsidy. 'It deserves and will receive the Government's full support,' he said.

Such vigorous support from a Government Minister must have

sounded ironic to BUA's senior managers. Despite all the promises to the private airlines, and the hopes raised, the Tory Civil Aviation Act of 1960 had secured only a handful of relatively unimportant scheduled routes to add to the traditional African flights.

Wyatt had fulfilled his part of the bargain in helping rationalize the independent airlines. There were obviously times when his disenchantment with the Government's contribution showed. But both he and Laker realized that BOAC's decision to withdraw from South America was an unrepeatable opportunity. At a stroke, it cut out the Government's dilemma of finding a way to help the private sector without being seen to undermine the stability of the state corporation and all the jobs and investment tied up in it.

Wyatt and Laker had no hesitations about seizing this opportunity. The route was a loss-maker and both men thought it would take a year to get into the black. But compared with the nail-biting insecurity of trooping contracts and the ups and downs of the charter market, the threat of short-term financial losses was mere turbulence on the way to cruising height. So overwhelming were the route's attractions that no one within BUA stopped for a moment to wonder quite how tough a job they were taking on. BUA had never had much contact with South America. Never mind. For the first time an independent airline was being offered the chance to operate a major scheduled international route.

Staff within BUA had long had to reconcile themselves to a secondary role, running services to 'second-city' destinations while the state airlines served foreign capitals. Even the African routes were shared with BOAC. Now they were to run services to the capitals of Brazil, Uruguay, Argentina and Chile. In their own right as an airline they were reckoned to be good enough to take over from BOAC, until this point barely challenged by private airlines.

Morale within BUA was never higher. The halo effect of this accolade helped burnish BUA's image generally with the public. The management recognized that they were doing good work to Africa, but these routes were never likely to win them the seven-column headline the *Daily Express* carried about the new service: 'Rolling down to Rio'.

When Buckingham Palace announced that Prince Philip would fly with BUA on his tour of South America, Freddie was delighted at this royal recognition of his airline.

As far as the British Government was concerned, there were no strings attached. For once the permit contained no commercially crippling small print to protect the state carrier. BUA could operate as many flights a week as it liked. There was no need to carry freight to make up for the missing first-class passengers reserved on the African routes for BOAC or to use obsolete aircraft to mute the independent challenge.

There were, however, some practical problems. BUA's VC–10s, the first of which had just arrived, were committed to trooping contracts and finding capacity for these, Africa and South America was going to be difficult. Julian Amery helped once again by announcing that he would allow BUA to substitute Britannias for the trooping flights.

It is entirely typical of the up-and-down history of independent aviation in the UK that these words were scarcely out of Amery's mouth before the Conservatives lost the general election. Hopes sank at BUA. When Amery had originally announced that BUA could have South America, he had been roundly criticized by the Opposition. In particular, the Labour Party had accused Amery of sharp practice and undermining the operations of BOAC. Firing a warning shot in BUA's direction, their spokesman on aviation added that the airlines should understand that 'a Labour Government will be in no way bound by this hurried and highly questionable deal'.

The bitter resentment felt within the Labour Party was reinforced when Fred Lee, Minister of Power after the Labour election victory, was forced to make an abject apology to Lord Poole, a director of Cowdray's merchant bank, Lazards, and of Air Holdings, BUA's holding company. Poole had issued a writ after a speech by Lee in which the latter had suggested that Poole's position as vice-chairman of the Conservative Party might have helped speed the decision to let BUA fly to South America.

Neither Laker, nor the rest of BUA's management, were ready to sit around waiting for the political bickering to end. The first proving flight with Captain 'Mac' Mackenzie, today British Caledonian's chief pilot, in command, left for South America on 12 October.

Freddie turned the second flight at the end of the month into a 28,000-mile, whistle-stop promotion tour of South America. Mackenzie and his colleagues treated the South Americans to an electric display of the VC–10's surgingly powerful takeoffs and thistledown landings.

Smooth arrivals on Montevideo's notoriously bumpy runway drew rounds of applause. At Buenos Aires, the VC–10 cocked a snook at its American Boeing 707 rival. The 707 was running up to maximum power, brakes hard on, ready for a takeoff using all the long runway. The VC–10 captain coolly upstaged them by asking the tower for permission to use the short runway. The British Embassy staff loved it all, a buccaneering comeback just as the British appeared to have given up.

In a period of remarkably intense flying, Mackenzie used every chance to get in as much crew training as possible. To this end the VC–10 did 168 landings, wearing out so many tyres that the aircraft carried extra ones. Over a thousand guests went up on demonstration flights and helped by nearly eight hundred bottles of champagne, they drank, whistled, stamped and applauded the VC–10's remarkable performance. The kerosene and champagne brew was as strong as ever.

By the end of October, Freddie had negotiated traffic rights at the South American end of the route after unbelievably hard work. On 5 November the service started, its future still in the balance with an avowedly hostile Labour Government in office. But when Laker appeared before the Air Transport Licensing Board in mid-November to seek conversion of the temporary permit into a full licence, it turned out to be scarcely more than a formality.

The sheer speed with which he had started BUA's service on the route, only a matter of weeks after BOAC's ended, helped him gain approval. His flair in promoting BUA's takeover as a signal example of British enterprise in action as well as extolling the virtues of the VC–10 decided the matter. It was in sharp contrast to BOAC's much-criticized decision to cut back its VC–10 order.

The new Minister of Aviation, Roy Jenkins, was politician enough to recognize a foregone conclusion when he saw it. After Jenkins had made it clear that he would neither oppose nor reverse any ATLB decision, the board at the start of December gave BUA a fifteen-year licence, the longest period for which it had ever awarded one.

Putting in BUA, which only had VC–10s, and was starting with a clean slate, strengthened the British negotiating hand in South

America. There was a stroke of luck when Brazil's international airline, Panair do Brasil, went bust. Britain was able to tell the Brazilians that it was either BUA and the VC–10 or a ban on their national airline, Varig, which now wanted to fly to London.

But BUA met rugged opposition almost all the way along the route. For most of the countries involved, it was a matter of practical politics. Each month the British airline was delayed was an extra month's revenue into the coffers of their own operator. It was almost a shock when right at the end of the route, the Chileans welcomed BUA with open arms. But they had no vested interest to protect.

With the passage of time, the story of BUA's South American venture has become a myth of private-enterprise dash succeeding where inefficient state industry floundered. To a degree this is true but more complex issues were involved. Some of Laker's own men recognized at the time that BOAC had never really stood a chance of getting the service into profit. The restrictions the Brazilians imposed on its flights in order to protect their own airline created bad blood between them and BOAC.

Munroe Blakemore, then general manager of BUA, lived almost continuously for six months in Brazil trying to negotiate better rights. Making the route viable was a tough, dour struggle. With the advantage of hindsight, it is easy to say that a moment's reflection would have convinced anyone of the folly of taking on this task. So golden did the opportunity seem, however, that no one at BUA thought twice about it.

George Carroll's starting point was Laker's basic formula for costing out services which he has applied to all his operations from the early Halifaxes to Skytrain's DC–10s. They worked out how much money two flights a week to South America should generate with a reasonable load of passengers. This was set against the aircraft's operating cost. What was left over was the sum available for overheads such as advertising and sales, and ultimately for profit.

Having done this, it was apparent that there was nothing to spare for lavish sales offices, homes with swimming pools for expatriate managers and chauffeur-driven cars. Carroll reasoned that all he had to do was get rid of the clutter that had been built up over the years by 'the Imperial Airways trainees'. Adopting such a simple approach soon cut down to size what had appeared to be a daunting task. It was a case of having a basic organization with a few key reservation staff, some telexes and a local manager.

Whatever the problems, the route was making a genuine profit in its third year, not so far adrift from Laker's own forecast that it would start to break even in 1966.

Apart from making profit for BUA, success on this route was a crucial one for independent aviation. The ability of a private airline to take over a major loss-making route from the state carrier and turn it into an operational, commercial and marketing success against great odds had a considerable influence on government policy in years to come. More than anything else, the principle of substitution was established: in certain circumstances, British air transport as a whole might benefit by replacing the state airline with an independent one.

Chapter 13

'A matter of principle'

BUA's position as the country's biggest independent airline was consolidated in 1965 when a number of domestic routes were added to its growing scheduled network. There were gains made, too, at the expense of BUA's traditional independent rival, Harold Bamberg's Eagle.

Four years earlier when the Civil Aviation Act had created the opportunity for private airlines to apply for scheduled routes, BUA and Eagle had agreed spheres of interest between themselves. BUA would concentrate on Africa and some European routes. Bamberg, who like Laker had got his break flying on the Berlin aircraft, would try to establish himself to some extent in Europe but mainly in the UK and on the North Atlantic.

After the disaster of the Airwork transatlantic cargo flights, BUA was only too glad to leave it to Bamberg to challenge TWA, Pan Am and BOAC on what was to them their busiest single route. Apart from a natural reluctance to open old wounds, it seemed to make more sense. Only the year before, in 1960, Bamberg had sold a majority stake in his airline to Cunard, anxious to get into air transport now that aircraft had eclipsed ships on the North Atlantic run. With a licence awarded to fly to New York and a £6 million fleet of new Boeing 707s, Cunard-Eagle was ready for take-off when Tory Aviation Minister Peter (later Lord) Thorneycroft supported BOAC's appeal against the newcomer on the grounds that 'too many seats were chasing too few passengers'.

Bamberg's bitterness at this shock decision was deep. He had found it difficult at the best of times to surrender any of his control or delegate authority at Eagle and found it harder still to get on with the management of the fading Cunard Steamship Company. When the Government's rebuff was compounded by Cunard promptly accepting an offer from BOAC to operate a joint transatlantic air service, he was furious. Bamberg's relationship with the stuffy Cunard board had never been happy and not surprisingly he decided to branch out on his own once again, buying back 60 per cent of Eagle in February 1963.

If that was the sort of treatment meted out by a Conservative Government, Bamberg and the other independent airlines were rightly wary of what Harold Wilson's new Labour Government might bring. The future looked bleak as the new Labour regime threatened to fall back on its traditional policy of protection for state corporations at the expense of the private sector.

The new Minister in charge of air transport, Roy Jenkins, soon confirmed these fears. The 1960 Act was so vague, said Jenkins, that there was no need for legislation. But there would be changes. There would still be opportunities for the private sector but their scope would be curbed. He would make it easier for them to obtain licences for inclusive tours and they would get his full support if they wanted to open a new route. But there was no question of this being at the expense of BEA or BOAC on international routes.

Bamberg's problem was more specific. The frequencies permitted by the authorities for his UK domestic flights were so limited that it was almost impossible to operate profitably. In the eighteen months before the Labour Government took office, Eagle was struggling. Losses up to October 1964 on domestic operations reached £300,000 and the London–Belfast flights were operating with a heart-breakingly low load factor of 13 per cent. (Load factor is the actual load expressed as a percentage of total capacity.)

When Jenkins's parting remarks made it clear that airlines like Eagle competing with BEA would not be allowed to raise the number of their flights and that they could take or leave it, Bamberg saw red. Overnight, in February 1965, he stopped British Eagle's domestic operations.

If it was a calculated attempt to overthrow Jenkins's new policy, it did not succeed. The alacrity of Bamberg's withdrawal, claimed Jenkins, suggested he was not altogether sorry to withdraw from his commitment. 'Bamberg must be the happiest man in Britain tonight,' said BEA chairman, Anthony (later Sir Anthony) Millward.

No doubt pleased at the withdrawal of his airline's only

competitor on the routes in question, Millward neglected to mention BEA's tactic of sandwiching Eagle's limited flights to Scotland between two of its own departures in an effort to clip its wings.

The history of independent aviation in Britain is that success has gone to anyone prepared to ignore the vagaries of official policy and seize whatever opportunity presented itself. Faced with a situation reminiscent of what had happened over South America, Laker was just as decisive. He promptly applied for Eagle's domestic route licences – offering to operate them with the 1–11, which was due shortly to get its certificate of airworthiness after the delays caused by the test-flight crashes. Bamberg as quickly said he would resume the flights. The Air Transport Licensing Board criticized him for 'disservice to the public'. The outcome was a period of remarkable competition with BUA flying to Scotland from Gatwick and BEA and Eagle running flights from Heathrow.

Domestic service was a significant addition to BUA's scheduled routes. The flywheel that provided the airline's main drive, this scheduled network had taken a big step with the inauguration in spring 1965 of the world's first passenger 1–11 services on the London–Genoa route. A few days later the 1–11 took over on the routes to Rotterdam and Amsterdam.

Travelling on the first flight to Genoa, a high-spirited Laker was delighted with the aircraft. 'They look like being a big success for us,' he told journalists. So enthusiastic was he that he added that BUA was thinking of spending £17 million over the next five years on another fifteen. Even BEA's former chairman, and a guest on the flight, Lord Douglas of Kirtleside, joined in the celebratory mood, calling BUA 'the best independent airline'.

Helped by Laker's growing flair for publicity and ability to ad-lib the eminently quotable remarks that still have journalists scrabbling for notebooks, BUA was the pace-setting airline as far as most of the public was concerned. By 1965, as well as the charter and trooping business, there was a more substantial scheduled network than any other independent had ever had. 'La BUA', as Laker had affectionately come to call it, was the undisputed second force in British aviation after the state corporations.

But within the airline, things were far from happy. Operationally BUA was a smart, well-run airline operating the most modern equipment to the highest standards – something that many independent airlines had been distinguished for. Yet like many British businesses that have grown rapidly by merger and acquisition, BUA had accumulated more than its share of problems – not least of which was that its own managing director and driving force, Laker himself, was becoming increasingly disenchanted.

Much had been done to integrate the various businesses. There had been a number of costly redundancies and some rationalization of the many different types of aircraft BUA owned, but more was needed to cut through the confusion. Each of the airlines acquired had brought in its own chief pilot and training captain as well as management. At one stage, BUA had seven base airports – Stansted, Southend, Gatwick, Heathrow, Hurn, Lydd and Blackpool.

Each part of the group had its own way of conducting its affairs. Reservations staff at the old Laker company, Channel Air Bridge, did not work formal overtime. They battled on when traffic was busy and took time off in the troughs of business. But other parts of BUA had paid overtime and when all the staff were gathered in the same building, the Channel Air Bridge people – at greater cost to the company – began to adopt the practice of working formal overtime.

Silver City, the last airline to be acquired, proved in the opinion of Douglas Whybrow to be 'a monster'. Despite losing money hand over fist its swollen staff operated out of lavish and expensive headquarters in Knightsbridge. A major redundancy programme had to be implemented.

The earlier acquisition of Hunting Clan had undermined the congenial atmosphere within the group. Though the African coach service had ostensibly been operated in partnership, Hunting and Airwork were always bitter opponents. More embarrassingly this particular merger provided an opportunity to compare the relative efficiency with which Hunting and Laker's company, Air Charter, had operated the Britannias they had owned. Hunting had lost a lot of money flying them compared with Air Charter's profit. When the two were put together, Whybrow, by now chief executive (commercial) of BUA under Laker, could see the differences. He realized that it showed Hunting up.

Some of the constituent airlines were unionized and others not. Freddie himself has never found it easy to get on with unions. Laker the Victorian entrepreneur likes to see himself rather than anyone else as the source of employee well-being and paternalism. Nor can he abide anything that slows up his fast-moving, off-the-cuff style of managerial decision-taking. There were occasions at BUA when his relations with some union officials were abrasive to say the least.

As early as May 1962, all BUA's 500 engineering staff were dismissed in a dispute at Gatwick. Laker bitterly claimed their demand for a £1 a week more was quite unreasonable. On yet another occasion, Laker himself loaded baggage at Gatwick during a strike of ground handling staff. Over the years the antagonism between Laker and influential union officials like Clive Jenkins hardened. Another significant factor was growing tension between Freddie and the pilots' union, BALPA.

Senior managers were not helped in the struggle to knock BUA into shape. The big shareholders often seemed more concerned about prestige than profits. They had taken the decision to move BUA into a large new office building near London's Victoria Station called Portland House. With two enormous and expensive reception areas, and more office space than was actually needed, Portland House was a costly burden.

Colleagues felt that Laker, essentially a one-man-band type of operator, was growing frustrated as BUA's organizational arteries began to harden. He liked to know everyone by name, right down to the doorman and it was no longer possible to do so. Not long afterwards, he suggested that it was not so much because he was restless but that he had an idea that, 'I may really be creative or I want to be creative. I find out that when I have done what I set out to do, there's a tendency for me to go and create something else.'

While Laker had plenty of opportunity and a great deal of freedom at BUA to exercise his flair for major decision-making and innovation, he had no personal financial stake in the venture. He had become a major public figure. He regarded himself as the creator of what was probably the biggest success story in aviation since the war. But to the shareholders, and to Wyatt, he was still their paid hand. There were times when it rankled, especially in the last year or so at BUA. There was more than one argument with Wyatt over who was boss.

There was an occasion when it seemed possible that a Southend-based charter airline, Channel, might join BUA. Its founder,

Squadron Leader Jack Jones, had one abortive round of negotiations with Laker. Then he went to Wyatt and said he was interested in talking but not with Laker, who was trying to drive too tough a bargain.

Wyatt decided to pay Jones a visit in Southend. Inevitably Freddie's men at Aviation Traders spotted Wyatt's Rolls at the airport and asked Laker what was up. Hopping mad, Laker went storming in to Wyatt and demanded to know what was going on. Wyatt accelerated the parting of the ways between the two men by simply reminding Laker who was chairman.

Much appreciation of other people's feelings never seems to have been one of Wyatt's stronger points. He used to wonder in the early days why Laker had not moved into Airwork's head office. When one of Freddie's colleagues told him it was because he had not actually provided his bright new protégé with an office, Wyatt was puzzled. He should come and take one, he said. You don't understand Freddie, was the reply. He wouldn't come barging in and take someone's office like that.

The would-be deal with Channel was not the only time Wyatt had left Laker out in the cold. When Silver City was purchased, Sir Donald Anderson, chairman of P&O, one of Silver City's major shareholders, would only discuss the deal with Wyatt and refused to talk to Laker, who was never even consulted. Again this led to a row and another assertion of 'I'm the boss' from Wyatt.

Such disagreements seemed inevitable. Wyatt believed he had held Airwork together through thick and thin and maintained the support of the shareholders for the strategy of expansion. Laker was an ambitious, self-made man from a poor background, in direct contrast to Wyatt with all his robust, upper-class confidence. What accentuated the difference was Wyatt's unwillingness to concede that Laker, whose immense aviation expertise had been so important to BUA, might take over as chairman one day.

After his departure from BUA, Laker strenuously denied that there had ever been any rift between him and Wyatt over policy. In a simple sense this was probably true but skirts round the growing personality conflict. This alone seems to have played the major part in disrupting the plan for Laker's peaceful departure from BUA. Originally Laker planned to leave, take a seat on the board of Air Holdings and start up a business, possibly in the travel industry, with his son, Kevin. Kevin's death in a car crash in July 1965, just after the announcement of Laker's resignation, shattered that hope.

In the end, Laker quit abruptly six weeks before the planned date of his departure on 31 December, after what Wyatt described as a 'petty squabble' which Laker in turn insisted was 'a matter of principle'. As far as any of the insiders could tell, it was a petty squabble. Laker had fired a long-standing employee of Airwork without consulting Wyatt who once again asserted his authority as chairman.

Chapter 14

'I just did a few sums on the back of an envelope'

Freddie Laker was planning to start up again with his own airline at least a year before his much-publicized row with Sir Myles when he walked out of BUA six weeks early. Three months before his decision to resign was announced mid-way through 1965, he was sounding out a few trusties from Air Charter he wanted to go with him.

One of these was George Forster, who had stayed in charge of trooping and *ad hoc* charter work in BUA. To the world at large, and to BUA, however, Freddie had only indicated that he wanted to start up on his own to build a family business for his son Kevin to share. A few hotels, perhaps, and an investment trust or two.

The subterfuge was fairly thin. Freddie had quiet talks with Geoffrey Knight and others at British Aircraft Corporation about the possibility of placing orders for BAC 1-11s and what kind of prices and delivery dates would be likely.

The moment he left BUA he started planning his new airline at his home in Epsom. He was still blighted by his son's death, but he was comforted by involving his daughter Elaine and Kevin's friend John Jones in his plans, as well as his wife and his close intimates.

One of the first moves was to set up his holding company in the 'offshore' tax haven of Jersey. Laker Airways was formed with 90 per cent of the shares in Freddie's name and the remaining 10 per cent in Joan's. In the UK he formed Laker Airways (Leasing) Ltd as the operator with the same share split. Then he announced to the public that he was setting up under his own name and that he had ordered three BAC 1-11s from the British Aircraft Corporation at a cost of around £4 million. He put £211,500 of his own money into the business and had arranged to borrow the rest from various City banks, led by Clydesdale Bank. Knight repaid Laker's years of support by arranging for BAC to underwrite some of the loan – help he was prepared to offer only to a handful of customers.

Freddie was disarmingly casual about how he had persuaded the City to cough up so much money. 'I just did a few sums on the back of an envelope,' he said disingenuously.

In fact he had thought through how to finance the purchase of the planes and then guarantee that they would make money in the greatest detail. He had calculated that he would need to carry between 65,000 and 70,000 passengers a year to make a profit, equal to approximately 7 per cent of the package-holiday market, which was growing at an explosive rate in the mid-1960s.

He had devised two radical ways of obtaining this business. One was by creating winter traffic to the popular Mediterranean resorts by offering 30 per cent discounts. The second was more original. Laker called it 'time charter' and it was one of the planks on which he had built his case to his backers.

But to begin with he had to create his airline. As soon as he announced his plans, he was deluged with applications to come and work for him. Over two thousand people applied for jobs.

His first paid recruit was one of the staff at BUA to whom Freddie had dropped a quiet word. 'Atty' Atkinson had met Laker when he was one of three Hunting administration staff sent down to Gatwick after the merger into BUA. He later crossed BUA's agents in the Canaries, who were long-established adherents of the Airwork faction, and he could see his future in the group was going to be short. Freddie told him that he would always have a job for him. When Laker Airways was formed, Atkinson was already out of work.

To begin with he stayed briefly at Freddie's Epsom house, Charters. The two drove down to Gatwick airport, south of London about half-way to Brighton, and Freddie drew up outside three empty offices on the outskirts of the airfield. They were each about fifteen feet square, and contained nothing except Freddie's desk with a couple of telephones sitting on it. They sat down on some empty orange boxes, naked lightbulbs hanging over their heads. 'This is Fredair,' said Atkinson's new boss.

Fredair was Laker's favourite description of his embryonic business. He always said he had only decided to call the airline Laker as a tribute to his mother, for whom he had a tremendous affection. If it is true that behind every successful man is a woman, in Freddie's case it was his mother, who had all the strength of character and drive that her son inherited. When Freddie was small she went out cleaning and during the war she worked in a salvage unit, reclaiming metal for munitions. She ended up running it. After the war she opened a general store in Canterbury with her second husband, who had taken the place of Freddie's real father who deserted them when Freddie was five. Freddie's stepfather changed his name by deed poll to Laker and Freddie developed a deep affection for him, calling him 'Dear'.

His mother was intensely ambitious for her son. Even when they had little money, she made sure he sat down to a carefully laid table for dinner as preparation for making his way up the ladder.

His stepfather died in 1967, but Freddie's mother, whom everyone at the airline called 'Gran', died in May 1979. Laker was at her funeral the day he heard about the DC–10 disaster.

The day after their visit to Gatwick to look at the offices, Laker and Atkinson shopped for cheap stationery at a bankruptcy sale in Reigate a few miles to the north-west of the airport. Atkinson is still using a cheap, battered notebook he acquired from that sale for his list of personal phone numbers. Freddie ordered some typewriters and other essentials for his offices and gradually they were painted and furnished, with Laker enlisting his family and friends as well as newly arrived recruits to his staff, as freelance decorators. The results were bleak and businesslike, with an almost aggressive lack of frills. The present offices at Gatwick, built on the corner of a hangar, are next door to the originals and share their utilitarian appearance. There is no lift and the uncarpeted concrete stairs are lit by naked lightbulbs, with the offices containing only cheap deal desks and chairs and plain steel filing cabinets.

Atkinson's first job was as operations manager, which meant coping with the 2,000 applications for jobs. Most were from aircrew, many of them at BUA. With few exceptions they were headed by young, ambitious first officers defecting from BUA for the chance of their own commands.

Only a few of the old guard joined Freddie in his new venture. Jack Wiseman stayed as director in charge of Aviation Traders Engineering, which was by now a major industrial organization incorporating all BUA's manufacturing and engineering subsidiaries. Alan Nicholls remained as group accountant. Bob Batt also stayed on.

Freddie had offered them the opportunity to join him, but had made no promises of large salaries or security. They were most of them approaching or already in their fifties and with too many commitments to want to face up to a second career under a man they knew only too well as a hard taskmaster. In any case, Freddie did not really need them. He planned a tight operation with no more than six planes. He used to tell people that if it grew any larger they could kick his arse.

When Freddie unveiled his new airline to the press at the beginning of February 1966 he called it 'contract carrier to the package-holiday trade' and 'a personalized airline'. He announced that he had arranged to take over BAC's 1–11 demonstrator for crew training late in the year, prior to taking delivery of his first new plane in December.

He revealed that his total staff was going to number about 120. He envisaged eighteen pilots, twenty-seven stewardesses, forty-eight engineers and twenty-six administrative staff. And he said that he planned to concentrate on inclusive-tour operations, with the emphasis on medium-range destinations like the Canary Islands, North Africa and the East Mediterranean.

The aviation industry found it difficult to work out Laker's sums. He suggested that he only expected to get a little over 5,000 flying hours from his three new jets in the 1967–8 holiday season, which the conventional pundits worked out as producing about £1.5 million in revenue – a low figure to cover overheads and begin paying off nearly £5 million in debts.

Reliance on inclusive tours, in the experience of most of the major airlines, usually produced utilization rates too low to cover depreciation and interest on new jets. Coupled with the low revenue rates of about 3d per seat-mile that the experts calculated were all that could be obtained for a 1–11, this had stopped anyone else thinking they were remotely suitable for inclusive tours. How was Freddie going to prove them wrong?

To begin with, he gave few clues, apart from one in his choice of livery for his new planes when they arrived. He planned to paint them in his racing colours of red and black along with a Union Jack. On the tail the name Laker was writ small. The red and black also ran in a broad stripe right down the side of the fuselage, to provide a prominent advertising space for large tour operators to put their names.

Hardly had he made his announcement than Laker was off on a diversification. Only three weeks after unveiling his long-term plans, he took delivery of his first plane – not an amazingly off-the-shelf 1–11 but one of a pair of Britannias which he had been unable to resist buying at a knockdown price of £373,000 from BOAC. Delays in deliveries of the Britannias had meant the nationalized corporation was already moving on into its first Boeing 707s and the older designs were obsolete for its transatlantic plans. The purchases were an ideal opportunity to turn his airline into a working outfit before his new jets were delivered. Most of the flight crews joining Laker Airways were trained on Britannias, so they could fly the new purchases while they waited for the BAC 1–11s. Laker and his management team, which had grown to include Cliff Nunn, originally from Transair, Bill Townsend as technical director and Peter Yeoman as chief engineer, both from Aviation Traders, and his son-in-law John Seear, could prove the tightness of their control on the engineering and administration sides.

When Freddie set up on his own, more than half the booming package-holiday market was in the hands of less than ten companies. What he badly wanted was a deal with Thomas Cook, the best-known of all and a subsidiary of British Rail, to give a seal of respectability to Laker Airways.

He did not get it. In spite of his formidable salesmanship, he could not wring an agreement out of the cumbersome, increasingly bureaucratic corporation. All they could see was that it meant a considerable commitment, which in their cautious minds immediately respelt itself as 'risk'.

The only inquiries Freddie was getting were from smaller operators and to begin with he treated them disdainfully. When Stuart Alderman of Wings Ltd telephoned for details he got through to George Forster, who was offhand to the point of rudeness. It was obvious to Alderman that Forster thought he was merely being inquisitive and that Wings was not big enough to be a serious customer.

Wings was a relatively youthful offshoot of Ramblers, which made its name in 1931 when it organized mass marches across the Derbyshire Peak District by slum dwellers from the industrial conurbation of Manchester in defiance of the landlords who owned the beautiful but bleak uplands. The flood of marchers organized by the idealistic Ramblers Association defeated the landowners, helping establish new rights to enjoy the country.

The Ramblers stayed a left-wing and altruistic organization after the Second World War, when Ernest Welsman became London regional secretary of the Youth Hostels Association, which had close links. Slowly, Ramblers became aware of new opportunities for its members abroad and began to plan a few discreet commercial operations. Ramblers Association Services started to organize charter flights and set up Wings Ltd with Ernest Welsman as managing director.

Welsman was a perceptive man with a natural business talent. Under his control Wings grew carefully, expanding its range of holidays, always insisting on high quality and good value. There is a certain irony in the comparison between the socialist Ramblers Association which owned Wings and the middle-class conservatives who were for the most part the tour operator's actual customers, but this did not stop the company thriving under Welsman's management. In 1961, Wings had become a member of ABTA, the Association of British Travel Agents, and by 1966 it was running tours to Corfu, Rhodes, Turkey and Greece, chartering aircraft from British United Airways and Transglobe Airways.

When Alderman, effectively Welsman's personal assistant, finally received details from George Forster, Laker's basic concept was simple: Laker Airways would provide a new BAC 1–11 for the exclusive use of one tour operator who would have to guarantee a minimum of 1,700 flying hours a year. Welsman and Alderman thought the idea attractive. They could see the risk of losing money, either through penalty payments or uneconomic fares, but their plans for 1967 convinced them Wings would be able to make full use of a plane. It would also cut out the bother of arranging *ad hoc* or series charters. They decided on an approach to Laker.

It was nearly a month before Freddie appeared at Wings' offices. He carried a small briefcase which to Alderman's impressionable eyes seemed far too small to contain the facts that Freddie always produced from it. Stuart never saw Laker take a piece of paper out; he merely opened the lid and looked inside and lo and behold he had the exact information needed, however obscure. Laker knew every detail he was asked, from the cost of a gallon of aviation fuel at Gatwick to the number of flying minutes to Istanbul.

Freddie impressed Wings enormously with his frankness and his knowledge of aircraft economics. He explained to Welsman and Alderman that, in the US, airlines operated to hours and minutes. In Europe, he pointed out, they referred to hours and 'round minutes'. When BOAC or BUA announced flight departures and arrivals they were always 11.00 hours or 12.15 hours. In the States, planes left at 11.02 and arrived at 12.13. 'A BAC 1–11,' said Freddie, 'costs £8 a minute to fly. If you add up all those odd minutes over a year, you are paying for a lot of extra flying.'

Freddie was disingenuously concerned about Wings' ability to take on a plane. He was aware that if the tour operator could not make good use of his plane, its failure would hit him just as severely. But he was also remarkably unready when Welsman said he was quite confident that Wings could keep its side of the bargain. Laker kept Wings waiting for some weeks – Alderman suspected him of still trying to secure a contract with Thomas Cook – and then did not have a contract ready. Welsman drafted one for him which Freddie was largely happy to accept.

The contract ran for a year beginning on 24 March 1967 and defined the flying hours as the time estimated by BAC to elapse between the moment the aircraft departed for a flight from the terminal building at one airport to the moment it came to rest at the terminal at another. Freddie demanded fifty minutes turn-round between each flight and two hours in every twenty-four to carry out daily maintenance, plus a sixteen-hour stretch at least once a week for more extensive overhauling.

Ernest Welsman wrote in several safety clauses, including one that enabled him to renegotiate prices if sterling fell in value by 15 per cent or more. In 1967 the pound dropped by 14.7 per cent. Luck could hardly have been more accurately on Freddie's side. Laker offered a rebate of £100 a flying hour for every hour over 1,700 flown for Wings and put a limit of 2,300 hours on the total the tour operator could use the plane. This was not meanness: it reflected Laker's tight manning which restricted the total number of hours his crews could physically manage in a year.

While he was negotiating with Wings, Laker had also been talking to another up-and-coming tour company called Lord Brothers. Coincidentally, this had been started at almost the same time as Wings. In 1957 Christopher Lord had just left Oxford University and taken a job as a courier for Wings in Yugoslavia. His brother Basil was training couriers for Swan's, another travel company, and towards the end of the holiday season their third brother Stephen joined them. They decided there did not seem to be much to the travel business that three bright, well-educated young men ought not to be able to manage for themselves. They treated themselves indulgently to a dinner of lobster and champagne and Lord Brothers was born.

For their first two years, they lost money, but then they began to grow fast. They were big enough to be accepted as ABTA members in 1961, the same year as Wings, and the following year they chartered their first flights with British United Airways, which was a big status step forward for Lord Brothers.

That was when they met Freddie Laker. The brothers found themselves condescended to by Sir Myles, but Laker's all-embracing attitude charmed them. They were invited to lunch and then dinner with him and began to feel they were becoming personal friends. When he arrived at their sixth-floor office in Regent Street in 1966 and offered them the chance to take on one of his new 1-11s, the brothers were flattered and excited. Laker told them that if they did not like the idea he would go elsewhere, but that he had chosen them because he thought them among the best. They gave little thought to the prospects of failure. Business was booming and they were confident that 1967 was going to be even better.

The contract the Lord Brothers signed with Laker was the same as the one that had been drafted by Welsman. The only difference was that it was due to begin one day later than the Wings contract.

Freddie had already announced in April that he had sold all the space on his new planes for the whole of the following year. In June he revealed the Lord Brothers contract, which he valued at £500,000, with a fanfare of publicity.

In the meantime, however, he had to find something for his new staff and his new Britannias to keep them busy. He had taken delivery of the two planes by May and in July he sent the first on a series of training flights from Gatwick to Hurn and Stansted. On 29 July the Britannia took off on Laker Airways' first paying flight, a contract for Air France.

For the next four months Laker's Britannias flew a mixture of training flights and *ad hoc* charters to Orly, Cologne, Rimini, Venice,

Dubrovnik, Rome, Dublin, Cherbourg, Athens, Amsterdam, Valencia and Las Palmas. The stewardesses wore Laker's new uniform, a petrol-blue creation designed by Winifred Ready, a former student from Accrington School of Arts and Crafts who taught needlework in Middlesex and was a friend of Freddie's chief stewardess, Nina Griffin. By the end of the holiday season, Laker's Britannias had carried 9,798 passengers. It wasn't a fortune, but the revenue was significant to the company which had budgeted on going through the period before the 1–11s were delivered as a dead loss.

Alan Hellary was responsible for the economical way in which Laker's aircraft flew. He was one of the very few long-serving Laker employees to leave BUA to join him. He had joined Freddie in November 1951 to fly on the contract from Berlin to Hamburg and then Hannover, sometimes flying a Bristol freighter, a York and a Tudor on separate flights in the same day. He had spent three years flying Tudors on the Australian run from Stansted to Adelaide, taking eleven days for the round flight and logging 110 flying hours. At BUA he had become one of the airline's senior VC–10 pilots on the South American routes.

When he heard that Freddie was resigning from the group Hellary wrote to say how sorry he was. When he read later in a newspaper that his ex-boss was starting up his own airline he telephoned Laker from his home at Bournemouth. Freddie asked him to come to his house at Epsom directly after his next flight arrived back from Aden. Hellary said that would be 4.00am. 'That's okay,' said Laker, 'I'll see you around 6.00am and we'll talk.'

Alan Hellary followed the man. He felt that without Freddie BUA stood no chance of becoming a unified operation. He had suffered himself from the still unhealed divisions between the companies that made up the group, with job titles still being duplicated and no prospects of promotion. But he was still taking a big step down from his secure and highly paid job as a VC–10 captain.

Freddie got the man he needed. Alan Hellary selected all the aircrews who were queueing up to join the new airline and then saw to their training, first on the Britannias and then later on the new BAC 1–11s.

He encouraged his new pilots and aircrews to become perfectionists. 'If you are going to be a pro, be a good pro,' he told them.

With the Britannias, he was training his new crews on planes he knew as well as anyone in the business. At Air Charter he had been flying them round the world to Christmas Island and on direct flights from Stansted to Entebbe, which BOAC said couldn't be done non-stop. Laker has always insisted on flying aircraft to the limit of their capability and Hellary had learned the lesson by heart.

The early charter for Air France went extremely well. There was one embarrassing moment when Hellary feared that a fault on his Britannia would delay an early flight out of Orly The Air France operations manager said that he was sure Laker would make arrangements for another plane to be flown over. Hellary did not have the nerve to tell him there wasn't one.

At the end of the summer, Freddie Laker found some new business for his two Britannias in Africa. The United Kingdom and the USA had imposed a joint embargo on sales of oil to Rhodesia on 17 December 1965 – and immediately the RAF had to begin flying supplies of oil into Zambia, firmly landlocked to the north of the rebel colony and hitherto dependent for most of its supplies on rail routes through its southern neighbour. The wry joke in Lusaka, the capital of Zambia, soon became that British Government sanctions were working: in another few weeks, all the measures taken against Rhodesia should succeed in bringing Zambia to her knees.

Freddie Laker missed taking part in the early British Government-financed airlift largely run by BUA and Caledonian, but almost as soon as it ended, the newspapers began carrying stories of Zambia's continuing plight. President Kaunda had been forced to resume exports of Zambian copper along Rhodesia's railways and his country was still critically short of fuel and other supplies.

Laker took his wife to Zambia on what was reported as a holiday. He arranged a meeting with Kaunda and told the suspicious President that he would like to take over the airlift. It took him four weeks to pull off the deal, but in the end he left with a contract which he reported was worth £250,000 to carry fuel and general cargoes into Zambia.

Apart from providing some charter work for his Britannias, the Zambian adventure had another outcome for Freddie Laker and his wife Joan. In Lusaka he met an attractive South African called Rosemary Black, with a growing family but without a husband.

Barely eighteen months later Joan had divorced Freddie and he had married Rosemary.

There was one final product from Laker's African interlude. In spite of his optimistic statements to the contrary, he still had no taker for the third of his BAC 1–11s, which was soon to be delivered, but he negotiated a lease with Air Congo. The third BAC 1–11 was painted in Air Congo's garish red, yellow, black, dark blue, grey and white colours, with a large leopard on its tail, and handed over to the African airline on 13 May. With it went flying crews and mechanics to keep it in the air on its one-year contract.

Air Congo had a massive fleet of ageing Dakotas, plus one Caravelle jet, badly damaged in a thunderstorm. Air Congo pilots apparently believed the correct method was to fly direct for the blackest area of a storm, exactly the opposite of the safe procedure. The BAC 1–11 was leased to take the Caravelle's place and its main run was from Kinshasa to Lubumbashi in the interior of the Congo.

Alan Hellary captained the plane on its first flight out of Kinshasa and when he taxied out for take off he found himself refused flight clearance because he carried no radio officer. He told the control tower that he was flying a British jet equipped to British international standards and that under British regulations he did not need a radio supercargo. He got nowhere. He taxied back off the runway and called up Freddie, who was staying in Kinshasa. Freddie roared into the airport and demanded clearance for his plane. He was told that the only man who could give it was the Aviation Minister. It was a Congolese national holiday and he was somewhere in the country. Freddie bullied the address out of the airport authorities and shot off into the countryside in a hired car. Three hours later he zoomed back waving a piece of paper signed by the Minister.

The hostesses on the 1–11 were Congolese, but flying and maintenance was done by Laker employees. The crews used to leave England for three-week tours. At first Hellary found them reluctant but gradually they established a comfortable base in Kinshasa and the posting became more popular. It made a change from European inclusive-tour flying.

The Air Congo contract lasted for a year and then lapsed, although Freddie had initially hoped that it would be a two-year deal.

Chapter 15

'I have my name on the side of the plane'

Laker operated his small fleet immaculately. Everything on the planes was run by the book, with the flying crews eager to prove their expertise and the cabin staff imbued with the special enthusiasm that Freddie seemed able to impart to anyone who fell under his overbearing charm. He was determined that Laker Airways would earn itself an unmatched reputation. In the first season he flew on many of the flights himself, mingling with the passengers and flattering them with his attention to detail.

When delays occurred he had an almost miraculous capacity for soothing passengers. Anxious Wings' or Lord Brothers' couriers, aware of a five-hour delay, waited nervously for their irate, sweaty, thirsty, tired cargoes of disillusioned holidaymakers to disembark. When Freddie was on the plane, the passengers emerged smiling, forgiving, relaxed. He used to tell them, 'I have my name on the side of the plane. It has got to do well,' and they loved it.

He did achieve remarkably good performance. Over the first year he outperformed BAC's figures by 2 per cent, partly by rigid attention to weight and partly by flying higher than 30,000 feet, which was the altitude at which most of BAC's calculations had been based. He also made the most of the 5 per cent tolerance in fuel figures allowed for in BAC's estimates of performance.

His biggest coup was flying his planes direct from Gatwick to Tenerife. This was at the very extreme of the 1–11's range. Freddie worked out that with seventy passengers and forty pounds of luggage each to give a total weight of 14,580 pounds, the BAC 1–11s would make the Canary Islands without a halt, provided the weather was favourable. He told Wings and Lord Brothers that if they only loaded the planes to that capacity, he would pay if conditions forced a stop at Lisbon to refuel. If they loaded past that point up to the maximum of eighty-four passengers then the travel companies bore the cost, which was £157 for airport charges and time lost.

For his own financial benefit, Laker encouraged his aircrews to fly his new planes as economically as possible. A lot of the savings were just good housekeeping. Why make unnecessary landings just because of careless flying techniques, Laker used to argue.

One of his pilots' techniques to save fuel was to get their planes to their optimum height of 35,000 feet as soon as possible without using too much power. There was nothing special about that. There was nothing unusual, either, in the pilots chatting to other aircraft going in the same direction. But Laker's pilots used these communication channels purposively. A Boeing 707, for example, had a flying ceiling of 41,000 feet. If one took off in front of a Laker 1–11, the latter's pilot would call the Boeing captain and encourage him to climb to his upper cruising altitude as quickly as possible so the 1–11 could in turn reach 35,000 feet rapidly.

The new airline also negotiated favourable flight paths across the countries it traversed.

More radically, Laker Airways pioneered the reduced-thrust takeoff technique which is now standard practice for major airlines. It was the inspiration of Freddie's chief navigator, Ron Bradley, whom Alan Hellary reckoned was half a genius. Bradley calculated the minimum amount of power needed for takeoff at every airport the Laker planes were operating from. He allowed for runway length, height above sea level and its effect on atmospheric pressure, temperature and wind strength from any direction. Then he produced a graph which showed the pilots exactly how much power they would need to take off from any airport at any given total flying weight. It was all reduced to one page.

Reducing power on takeoff had a major impact on engine wear. Takeoffs are when engines are under most stress. Rolls-Royce commented on the fact that Laker's Spey engines were in the best condition of any they received for reconditioning and the company earned the double bonus of paying for fewer overhauls and getting longer flying hours between each reconditioning.

Nineteen-sixty-seven was a lousy year for the travel industry. There was the brief but bloody war between Israel and the Arab states, the King of Greece was effectively usurped by a group of fascist colonels, the Spanish, still ruled by General Franco, intensified their hostility to British ownership of Gibraltar. British airlines managed to increase their inclusive tour business, but only by 12 per cent to just over a million passengers. After three years of spectacular growth a levelling-off was inevitable, but it did not make life easier for Laker Airways.

Nor did the fact that one of Freddie's deals went sour. After the winter in Africa, Laker had leased one of his Britannias on a time charter to Treffield International, a Midlands-based airline owned by Lord Trefgarne, now a junior minister in the Government, and his younger brother. Operating from Birmingham airport, Treffield's business was supposed to come from the North and Midlands, cutting out the trek to the main London airport.

It was only a matter of weeks before George Forster became aware that Treffield was not paying up as promptly as it should. He let the delays run for a time, but in the end he went to Freddie. Laker brought the contract to an abrupt halt. Treffield went to the wall, taking with it Youth Travel Company, the weakest of the three tour operators operating a consortium to share aircraft space. The two who survived were another small company, Cathedral Touring Agency, which was also seriously embarrassed, and a much more substantial concern, Arrowsmith Holidays.

Arrowsmith belonged to one of the pioneers of inclusive tours, Harry Bowden Smith, responsible more than anyone else for starting package holidays from the North of England. As the business grew, Arrowsmith used a variety of airlines including Treffield International. His first programme, when he founded his company in 1946, was to Yorkshire and Scotland, and was just profitable, but not so much so that he did not have to help make ends meet by a little trombone playing. The name of the company was a play on his own – 'Arry Smith. Two years later he started the first holidays abroad from war-weary Britain, to Ireland, where the greatest attraction was the absence of rationing.

Harry was intimately involved in Treffield's financial crisis. In the closing stages, he was visiting Castle Donington daily with pound notes in envelopes for the pilots to enable them to buy fuel abroad to bring their charter passengers back to the UK. When the company finally folded, leaving Laker with a bad debt of £16,000, and bringing the Manchester consortium to its knees, it was Bowden Smith who found other aircraft to carry the inclusive tour business.

One of the airlines he used was Laker Airways.

It was a particularly soul-destroying time for Harry Bowden Smith. Another chartered plane, an Argonaut, full of Arrowsmith holidaymakers, crashed at the end of its return flight from Palma in the middle of Stockport. It was afterwards discovered that the pilot had run short of fuel and had switched to an empty tank. And at about the same time Harry's wife died after three years suffering from brain cancer. He was nearly a broken man.

He had been thinking of selling his business for some time. Laker was impressed by Arrowsmith's profit record and the business, which was one of the best in the travel industry, and made an offer which Harry Bowden Smith accepted. The day after the deal was completed in November 1967, Harry went into hospital with heart trouble. He had been worn down by five years of stress. He was operated on and spent six weeks in hospital, followed by another four and a half months' recuperation. Freddie in the meanwhile delightedly announced his new acquisition, putting an inflated price tag on it of £500,000 and revealing to a slightly surprised world that 'our declared policy on formation was vertical integration – vitally important to stabilize and if possible lower the cost of packaged holidays'. Cliff Nunn became managing director of Arrowsmith, with Harry Bowden Smith a temporarily incapacitated chairman.

Three months earlier Laker had leased eleven acres of land from the British Airports Authority at Gatwick for a £1 million jet centre and in the spring had ordered a fourth BAC 1–11, to be delivered in April 1968. Laker Airways, according to Freddie, was worth £6 million and he was thinking of a share quotation on the London Stock Exchange as soon as he had been in business long enough to put up the minimum three-year profit record.

Both Wings and Lord Brothers had been successful with their time charters, even if the sums had not worked out quite as they had expected, and Lord had done so well it decided it could use another jet next year. Laker had also arranged to sell his two Britannias and the advance payment on the deal had meant that Laker Airways had made a small profit of £39,000 in its first fifteen months of business to 31 March 1967. And he had also begun negotiating with BAC to buy its prototype VC–10 which it was hoped would be available in the spring of 1968. There was no denying that his new airline had got off to an impressive start.

However, in spite of announcing a profit of £305,000 for the 1967 summer season, Freddie warned that the second half of his current financial year looked bleak. 'It looks as though 1968 will be very tough indeed. I doubt if we shall show a full year's profit of more than £100,000. Not only is the December–May half much quieter, but we don't know what may happen to travel allowances or the economy generally in the New Year.'

He boasted that the key to his whole operation was red-hot auditing. 'I don't want to know that I'm losing stacks of money three months after it has happened, so I've an auditor here almost full time. The half-yearly figures up to 30 November were on my desk by 14 December.'

Just as important, though, was Freddie's determination to keep his aircraft full. One new line of business that was already proving very helpful was flying inclusive tours from West Berlin. Laker had recruited a German from the accounts department of BUA who had suggested there was a market for Laker Airways in the isolated German city. Lufthansa was excluded from the market because of the West German Government's refusal to acknowledge the existence of East Germany or its right to dictate flying over Germany and the city's tour operators were dependent on British and American airlines to fly their customers.

In 1968 Freddie succeeded in selling a version of his time charter to Flug Union, a new tour company. The holiday traffic only occupied the plane to capacity in the summer months, but out of season Laker Airways found a ready market flying thousands of Turkish 'guestworkers' home.

Flug Union's founder, Rolf Teichmann, was nervous about his contract, which committed him to a twelve-month charter. He was attracted by the 1–11 because it was modern, but he was afraid the static West Berlin population would leave him with surplus capacity, unless he carved deeply into his competitors' business. Fortunately for him and Laker his worries proved unfounded. By 1973 Freddie had three 1–11s flying out of Berlin out of a total of five and his contract with Teichmann has run for ten years. Flug Union is also a probable user of at least one new Laker Airbus.

Another source of off-season business for Laker Airways was for the British India Steam Navigation Company, flying cruise passengers to and from Mediterranean ports. Like most off-season business, the rates were marginal, both for the shipping line and for the airline, but provided useful revenue in the slack period. So did another hardy annual, transporting hundreds of thousands of pilgrims to Mecca for the Hadj, the Muslim holy week.

From the start of Laker Airways Freddie was keeping a careful watch on possible planes to buy for the future. With the help of his chief pilot and his engineering department he undertook studies of the Boeing 727. To begin with Laker was interested in this plane, which he estimated could fly to Nairobi in three stages and which was in fact flown across the Atlantic by Wardair of Canada. His interest waned sharply when the authorities insisted that the 727s be fitted with stick shakers, an expensive modification at an estimated £100,000 per plane, to give warning of stalls.

Freddie then turned his attention back to BAC, which had a successor to the 1–11 on its drawing boards. In 1967 Laker announced that he would be buying three 2–11s when they were built. In December, the Government decided that the project was too expensive. Then at the beginning of February 1969 Freddie signed letters of intent to buy BAC's next effort, the 3–11, at a total cost put at £20 million. The 3–11 was a wide-bodied 270-seater which could have been in service in 1974 if it had been given the go-ahead. Freddie's order was a shot-in-the-arm for the 3–11 and in view of his close relationship with Geoffrey Knight obviously was designed to help tip the British Government away from the Airbus, the 3–11's direct competitor. He turned the screw by adding that he would have to buy American unless the Government decided what it was going to do by March.

In practice, his purchases were more modest. A fifth 1–11 was added to his little fleet in April 1968 and the Britannias were replaced with two leased 707s early in 1969.

Although the outward image of Laker Airways was of untrammelled achievement, at the end of 1967 one of its major props had been on the verge of collapse and Freddie was forced into decisive action to shore it up. His quick purchase of Arrowsmith was influenced by this crisis, which brought home to him only too clearly just how important vertical integration really was.

The weak link was Lord Brothers, which on the surface appeared the more successful of Freddie's main time charterers with its plans to take on a second 1–11 for its 1968 season. The travel firm had got its sums dramatically wrong. Far from being able to fill two jets, it would have been quite adequately served with one.

Christopher Lord blamed the debacle on the company's new computer. Lord Brothers had bought one of the first to be used in the travel industry from ICL and he claimed that they had been a guinea pig. Ernest Welsman had a different opinion. He told Stuart Alderman that the first figure Lord Brothers ran off their new computer was the projected profit for the year. It seemed success had gone to their heads. Their personal relationship had also deteriorated to an untenable level. They had all but stopped talking to each other. Their business was running rapidly downhill.

Freddie did what he had jokingly threatened in the beginning. He took Lord Brothers over. He first of all contacted Gellatly Hankey, the sleeping partner in the City with 49 per cent of Lord Brothers' equity and bought its stake.

Then he cornered Christopher and made him an offer for his 25½ per cent holding. Lord took a fortnight's holiday in Majorca to decide, but Freddie did not give him much option. He sold out on 26 January 1968, ten years to the day since Lord Brothers took its first booking.

Stephen Lord remained to run the business. Freddie's worst fears were realized. Bookings for Lord Brothers stayed on the level of the previous year, fulfilling Laker's forecast that 1968 was going to be tough and only making full use of a single 1–11 to its capacity. The other had to be found different business. On paper Lord Brothers owed Laker Airways something in the region of £500,000 at the end of the season.

Laker was not helped by a relatively poor performance from Arrowsmith. Due to the after-effect of the Treffield disaster and the collapse of the Manchester airport consortium, Arrowsmith's flying holiday total fell to 32,000 passengers from the record 37,000 the year before. Recovering from his operation, Harry Bowden Smith felt that if only he had been there to prepare the brochures the previous winter and fight for customers himself, this would never have happened.

In spite of Freddie's forebodings, 1968 was a year of further expansion for his group. The inclusive-tour industry was back on its growth path, with a rise of 27 per cent in the number of passengers carried by UK airlines. Although Harry Bowden Smith was not exactly thrilled about it, Arrowsmith made considerable use of Laker's Britannias as well as helping mop up the surplus capacity for the fourth BAC 1–11. Demand for package holidays was growing at an astounding rate, with Laker just one – and not a very big one at that – of the independent airlines operating fleets of 1–11s, Britannias and Boeing 707s.

The competition between the inclusive-tour operators was becoming increasingly fierce. Along with expansion, particularly to Spain, came price warfare. While the planes were full, Freddie's new travel subsidiaries, Lord Brothers and Arrowsmith, were finding the margins on their package holidays cut to the bone. Not only were they forced to sell their holidays as cheaply as they could, but they were also having to invest in hotels in Spain in order to make sure they had beds to offer their customers.

Leading the cut-price campaign was Clarksons Holidays, under the management of Tom Gullick. Gullick blazed a trail of low-price holidays to the sun that brought Clarksons, a subsidiary of the giant Shipping and Industrial Holdings conglomerate, an apparent bonanza of new customers. In 1968, four years after its formation, its customers had grown to 175,000 and five years later it handled 1.1 million holidaymakers, almost as much as the whole 1968 industry total.

Tom Gullick's slogan was volume and to win it he was prepared to undercut anyone else's prices and overbid his competitors ruthlessly to tie up accommodation in which to package his new cheap business. To the rest of the tour operators Gullick seemed to be able to walk on water. They could not see how he could hope to make a profit at the crazy prices he was quoting, but they either had to leave the market to him or compete.

Chapter 16

'A second force'

If life was tough for Laker Airways in the growingly competitive inclusive-tours market, events in the next couple of years proved that Freddie had still got his sums right. The first proof came at the end of 1968, when Harold Bamberg's British Eagle went bust.

It is impossible to resist drawing comparisons between Bamberg and Laker. They were almost exactly the same age. They had both made their first fortunes in the Berlin airlift. They had been contemporaries throughout the fifties when the independent airlines were little more than sky tramps. They had competed for government trooping contracts. They had done aircraft and company deals with each other. They had both sold out to shipping groups for 'a million'. They were the two outstanding entrepreneurs in the industry. Now Harold Bamberg had failed spectacularly, owing Rolls-Royce £630,000 and Esso £300,000, among a list of creditors owed £5½ million.

What had brought Bamberg to his knees was a combination of circumstances and personal characteristics. Bamberg was reportedly demanding and bad at delegating authority. He was also slow to take advice from his subordinates. Although Freddie could be accused of the same faults, he had a sharp ear for suggestions from his staff or anyone else, even if he sometimes appropriated them as his own.

Both of them had exceptionally wide visions of the potential for air travel, but Bamberg was the more extreme, pushing his ideas further and faster than Freddie. When they failed, he pulled out, dramatically and sometimes painfully, where Laker tended to pick up the pieces and make them into something else.

Among the astute operators who picked juicy plums out of the wreckage of British Eagle was Freddie Laker. He needed replacements for his two Britannias and there for the taking were the two Boeings that Bamberg had just bought from Qantas with the help of merchant bankers Kleinwort Benson. The bank wanted them off its hands and Freddie was happy to lease them for Bermudan $8,500 a month.

There does not ever seem to have been an easy time for the independent airlines. By 1960, only eleven of the fifty-seven companies that had been set up since the war to try to run UK domestic services had survived, and nine of those had been taken over.

In spite of the 1960 Civil Aviation Act and the lip service paid by successive governments to giving independents a better chance, the sixties had been hardly any better. When British Eagle went to the wall in 1968, it was only exceptional in being the second largest private airline with 2,300 staff, including 220 pilots and 25 aircraft. In the previous two years nine independents had gone out of business and in the next five years fourteen more went to the wall. Most of them were tiny, ramshackle affairs trying to cash in on the boom in holiday traffic, but that did not alter the fact that they were operating in a hard world.

Ironically business was booming in air travel. But to win a share of it meant new jets costing millions of pounds that had to be paid back out of profits cut paper-thin by tough and at times desperate competitors. Staying ahead in this multi-million-pound poker game required talents of a very high order.

They were talents that had been running out for a long time in Britain's biggest independent, British United Airways, ever since Freddie left. With the benefit of hindsight, it is clear that BUA never managed to weld all the companies it took over into a homogeneous whole. There was never a unified management team and even the shareholders never fully shared an ambition to make BUA work.

It was beginning to lose shareholders as early as October 1965, at the same time as Freddie was preparing to go. Hunting Aviation, Guinness Mahon and Blue Star sold out their holdings, on some estimates as high as 37 per cent, to four of the five remaining major shareholders, and stole amicably away. The next year the UK airline division of the group lost £330,000 and by the middle of 1967 it was forecasting a loss of £532,000, rising to £1.1 million in 1968 and £1.4 million the year after. Its domestic trunk services were heading for disaster and BUA was in the thick of economies, including moving its office staff from London to Gatwick.

Efforts were made to rationalize the regional carriers in the group by merging BUA Channel Islands, itself a grouping of Jersey Airlines with Silver City's Northern Division, with BU Manx Airways and Morton Air Services in spite of considerable employee protests. There was a series of strikes during 1968, including one by the group's pilots that was the most acrimonious pilot-management conflict that the UK civil aviation industry had ever known.

By the end of 1968 BUA had begun to make a modest profit on its South American routes after four years' hard work and had acquired a large slice of the inclusive-tour market, working for Lord Brothers, Horizon Holidays, Global and its own travel subsidiary Leroy Tours. But internally the situation was far from good. In fact the group was already breaking up. The Cayzers had decided to split the main airline activities from the rest of the group and had paid the other shareholders £16 million for the overseas and regional scheduled routes, 51 per cent of Bristow Helicopters, and the controlling interests in Sierra Leone Airways, Uganda Air Services and Gambia Airways. The other parts of the group, Freddie Laker's old company Aviation Traders, British Air Ferries and one or two other interests, were hived off under the umbrella of the original Air Holdings.

Late that summer Sir Nicholas Cayzer asked BEA to buy BUA for £9 million. The answer was no. BUA was forced to go on trying to put its own house in order. Alan Bristow had been given the job of managing director with a brief to cut losses. It was a task that appealed to his hard-hitting personality. Within days he was carving into the soft underbelly of BUA's management perks, giving staff a week to decide whether to buy their company cars at valuation or have them sold.

The publication of the report compiled by a parliamentary committee inquiring into civil air transport created a diversion. The committee was headed by Professor Sir Ronald Edwards, then chairman of the Electricity Council and professor at the London School of Economics (later chairman of the Beecham group and briefly of British Leyland). The Edwards Report had a major impact on everyone's thinking about flying in almost every area, with its forecasts of traffic growth, its analysis of supply and demand for airline seats, its studies of airline economics and its views of how the industry should be regulated. For BUA, its most striking recommendation was the creation of a 'second-force' independent airline, which in essence was the resurrection of Duncan Sandys's idea.

BUA promptly pitched for the role of second-force airline, presenting a six-year plan for route expansion, including London–New York services of unlimited frequency from 1974 onwards and the progressive transfer of BOAC's African trunk services. It argued that this would give it the rational route network and the minimum output on long-haul services of 4,000 million scheduled seat-miles that the Edwards committee had decided was necessary to make the second-force airline a viable international operator. BUA estimated that it needed £60 million for new aircraft and £25 million for ground facilities and working capital.

With an election only a year off, the Labour Government of Harold Wilson equivocated about implementing any of the suggestions from Edwards and at the end of 1969 Sir Nicholas Cayzer approached Keith (later Sir Keith) Granville, managing director of BOAC, this time asking only £8.7 million. BOAC, threatened, if only on paper, with losing a large slice of its scheduled services to a new second-force airline, was interested. If it bought BUA, it would get back its South American routes, plus a large slice of African business, a base at Gatwick and a fat infusion of non-scheduled charter business. Under Bristow, BUA's business had jumped in 1969, with the scheduled passengers increasing by 40 per cent and the non-scheduled by 58 per cent.

The nationalized airline was not the only one interested in BUA. Alan Bristow had tried to buy control before Sir Nicholas went to see Granville, underwriting his offer with the 49 per cent he still owned in Bristow Helicopters. Bristow did not get on well with the Hon. Anthony Cayzer, Sir Nicholas's nephew and chairman of BUA. A second offer from Bristow after the initial talks with BOAC was turned down.

Also interested was Caledonian Airways, which saw a merger with BUA the logical way to create a major independent airline. Adam Thomson, chairman of Caledonian, began serious negotiations with BUA and on 5 March 1970 was on the point of making an offer. He met with BUA management in a rented flat in Dolphin Square, London, to thrash out details.

The next day news of proposals for a merger between BOAC and BUA leaked to the press. The astonished Thomson discovered that Sir Nicholas had agreed a price of £7.9 million with BOAC, with the Board of Trade asked to approve the deal at the end of January. Roy Mason, President of the Board of Trade, had met Sir Nicholas early in February and been assured that there were no prospects of a merger with another independent. On this understanding Mason had approved the deal.

Thomson was not the only independent to be furious. Freddie Laker burst out with, 'the death knell of British independent aircraft operators is now being rung, unless this BOAC–BUA takeover is stopped in its tracks'.

Within a week Freddie had delivered a letter to Sir Nicholas making it clear he was interested in buying BUA. His offer ran straight into opposition from the airline unions, under the strident leadership of Clive Jenkins, who was a confirmed opponent of Laker. At a mass meeting of BUA's employees at Gatwick, Jenkins dismissed Freddie's intervention as irrelevant.

'He's just an old film star trying to make a comeback,' Jenkins said. And he followed this up with a bitter article in the *Daily Mirror*.

Caledonian reacted more subtly. Apart from announcing that it was applying immediately for all BUA's scheduled routes, it leaked to *The Observer* the details of how close it had been to doing a deal. After a carefully worded story appeared in the Sunday newspaper, Sir Max Brown, the senior civil servant at the Board of Trade, quizzed the author of the article – one Roger Eglin – about his facts. On 18 March, as Thomson and John de la Haye, Caledonian's co-founder, listened anxiously, Mason told the House of Commons that he had been misled by British & Commonwealth Shipping about the prospects of forming a second-force airline and that he had not known that the negotiations had been still in progress with Caledonian. As a result he was withholding his permission for a merger with BOAC until other offers could be assessed. It was a dramatic moment. The Tories voluntarily withdrew their motion censuring the Government and Thomson and de la Haye had the satisfaction of hearing a Labour Minister describe the independent airlines as a national asset.

Cayzer set a deadline of 21 May for further offers. Freddie was not able to put forward a bid and on 22 May announced that he had dropped out. Caledonian, on the other hand, pushed ahead. In June, the Labour Party was ousted by the Tories at the general election and four months later it was announced that Caledonian was to purchase BUA as from 30 November for £6.9 million as well as agreeing to buy three BAC 1-11s from British & Commonwealth for £5 million. With funds of £12 million, a staff of 4,400 and a fleet of 31 aircraft, the new group was as big as Swissair, Sabena or Qantas and overshadowed every other airline in the UK except for BEA and BOAC.

Its founders gave a sigh of relief. For six hard, grinding months, Thomson and de la Haye had combed the City of London to obtain finance to launch the second force. Even their colleagues had begun to resent their absence from the airline, asking when they would next see them in the airline's offices at Gatwick.

That this was the direct result of the Tory acceptance of the Edwards Report's recommendation of the need for a second force was made crystal clear when the new Government announced that British Caledonian, as the new group was named, was to be given BOAC's lucrative but politically volatile West African routes, its service to Tripoli in Libya and a share of the London–Paris run. BCAL also applied for a scheduled service to New York and was granted a fifteen-year licence from 1 April 1973.

Chapter 17

'What we want is something simple – like a train'

The driving force in the new group was Caledonian. Since 1970 it has successfully become a competitive yardstick to British Airways and its tartan-clad stewardesses and blue and gold-liveried jets with the Scottish lion on the tail have become almost as well known as the nationalized airline's red, white and blue. But in 1970 Caledonian had come from nowhere. It had been in operation for less than ten years but had emerged as by far the most financially secure independent airline in the UK, with a long list of institutional investors, particularly in Scotland.

Its success was based on exploiting the pent-up demand for cheap travel across the Atlantic. Ironically, it was an opportunity that Harold Bamberg could have had for the asking. It was Bamberg who first dreamed up the idea of very low fares in the fifties, although his applications to the ATLB were for services on British colonial routes. The pamphlet he published to support his case proposed fares to the West Indies and the Far East less than half the then current tourist fares. Prophetically, Bamberg wrote: 'The airlines of the world have developed, and by now fully exploited, the market represented by the wealthy and the business traveller. It must find new markets among more modest travellers. The answer is to reduce the cost of air transport. . . . If fares were reduced many more people would travel.'

But when Eagle Airways Bermuda's New York charter superintendent, John de la Haye, went to Bamberg with a plan to apply to the Americans for a new kind of licence to permit the operation of charter-only services between London and the US, Bamberg did not seize the opportunity.

De la Haye was convinced that there was tremendous potential for charters across the Atlantic being deliberately ignored by the big airlines who were afraid cut-price fares would merely dilute their existing business. He spent two and a half frustrating years working for Eagle, but on Christmas Eve 1960 he flew across to Britain from America to meet Adam Thomson, then an airline pilot, in a hotel in Windsor on Christmas Day. Thomson was a senior pilot with Britannia, which had been taken over by Silver City. He too was disenchanted and wanted to run his own airline.

This was their second meeting and it proved to be crucial. De la Haye flew back to the US that evening, spending twenty-four hours in the hold of a freighter inches from a snarling, caged Alsatian and landing at Gander in a snowstorm, but committed to starting up a new business in partnership with Thomson.

The partners faced two critical hurdles. They needed money to back their plans, and they needed a permit from the Civil Aeronautics Board of the United States, backed by a licence from the ATLB in the UK. Of the two, the permit was the more important.

Their application proved very unpopular in the UK. The essential principle that the Board of Trade objected to conceding was that the US had a prior right to traffic originating in America. The big airlines disliked the idea for other reasons. The principal objector at the CAB hearing in the US was Pan Am, but right behind its lawyer stood one hired by BOAC. They feared that Caledonian's charter licence would open the floodgates to low-cost travel over the north Atlantic. They were right.

It wasn't until 20 May 1963 that the CAB finally granted Caledonian Airways its foreign air carriers' permit for a three-year period under Section 402 of the Federal Aviation Act. It was signed by President John F. Kennedy on 17 June. The 'Caledonian Case' was a breakthrough that has been the stepping-off point for every other airline, including Laker Airways, wanting to fly charters to and from the US and similarly to Canada.

The partners' marketing strategy centred on exploiting the strong ethnic ties between the big expatriate Scottish communities in Canada and North America and their home country. One reason was that Thomson found Scottish investors more interested than capitalists in London.

The second more important reason for the Scottish link was that Caledonian had decided to make use of a neglected provision in travel regulations in order to be able to offer cheap fares. IATA members' main obsession had always been to protect their scheduled traffic. In 1953, though, IATA had adopted a resolution allowing its members to negotiate cut-price charters, 'with one person on behalf of a group whose principal aims, purposes and objectives are other than air travel and where the group has sufficient affinity existing prior to the application for charter transportation to distinguish it and set it apart from the general public'. In other words, not the general public and not anyone who intends to fly in any case.

There were other rules. The agent could not take more than 5 per cent commission, the membership of the affinity group must not be more than a totally arbitrary 20,000 and anyone flying on a cut-price charter must have been a member for six months – these were the important ones

It was de la Haye's and Thomson's inspiration to realize that affinity of interest embraced ties of blood as well as a whole range of shared interests.

They played heavily on the Scottish image. On the planes the Caledonian name was supported by the slogan 'The Scottish International Airline'. To begin with the stewardesses were dressed in the ancient Black Watch tartan, neutral in colour and non-sectarian, but later de la Haye selected fourteen different tartans and let the girls choose the ones they liked. He also let them wear jewellery and their hair long, although he never let them shorten their skirts more than five inches above the knee. The rules said four inches, but he knew they would cheat.

Not that Caledonian's air hostesses were chosen for sex appeal. They were nice, sensible girls who could mother the passengers who in many cases had never flown before. These were the members of the clubs and associations to which the new airline went to find its affinity groups and they were very naive. Caledonian's army of tartan-clad young ladies spent their evenings in draughty drill halls guiding organizations with names like Friends of Clan Albion, the Anglo-Scottish-American Group, the Anglo-American Families Association, the Rose and Maple Amity Club, on how to amend their constitutions to meet government affinity rules, and how to administer their travel arrangements and safeguard their funds. The girls demonstrated meal trays, explained about onboard lavatories and then personally saw off the groups they were looking after. Sometimes they even collected the money. One of the biggest affinity groups was called the Paisley Buddies. It was totally genuine, sending huge groups of Glasgow mums and grandmas over to the States.

Similar organizations were fostered in Canada, New York and the west coast of the US. There was a British American Club based in California, and a Canadian US Pacific Association. In New York tour organizer Murray Vidockler put money into Caledonian and marshalled the ethnic Scots into affinity groups for a trip to the old country.

Caledonian piped them onto its planes and gave them free meals, free drinks and overnight bags as well as their cut-price travel. Its reward was booming business. By 1970 Caledonian was flying 800,000 charter passengers a year and it was the dominant UK carrier in the affinity business.

When Freddie Laker snapped up the two ex-Qantas Boeing 707s from British Eagle's receivers early in 1969 it was for the booming transatlantic charter business that he wanted them. He had never been involved in carrying passengers to and from North America before, but he was never slow to grasp the main chance. His first move after collecting his new Boeings was to find himself a good lawyer to obtain Laker Airways a licence to operate charters.

The man he picked was a lanky Philadelphia lawyer called Bob Beckman. Beckman did all the work preparing an application for a permit from the Civil Aviation Bureau that would authorize Laker Airways to operate transatlantic charter flights. Freddie planned to fly over to the United States a couple of days before the CAB hearing into his application. Beckman went to the airport at Washington to meet his new client, who did not show up. The lawyer only learned why the next day, when Laker finally arrived. Freddie had gone to Heathrow to catch a scheduled flight to America and because he was well known, BOAC's public relations staff had spotted him at the ticket counter and whisked him along to their VIP lounge for drinks. Freddie bypassed most of the formalities and only when he actually tried to board his flight did anyone remember to ask to see his passport. He did not have it.

Instead Freddie went racing to see one of his horses win and the next day the story made headlines in the sports pages of the national newspapers.

When Laker finally arrived in Washington Beckman met him for the first time in Laker's hotel, the Hay-Adams. It is a handsome hotel built in the grand style, with high ceilings and ornate mouldings as well as the inflated prices that go with such adornments.

Beckman joined Freddie for breakfast. Laker opened the menu and scanned it swiftly. 'Two dollars and fifty cents for scrambled eggs!' he said indignantly, his voice ringing across the dining room. He was getting across to his new American lawyer that he did not like being hit too hard with high bills.

They went afterwards to the CAB hearing, where Laker expected proceedings to follow British lines, where everything was considered on the day. Instead the American procedure was to submit everything in writing in advance, with the hearing itself confined to those matters that require exploration. There was no objection; by 1970 the right to operate charters across the Atlantic was virtually open to any airline with the necessary expertise and equipment; and the whole hearing was over in about twelve minutes. Standing outside the CAB headquarters, blinking in the Washington sunshine, Freddie turned to Beckman and said, 'You damned American lawyers, you work by the minute and charge by the year!'

Afterwards he always referred to Beckman as his expensive American. It became one of his standing jokes. He wasn't above using it to his advantage, either. Years later Beckman had him on the witness stand at one of the Skytrain hearings and asked him how much he had spent on trying to bring it into service.

'Well,' said Laker, 'my legal fees have been $400,000.' Beckman nearly went through the floor in embarrassment. He personally had not received anything like that from Laker Airways.

Laker won his licence to fly to the United States and back and in the spring of 1970 he began operating affinity charters. He walked smack into one of the biggest scandals ever to hit the civil aviation industry.

One of Freddie Laker's most impressive qualities has always been his essential honesty. At times he seems to slice his interpretation of the whole truth somewhat fine, especially when he is negotiating a deal, and there is no question but that Freddie believes in the old idea of *caveat emptor* – let the buyer beware. But all the time he is influenced by a strong moral conviction that an ordinary man does not lie. He has always thought of himself as an ordinary man. This meant, in the context of affinity group travel, that ordinary men and women would not perjure themselves in order to obtain cheap air travel. Freddie was to be swiftly disillusioned.

Of the 8 million passengers who flew across the Atlantic in 1970, approximately 1.4 million were flying as members of affinity groups. Possibly as many as half the affinity-group passengers were by then phony. As a latecomer, Laker Airways was picking up the least creditable business.

The lure of less than half-price fares to and from the States had by 1970 irretrievably corrupted the affinity-group concept. As early as 1964 the Midlands Dahlia Society had been forced to cancel its planned excursion to the United States for a return fare of £66 because it had advertised in the personal columns of *The Sunday Times* for people to fill its empty seats. It received a letter back from a Mr Hamilton asking for details and inquiring whether he could join at Manchester or would he first have to journey to London. It could scarcely have been more effectively worded to make clear that Mr Hamilton's sole reason for joining the Midlands Dahlia Society was to obtain cheap travel to the US and that he was not yet a member, far less one of more than six months' standing. The dahlia growers accused Hamilton of being an agent provocateur from a rose-growing society – how else could BOAC have learned of the letter? The breach, however, of government regulations covering affinity travel, was in the Midland Dahlia Society's advertisement.

It did not take long before unscrupulous organizers were in on the act, creating fake societies, backdating memberships, suborning airline staff and even receiving stolen tickets. The extent of the corruption only started to come to the surface at the same time as Laker Airways' 707 began flying. One of the first hints came in an article in the *Financial Times* of London by its travel correspondent, Arthur Sandles. It began: 'An American girl I know in London has a sick mother in the United States. She almost commutes between Heathrow and Kennedy Airports – and has yet to pay the full fare. Membership of numerous "affinity groups" gives her access to regular flights at rates upwards of £40. When one of her groups does not happen to have a suitable trip she knows the ropes well enough to pick up a ticket from someone else's charter.'

The only way she could pick up a ticket from someone else's charter at short notice was by breaking the rules about membership duration. It was easy enough. Knowing the ropes meant knowing a 'charter consultant' like Aitex Travel, which was offering economy travel to Europe, North America, the Middle East, the Far East, Australia and Africa. Once in its Regent Street office, inquirers were told they could buy return tickets to New York in about one month's time.

'Technically speaking,' they were informed, 'you have to be a member of a club, but we can arrange that. We have several clubs and we can backdate your membership to six months. You do it our way and everything will be all right.'

Strictly speaking, they were committing no offence, until the charter flight took off. The responsibility for policing charters rested on the shoulders of the airlines.

Watching to see whether they carried out their police work was the Department of Trade in the UK and the CAB in the States. The CAB was already extremely disillusioned about the whole business. By the beginning of 1970 its enforcement bureau chief, Richard O'Melia, had come to the conclusion that all but the closest affinity groups, like nudists or bishops, existed entirely for cheap travel and were being widely misused. All the Department of Trade inspectors could do in the UK was warn the airlines when they were tipped off that some or all the members of so-called affinity groups were not legitimate. It was then the responsibility of the airlines either to take the rule-breaking passengers off, or face the fines that either the British courts or the CAB might impose.

Freddie was extremely disturbed. He telephoned Beckman from one of his instant Laker board meetings at Gatwick and asked for his advice on how to protect Laker Airways against the illegal operations.

'Stop operating,' said Beckman.

'That's the kind of advice I'm getting from my expensive American,' Freddie quipped. Beckman did not hear from him again for a year. Freddie contacted Raymond Colegate at the Department of Trade who was in charge of enforcing the air transport regulation. He suggested to Colegate that the airlines should keep a blacklist of bent charter operators. Colegate told Freddie that he could not do that. It amounted to boycotting. Beckman also told him it could expose him to the charge of violating US anti-trust laws.

In spite of Colegate's warning Freddie did put the blacklist idea forward in a paper to the Government proposing eight suggestions to tighten up on illegal charters, including making charter clubs submit full passenger lists six months in advance of takeoff and stamping tickets with warnings that in order to be on a specified flight passengers must have been members of the chartering organization for at least six months; otherwise they risked being refused a seat. None of them was adopted.

So Freddie decided to clean up his business himself. He put his faith in his belief that the ordinary man or woman did not lie. He asked every passenger on his flights to put their hand on the Bible and swear they had been members of their affinity groups for a year The rules required only six months, but Freddie decided to demand a year. They also had to swear they had not joined for purposes of travel. Beckman had box-loads of affidavits in his office. No one flew on Laker Airways unless they signed these affidavits.

How much this reflected Freddie's genuine belief in the essential honesty of the common man and how much his hope that these elaborate precautions would convince the CAB that he was not condoning illegal flights can only be guessed, but whatever the motive the idea did not work. Everybody happily perjured themselves. Lawyers, doctors, accountants, everyone signed the affidavits. One of Laker's US-based staff watched a group of priests lining up to check in for a flight to the UK. He went across to one of them and said, 'Father, do you know what you are going to have to do when you get to the check-in point?'

'Yes, I do.'

'You are going to have to swear that you have been a member of this organization for a year and not joined for the purposes of travel.'

'Yes,' said the priest, 'I know.'

'Father, don't you feel in danger of committing a mortal sin?'

It did not take Freddie long to learn that his natural-honesty premise was a waste of time. Crooked charter organizers in New York were selling tickets to any takers, arranging for them to join their groups at mid-town hotels, issuing them with backdated membership forms for genuine but all-embracing affinity groups with large and unpoliceable membership, putting them in buses and spiriting them to airports at the last minute – in short doing anything to get them onto cut-price flights.

In London the centre for illicit trade in charter tickets was the

Earls Court Road and Haymarket. Noticeboards appeared covered with cards advertising cheap tickets. Most of the buyers were students with a youthful contempt for bureaucracy of any kind. They regarded cheap air travel as a right and breaking the regulations as about as serious an offence as smuggling a few cigarettes in from abroad.

What was disillusioning to Laker was not the immorality of the charter operators but the avidity with which the 'ordinary man' connived with them for cheap travel.

At the end of August the CAB and the Department of Trade began to crack down on the illicit charters. Two consecutive charters by the Bexleyheath Theatre and Music Appreciation Society were cancelled after the DoT was given a tip-off that not all the passengers were bona fide members. Lloyd International Airways cancelled the flights. At nearly the same time Caledonian Airways put forty-two passengers off one of its flights to New York for the same reason. A month later eighty-four passengers were turned off a BUA VC–10 at Gatwick after the DoT had warned the airline that not all the passengers flying as members of the Contemporary Cinematic Arts Club might be genuine.

In the US, the CAB began compiling lists of dubious charters by all the major operators, including Caledonian, BUA, World Airways and even the national airlines like BOAC, Pan Am and TWA. The CAB began demanding more details and imposing fines on airlines which were proved guilty of infringing the rules or even who failed to provide proof of their innocence.

Laker Airways was hit twice early in 1971. On 27 March it had to take thirty-eight passengers off a flight from Gatwick to New York after a warning from the DoT. The Department had been tipped off by a travel agent who had a particular dislike of bent affinity groups. The Laker 707 had been chartered on behalf of the European Immigrant Families Association and the Inter-University Student Programme, two typical umbrella titles that neatly embraced the two main sources of cut-price travellers, older people visiting friends and relatives and young students off for a subsistence holiday across the Atlantic.

Two months later Laker was raided once more by the Department, again due to a tip-off from the travel agent. This time a spot check of the 158 passengers on Laker's Boeing revealed forty-six of them were not bona fide members of the US Left Hand Club, which had chartered the flight through a New York agent. The aircraft left with the remaining 112 after a three-and-a-half-hour delay while the Department's inspectors interrogated the passengers.

The raid was filmed by Independent Television News, which had also been tipped off. As the bewildered passengers stood there, among them an old lady in tears, Freddie was furious. He accused the Department of telling the television company of its plans and said that if it had not been responsible it should have called off its investigation when it saw the TV cameras. The Department was equally perturbed at the presence of the TV cameras and realized that its officials, too, had been 'set up'. It was the last such formal 'raid' officials made.

After his last brush with the Department Laker had overprinted his tickets with the regulations applying to charter flights, but he must have realized that all passengers on his flights were not qualified. His sense of outrage was fuelled by the adverse publicity, but it reflected the fact that his own attitudes towards cheap travel had already undergone a subtle change. From being shocked at the duplicity of most travellers, Freddie had come to accept the philosophy being widely promoted not just by the bent charter operators but by people in the respectable end of the travel industry and in major airlines, including British Overseas Airways Corporation, and even in the Department of Trade and Industry itself. This was that the regulations needed reform and that everyone was entitled to cheap travel without having to belong to irrelevant affinity groups.

The previous November Colegate had told delegates at a conference of the Association of British Travel Agents in Rotterdam that the rules governing cut-rate charter flights by affinity groups were 'the biggest can of worms on the travel scene'. BOAC had already put up proposals for an 'Earlybird' booking system and it and British Caledonian were being granted special charter rights to the Far East that took them clear of the need for affinity traffic.

At the same time the charter racketeers had achieved near-respectability following a little-publicized case at Great Marlborough Street magistrates' court, London. Ian Tollemache, founder of the Seven Seas Fellowship, one of the earlier group operators, was convicted of contravening the ATLB's civil aviation licensing regulations. He was fined £5 and the magistrate delivered his opinion that since cheap transport was to the public good he could not see where any vice lay.

By the spring of 1971 operators like Tollemache were running what amounted to cheap scheduled travel. A string of cut-price ticket agencies had opened. Jet Travel Concessions, Seat Centre, Charter Flight Facilities, Expo International and Travelscene were all openly selling backdated memberships along with cheap tickets and more and more affinity groups were cheerfully admitting instant members.

But at the same time Laker was being harassed by the authorities for something he could not control and which was apparently increasingly being publicly condoned. The worms were out of the can and crawling all over Laker Airways' transatlantic business.

When Freddie had finished shooting his mouth off at the Department and the television companies, he called a meeting of his top management, including Robin Flood, his public relations chief. Once his anger had subsided, he started talking about how they could break out of the trap that affinities created.

'What we want,' he said, 'is something simple like a train.' It was not a new idea. He had registered the name of Skytrain the year before, when he first started to try to find a solution to the affinities problem. Now, however, he was in earnest.

Six weeks later Freddie Laker lodged an application with the ATLB for a new, simplified, no-booking, walk-on scheduled service across the Atlantic at fares of £32.50 each way in the winter and £37.50 in the summer. The battle for Skytrain had begun.

Freddie announced Skytrain at a press conference at the Savoy Hotel on the last day of June 1971. He told the press and television reporters that its £37.50 single transatlantic fare was a direct challenge to government, both in the UK and the US, to liberalize air travel and reduce fares. He revealed that Laker Airways had net assets of £1.68 million and tax equalization reserves of £450,000 – a total of over £2 million which could be looked at two ways. It was not at all bad as a measure of five years' hard work from a standing start in one of the toughest commercial arenas in the world. But it was not much compared to the might of the national airlines or even Britain's new 'second force', British Caledonian. However, Freddie said confidently that he had the financial structure to back Skytrain.

Launching it would not need any extra capital, he told journalists.

Laker's application for Skytrain was not heard until the end of October, which gave him time to put together a more detailed case.

In the meantime the authorities on both sides of the Atlantic, far from accepting defeat over bent charters, had merely been nurturing new methods of control. In Britain, the first blow was struck with a £200 fine imposed by a magistrate in the small country town of Dorking on the head of a local air charter firm for breaking air-licensing regulations. The message was clear. The period of *laissez-faire* was abruptly over. At the same time the ATLB introduced tougher regulations. Individual charters had to be filed in advance and doubtful cases had to undergo a hearing. A whole flock of hearings began, with the ATLB throwing out an alarming proportion.

The airline was also in trouble in the States. At the end of the year the CAB revealed that Laker Airways was the first foreign charter airline to fail to give it the information it was demanding about flights to and from America. The board said it was concerned about Laker's 'indifference' to repeated requests for information on flights over the past six months. The CAB gave Freddie a twenty-day time limit to produce the details it wanted.

The CAB's enforcement branch had compiled a list of 217 charter flights by Laker Airways which it claimed had included bogus affinity groups. Freddie proved remarkably uncooperative. In Britain Laker said that he was surprised that the CAB was behaving the way it was. The company said that its American lawyers had been discussing the question for some months and that the airline had not heard that these talks had broken down in any way.

'It's simply a matter of what we feel they have a right to know.'

What the CAB was entitled to know in Laker's view was not enough to satisfy the American Government agency. Three months after the CAB's deadline ran out it announced that Laker Airways and Donaldson International, which had also fallen foul of O'Melia, would have to submit supporting information to the CAB at least twenty-five days before each flight to prove they were abiding by the regulations. The board revealed that several CAB employees had responded to 'mass media advertising' and bought tickets on charter flights operated by the two British airlines. They were accepted as passengers and flown between America and Britain even though they did not meet charter eligibility requirements.

The effect on Laker Airways' affinity charters was drastic. Just how badly the airline had been hit was revealed by Freddie in evidence to the CAA in August, when he made his second formal attempt to win a licence for Skytrain. Under cross-examination by British Caledonian's lawyer Leonard Bebchick, Freddie said, 'Last year we did something like 150 flights – and these are round figures out of my head, but it gives you an idea of the size of the problem – about 150 flights last year. This year we are doing 12. Why are we doing 12? The passengers are there, the trade is there. The reasons are quite simple.

'Either the groups were not good enough for us to put out – I am prepared to talk about myself, but it is across the board – and then out of those we thought were good enough to put up, the CAA turned some of them down; and of those the Americans and the Canadians turned some others down. Anyway, the net result is that in Laker Airways we are probably doing something like 10 per cent of what we did last year.'

The north Atlantic was not the only long-distance route on which inclusive-tour and affinity-group charters had been developed. With his usual sharp eye for business, Freddie had watched how Lloyd International had flourished with its charters to the Far East and in 1970 Lord Brothers announced long-distance holidays in South Africa and India, as well as a round-the-world air tour in its new winter programme. The prices were keen. Fifteen days in India, for example, only cost £369 all-in.

In the summer of 1970 Freddie also began trying to obtain permission to fly to Australia. His first application was turned down but early in 1971 he flew to Australia with his son-in-law John Seear to try again. He talked to Sir Donald Anderson, director-general of the Australian Department of Civil Aviation. Laker campaigned on Australia's need for tourism and proposed fifteen-day inclusive tours from Australia to the UK, with full board at first-class hotels, for $A935.

In April Freddie said that the Australians were considering his application to provide inclusive tours for 9,000 Australians with a guarantee of an equal number of British visitors. His application fell on stony ground. One Australian source had estimated that BOAC and Qantas had lost £11 million revenue in 1970 due to charter operations, and Sir Donald, who for a period doubled as director-general and chairman of Qantas, was unlikely to be sympathetic to Laker.

In spite of the rebuff, Freddie has never stopped his efforts to win permission to fly to Australia. It is his ambition to extend Skytrain from California on around the world. So far Australia has vigorously resisted the proposals, but even the threat has appeared to result in a series of substantial reductions in fares between the UK and Australia.

At the time, Laker was probably fortunate that his application was refused. His tours would have coincided with BOAC and British Caledonian being given the right to fly exempt charters to the Far East.

A sideline that did come to fruition for Freddie was his participation in 1970 in a new airline called International Caribbean Airways. Freddie went into partnership with two Barbados-based businessmen, Norman Ricketts and Geoffrey Edwards, with the support of the Barbados Government, which was not averse, like most of the West Indies mini-states, to the idea of its own airline. The new airline began operating scheduled weekly flights between Barbados and Luxembourg and regular charters from Canada and West Germany with fares at roughly half the standard BOAC price at £131, roughly comparable to BOAC's new 'Earlybird' advance-booking fares. International Caribbean was a convenient outlet for one of Freddie's two 707s which was painted in striking colours as befitted a national West Indian airline. The colours raised a few eyebrows among conservative British tourists when Freddie made use of the ICA 707 on *ad hoc* charter work, which he had no compunction in doing whenever it paid.

In 1973 Freddie bought Ricketts and Edwards out and at the same time the Barbados Government took up its option to a 51 per cent share in the airline. In January 1975 ICA was designated the national carrier for Barbados by IATA.

Chapter 18

'Just in case'

It was cool, even by the standards of an English summer, when the Civil Aviation Authority's first hearing of the Skytrain case began in August 1972. But the weather could do nothing to dampen Laker's bouncing enthusiasm. As far as he was concerned, he was onto a winner.

He told Lord Boyd-Carpenter, chairman of the newly formed authority, that he thought Skytrain would be exceedingly profitable. 'If I may say so, I think it is the best idea I have ever dreamt up, certainly the most profitable. So far I have never seen anything quite so profitable.'

Laker has always been engagingly candid about the profit, or 'heavy sugar' as he sometimes likes to refer to it, to be made from championing the cause of the forgotten man. But a year before the CAA hearing, when Laker and his senior managers were beginning to thrash out the details of Skytrain, their immediate preoccupation was not so much profit as survival.

Laker is at his most inventive when under pressure. He feels all his best ideas have developed accidentally out of the need to solve some problem. And Skytrain was no exception. The concept, like many good ideas, was simple. All most affinity travellers wanted, he reasoned, was cheap point-to-point transport. They did not want the frills: reservations, hotel bookings, or even meals. Buying a ticket would be as simple as for a train. If it was full, people would simply have to wait for the next one.

Picking a name was a matter of the obvious. Laker had pioneered rail-air connections when he had persuaded the French authorities to build a spur line into Le Touquet airport to meet aircraft on BUA's Silver Arrow service from London to Paris, and Gatwick airport was linked to London by rail. Skytrain was merely a way of describing the route from London to New York.

The idea would need to be refined. Laker had already applied to the Air Transport Licensing Board for a ten-year permit for his novel Skytrain. The hearing had taken place in October 1971 – and the ATLB had taken some convincing that such a revolutionary idea, cutting across all conventional notions of scheduled and charter airline regulation, should be allowed to go ahead.

In Washington, Bob Beckman heard the hearings were coming up and offered to fly over and help. Almost before his plane had touched down at Heathrow, he was in a car on his way over to Laker's headquarters on the edge of the runway at London's other main airport, Gatwick.

They were all sitting round the boardroom table waiting for him: Laker; his right-hand man, Cliff Nunn; his son-in-law, John Seear, and most of the rest of the senior management. There was some chat about Beckman's flight, a little leg-pulling, and then Laker signalled the opening of business. 'Okay, tell us. Bring us the word from Mount Olympus,' he said.

Beckman had no simple message. Instead he had a lot of questions. When he had first heard of Laker's new idea for a way out of the morass of the bent affinity market, Beckman had begun floating the plan around. There was no better place to do it than Washington. The headquarters of the Civil Aeronautics Board were there – along Connecticut Avenue from Beckman's own office – and there were more lawyers expert in aviation in Washington than anywhere else in the world.

As Beckman described Laker's dream of a 'train in the sky' where passengers arrived at the airport, bought a ticket and stepped on board, his contemporaries were cynical. But they were sure of one thing. There would be plenty of work for the lawyers. The smart ones reckoned Beckman would put his young children through college on the fees from this brief.

The Department of Trade's civil servants were equally sceptical when Laker first tried Skytrain out on them, but some of them thought it had sufficient merit to be worthy of consideration. Beckman wanted to see if the idea could be developed to the point where it would have a chance of winning over the sceptics and defeating the certain opposition of the scheduled airlines. Whatever Laker might say, his rivals were certain to claim that Skytrain was no more than a clever way of repackaging cheap air travel legally.

After a few minutes' probing by Beckman, with his sharp line in cross-examination, the Skytrain was beginning to look shaky. Laker had been quick with his answer to Beckman's first question but the lawyer, although he did not say so, thought it a poor one. Insistently he led Laker on through the questions. Wouldn't Skytrain divert a lot of traffic away from the scheduled airlines? How great were the dangers of a chaotic price war breaking out? Surely all the other airlines would want to compete?

Laker, appreciating what Beckman was up to, began to spot the pitfalls as they opened up in front of him and became increasingly intrigued. He was more than intelligent enough to realize that while a few shaky answers were inconsequential in the privacy of his own boardroom, his case would have to be more persuasive if the ATLB was to be won over. Soon Laker was responding to Beckman's coaching and groping towards a reasoned case for Skytrain.

He insisted that Beckman cancel his hotel reservation and come to stay at his home. As they ate dinner, Skytrain seemed the least of Laker's problems. He was the genial host, laughing and joking. Beckman was puzzled. He had anticipated that they would continue chiselling away at Skytrain. He shrugged and joined in.

Later still, after midnight, he was in bed reading when Laker walked into the guest room in his pyjamas. Standing there, a rumpled, over-sized teddy bear, scratching himself, Laker said, 'About those questions you were asking.' Late into the night, they tossed ideas back and forth. By four in the morning, Laker had all the arguments and counter-arguments for Skytrain clear in his mind.

His objectives at the outset were modest. He wanted to get away from the chaos of affinity and secure a modest niche in the low-fare charter market. He saw Skytrain not as an attempt to break into the scheduled business but as a development of his existing charters and was genuinely surprised that Beckman insisted that it was certain to be regarded as a scheduled service. There was no suggestion that Laker's 158-seat Boeing 707 which would fly the daily Skytrain was taking off on a crusade against the scheduled airlines or was set on disrupting the north Atlantic market which by this time was over 12 million passengers a year.

Before Skytrain could fly, many verbal battles had to be won. The first was to convince the ATLB that a licence should be granted. The second was to persuade the Government to designate Laker as a

British carrier on the north Atlantic. And then this process had to be repeated with the authorities on the other side of the Atlantic. With so many arguments to come, the early rehearsals by Beckman and Laker of the case for Skytrain were all important.

After all the preparation, the autumn hearing at the ATLB was an anti-climax. The board listened carefully to Laker's arguments and then the following month, in November, announced that they had turned him down.

The rejection scarcely came as a surprise. The independent airlines had long ceased to have much conviction in the ATLB's willingness to lead or innovate. The Minister had reversed the ATLB's decision to give Cunard–Eagle a transatlantic scheduled licence after an appeal from BOAC. Ever since, the board, stripped of whatever bite it might have had, had become excessively timid. Beckman, who had acted for Harold Bamberg at Eagle, had had first-hand experience of this. Civil servants involved with aviation at the Department of Trade had learned to turn the board's weakness to their advantage. The common pattern was for someone, usually either BOAC or BEA, to appeal against ATLB decisions. If they felt it necessary, officials in the Department knew that they stood a fair chance of influencing the outcome of an appeal by selecting the 'right' commissioner to hear it. Should this fail to produce the desired result, the Minister was not bound to accept the commissioner's recommendation and often did not do so.

The ATLB's main argument for rejecting Skytrain was that the scheduled airlines, within the International Air Transport Association (IATA), were still arguing bitterly about the current fare structure for the north Atlantic. While the debate about these fares was so 'delicately balanced', the board felt it impossible to judge the impact of Skytrain on the existing airlines or vice versa.

The board fretted over whether Laker's 'forgotten man' actually existed, and over the service's chances of success. Laker's counter to this had been that his airline could afford to lose £400,000 if the worst happened. He would not allow 'the fabric of the company' to become involved. The operation carried little risk, anyway. If the results were unfavourable, the service could be withdrawn or cut back. Such an eventuality might inconvenience the public but, without an advanced reservation system, there would be no question of their losing their money if flights were stopped.

1 One Tudor and a line of Yorks queueing for takeoff in the Berlin Airlift.

2 Cockpit of a Tudor.

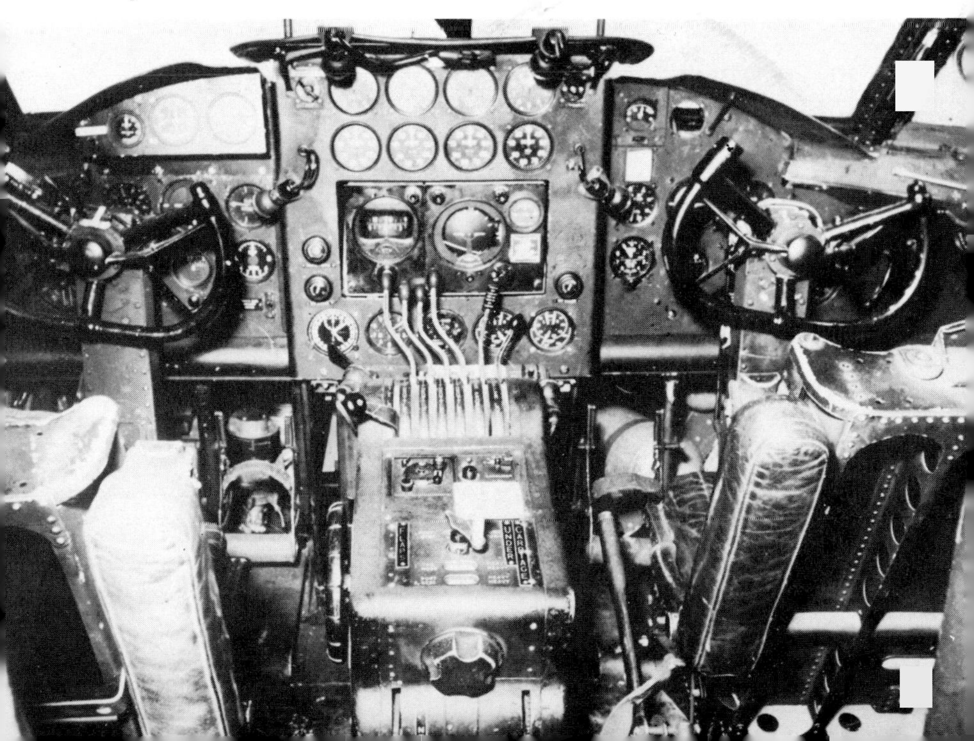

3 Freddie and Joan Laker in 1957.

4 Part of Aviation Traders' vast fleet of scrapped Hunting-Percival Prentices – ex-RAF trainers bought by Freddie to convert for civil use. In the middle stands a lone Tudor.

5 The Accountant at Southend Airport flanked by Freddie's Bentley.

6 Freddie and Jack Wiseman with the crew of the Accountant.

7 Freddie with Mr J.O. Death at the Newmarket Sales in September 1958. He spent nearly £20,000 buying three colts for his Epsom stud.

8 The Carvair, Freddie's ingeniously converted DC–4 and the scissor jack invented by his chief designer Arthur Leftley.

9 BUA's VC–10 having a cargo door carved in its fuselage.

10 Laker Airways is born. Freddie with his new chief engineer Bill Townsend *(left)* and 'Atty' Atkinson *(right)* his general manager with a model of their new BAC 1–11 passenger jet.

11 Freddie and Harold Bamberg, one of his greatest rivals.

12 BELOW The first Skytrain flight leaves Gatwick airport for America.

13 OPPOSITE Freddie celebrating winning his battle for Skytrain.

LAKER
LAKER
POL ROGER

14 Freddie and his third wife, Patricia, at London's Heathrow airport en route to America in June 1978.

15 Sir Frederick Laker outside Buckingham Palace after being knighted in July 1978.

Laker thought the risk minimal. To succeed, he pointed out, all he had to do was sell a hundred £37.50 seats per flight on his Boeing 707 aircraft – a load factor of 62.9 per cent. Based on US experience with stand-by fares and on the evidence of International Caribbean Airways' cheap flights Laker was running between Luxembourg and Barbados, he believed the load factor might be as high as 70 per cent.

His costs were much lower than conventional carriers. The 707's round trip to New York would only cost £6,600. Meals would be charged for: £1 for main ones, 50 pence for breakfast and 25 pence for tea. His promotional budget would be £30,000, and while this included launching costs, he felt that even this was on the high side.

Laker and Beckman thought they had prepared for every eventuality. Airlines usually worried about employees selling off expensive air tickets cheap. Laker realized he would have the opposite problem. There was a danger that people might buy, only to resell at a profit. He invented all sorts of ways of stopping this including stamping buyers' hands with ultra-violet to deter professional ticket touts. Despite all his careful preparation, the ATLB still caught Laker on the hop. How would he control the crowds of eager passengers?

Predicting the market had been one of the trickiest problems. In the end, Laker had simply worked out a continuum of load factors starting at 40 per cent and working up to 90 per cent. Then he had calculated the profit or loss figures at the varying load factors. But he had been so preoccupied with trying to define the market and whether there would be enough people to fill the seats that he had not got round to anticipating being overwhelmed by the demand. After the first day of the hearing, he and Beckman had to work late devising 'crowd-control' plans.

Successive governments had overridden its decisions so often, the ATLB had little reason to stick its neck out at the best of times. But autumn 1971 was no time to choose to be caught up in controversy. The ATLB's days were numbered and the board was being wound up. The new Conservative Government had accepted the views on civil aviation prepared by Professor Sir Ronald Edwards and his committee in a government-commissioned study of the industry It was already looking for a chairman to run the new air transport agency, the Civil Aviation Authority, which would implement the more liberal, competitive regime Edwards had called for. Only a month after the ATLB turned Laker down, John Boyd-Carpenter, a Tory MP, was given the job.

Still, even if the ATLB was being axed, its final verdict, though negative, was encouraging. 'It seems worth a trial in some form in the right circumstances, especially if it drew off some of the present illegal traffic,' said the board.

The hearing had been a good dress rehearsal. Many of the criticisms – that Skytrain would divert traffic from existing airlines and that their reaction might cause disruption – had correctly been anticipated. One of the most encouraging features was the attitude of BOAC. The state airline did not make a formal objection. Instead its representative pointed out that traffic was already moving at fares close to those proposed by Laker and that new low fares should be available within four months on scheduled flights.

Redrawing the customary battle lines between state airlines and independents, British Caledonian was the main objector. Since Caledonian had acquired BUA, the airline had moved in as Laker's next-door neighbour at Gatwick. British Caledonian's main witness was one of the senior managers acquired with BUA, Alastair Pugh. A decade earlier he had worked, at Laker's behest, to prepare BUA's scheduled route applications. Now he was planning director of BCAL.

British Caledonian had become equally disenchanted with the growing corruption of the affinity-group market and the ruinous rates being charged by the 'boom and bust' competition. Unlike Laker, however, the long-term goal of the airline's founders, de la Haye and Thomson, was to run fully-fledged scheduled services across the Atlantic. They felt this was the only way to break loose from the insecurity of the charter market and build an airline with a long-term future.

By demonstrating that there was a need for a 'second-force' independent airline, which on some routes might compete with the state airlines, the Edwards Report had created an opportunity which Caledonian had been quick to seize. Its successful takeover of BUA and the encouraging attitude of the Government had left British Caledonian with the ball at its feet. Laker could not have chosen a more inopportune time to step in and try to kick it off the field. The plum route between London and New York, by far the busiest long-haul international route, was the cornerstone of their long-term strategy. BCAL's own application for a scheduled licence to fly to New York was due to be heard shortly.

The ATLB's obvious hint that Skytrain might have some merit were more than enough to encourage Laker to appeal. The commissioner chosen to take the appeal, Sir Dennis Proctor, seemed ideal. His interests were many and varied. He was a trustee of the Tate Gallery, and only the year before he had published a book about Hannibal, a man who seemed to share Laker's refusal to give way to obstacles.

Sir Dennis had been a civil servant for over thirty years before retiring but he had also had a taste of the outside world. For three years, he had worked in industry, becoming managing director of the Maersk Company. Just before the appeal, he had been a director of another public company, Williams Hudson.

It is hard to believe that the Department's nomination of a man who had left the Civil Service for a spell, only to demonstrate that he could rise to the top in industry, was an accident. Laker was clearly a man after his own heart. He concluded crisply that he had 'no hesitation in recommending this appeal'. Where the ATLB had wandered round the houses, Sir Dennis dismissed many of the objections to Skytrain out of hand.

The uncertainties about IATA's current tariffs had been resolved, he said, and much had still to be settled before advanced-booking fares could be introduced on charter or scheduled flights. He agreed that Laker had demonstrated the need for Skytrain. He had also shown his ability and willingness to stand the loss if the experiment failed. It was not for the authorities to fret about potential risks facing Laker. It was for Freddie to decide how he would meet any competition that might develop. Nor, Proctor pointed out, should the ATLB have worried about the problems of designating Laker as a British scheduled airline. That was for the Minister to decide.

BCAL's objections were brushed aside. BOAC was so far the only authorized British scheduled carrier on the route and had not objected.

Highly encouraging from Laker's point of view was that BOAC's position, if anything, had shifted towards a degree of support for Skytrain. While they were keen to see cheaper advanced-booking fares, which they had pioneered with Earlybird to Bermuda, they could see the merit in trying out a new type of service.

Laker told Sir Dennis that if a licence were granted quickly, he thought Skytrain could be flying by August, only fourteen months after his first application to the ATLB in 1971.

But it was still too early to start popping the champagne. John Davies, the Tory Secretary of State at the Department of Trade and Industry, dismissed the appeal and requested that the new controlling body, the Civil Aviation Authority, reconsider the application. Laker was naturally indignant at this delay and went to see the Prime Minister, Edward Heath, at 10 Downing Street to argue that the appeal should be upheld. Heath was sympathetic and was on the verge of overriding Davies. In the end, he was reluctantly convinced that the CAA would have been irreparably weakened, almost before it had begun its work, if it were excluded from consideration of such an important case.

Laker was frustrated but had every reason for optimism about Skytrain's prospects. Twelve years earlier at BUA, he had seen a Tory Government pass a new Aviation Act, only to see the promises of a better future for the independent airlines remain largely unfulfilled. This time, there seemed every chance that the latest measure, the 1971 Civil Aviation Act, might achieve something more positive. He knew from his contacts with the Department of Trade through 1971 over the affinity problem that officials were willing to take a more constructive approach.

The origins of what was effectively a revolution in official policy went back to the period from 1967 to 1969 when the late Anthony Crosland was the Labour Government's President of the Board of Trade, the Department of Trade and Industry's predecessor.

Until then most of the arguments about civil aviation had really been about ownership. The Tories tended to back the free-enterprise independent airlines; the Socialists supported the state corporations.

While he was a Socialist, Crosland's contribution to the long-running aviation debate was to suggest that ownership wasn't really so important. What mattered was whether the business in question was efficient. And if the state airline was inefficient, the consumer was paying twice – once through high fares and then through his taxes. What gave Crosland's views added strength was that, unusually in Labour Party terms, his junior Minister, Bill Rodgers, who was on the right wing of the party too, shared them.

Crosland had a number of forceful advisers, not least of them Alan Day, an economics professor at the London School of Economics. As the Government's adviser on civil air transport reporting directly to Crosland, Day was well placed to advance his views in favour of more competition improving efficiency. Day believed the consumer mattered (he became chairman of the Airline Users' Committee for a brief period in 1979) and that more efficient airlines should help cut excessively high fares.

The Edwards Committee's inquiry was the immediate outcome of these influences. Edwards had become an industrialist but like Day he was a professor and held seminars at LSE. As a practising businessman, Edwards was not content to sit in isolation and pass judgement. He insisted that his inquiry get out and about in the industry. The committee visited California where competition had produced some of the world's lowest air fares. Edwards ordered a special investigation to confirm that BUA's route to South America was making a genuine profit. The results of this, as much as anything, helped convince him that independent airlines, given the opportunity, could play an important role in expanding British air transport.

To add to these two LSE men, there was a third, Raymond Colegate, the career civil servant who joined the Board of Trade's aviation department in 1967. Before this, he worked in the Central Statistical Office, the Treasury and abroad in Europe with the European Free Trade Association.

Colegate was the link man between the Department and Edwards. He originated a series of straight briefing papers plus some more imaginative 'think' papers. These raised a number of issues: one in particular was whether the system would work when scheduled airlines were tightly regulated and the rules covering affinities so loose. It was very much to the point. At the Department, Colegate had the unenviable task of policing the great affinity charade and realized that some reform was essential.

The trouble was that affinity, originally a 1930s idea for regulating bus charters, was purely arbitrary. There was no economic justification for it and it was far from clear how it had come to be applied to air transport. Why should people have to belong to a group of bird-lovers to get on an aircraft? Affinity rules were an anachronism and no more than a means of making sure that low-cost fares being offered by efficient airlines like Caledonian and Laker were not too competitive with the scheduled airlines.

The belief that change was needed spread beyond the independent airlines and the people associated with Edwards. One of the most radical thinkers of all, Hugh Welburn, was actually working for BOAC as assistant market research manager. Two months after the Edwards Report was published in May 1969, entirely on his own accord, but with the encouragement of his boss, Eric Hall, Welburn wrote a paper simply called 'Bonus' and circulated it within the airline.

Some years earlier, Welburn had left BEA, disenchanted by the complacency of the airline's senior management towards charter competition and its reluctance to recognize and cater for the rapidly expanding demand for low-fare travel. Something of an idealist, he still remembers the impact of a lecture in the 1950s by US aviation pioneer Eddie Rickenbacker which stressed the value of air transport in bringing peace and prosperity to the community. Welburn is a determined original thinker and admirer of Laker.

Welburn argued that the airline was not just selling a single product, travel. He told doubtful managers that they were not simply in the business of selling seats, they were selling a whole range of services: the right to cancel a seat at short notice without penalty; the right to book a seat at the last moment in the expectation that one would be available and the facility to inter-line – to make a series of bookings with different scheduled airlines right around the world on the same ticket.

Moreover, despite what BOAC staff might think, the airline market was no longer homogeneous. There were sharply differentiated groups of travellers. Businessmen would want to buy all these services; the holidaymaker or tourist, the VFR (visiting friends and relatives) traffic, had much simpler requirements. They only wanted a seat from A to B. The link between Welburn's VFR traveller and Laker's forgotten man is obvious. As Laker was trying to demonstrate, they were the travellers who didn't want the frills.

Anticipating Laker's ideas almost to the last full stop, 'Bonus' argued that scheduled airlines, 'do not really cater for the important and fast-growing segment which does not value these qualities highly and is willing to sacrifice them in order to save money'. Not only was BOAC neglecting the changing needs of the market, its average load factor was around 60 per cent. In other words, said Welburn, the airline was wasting 40 per cent of its output.

It was within BOAC's power to eliminate some of this waste. Using Boadicea, the airline's reservations computer, Welburn pointed out that the number of seats likely to be empty on any particular flight could be predicted well in advance. If these seats, normally part of the 'wasted' output, could be sold more cheaply to people willing to make firm bookings well in advance, there would be a 'bonus' for the airline as well as for the passenger.

Welburn had 'invented' APEX, or advanced purchase excursion fares, today one of the most popular methods of travelling economically by air. BOAC first tried these fares, then called Earlybird, in 1970 with great success on the London–Bermuda route, which was controlled by the British Government.

BOAC really wanted to try APEX on flights to America but gaining wider acceptance for this innovation was a struggle. Other airline members of IATA were either uninterested, simply could not understand the reasoning behind APEX, claimed it was too complicated, or could see practical obstacles. The German airline Lufthansa argued that its reservation computer did not have the capability to handle APEX.

The APEX argument showed IATA up at its very worst. The most common complaint against IATA is that it is a cartel. But few outsiders realize how woefully inefficient IATA's airline traffic conferences are at fixing fares. When IATA was re-formed at the end of the Second World War, its founder director general, Sir William Hildred, introduced the unanimity rule – no fare decision could be taken without approval of all airlines affected – to overcome the fears of the smaller airlines that they would be bullied into decisions by giants like Pan Am and BOAC.

The tariff managers who go to IATA have their instructions and orders to stick to them. It is not a system calculated to produce original thinking or reform. The veterans who have been at it for years are battle-weary. After his initial rebuff, before putting APEX to IATA again, Welburn made explanatory visits to twenty-two airlines.

Slowly, very slowly, APEX began to be noticed. But the decisions Laker could make during the course of one evening about Skytrain took IATA years to make about APEX. If IATA had been able to gear itself up more swiftly to reform fares with ideas like APEX, it is possible the market might have been closed to Skytrain.

At the Department of Trade, Colegate, still searching for an answer to the problem of regulating the charter market in a sensible fashion, realized the potential in Welburn's ideas. Making passengers book well in advance and ensuring that charter airlines filled their aircraft was a logical rule that could be justified by sound economic arguments. Everyone would get a bonus. So out of APEX, Colegate constructed its charter equivalent, ABC, for advanced booking charter, beating IATA in his application of the basic advanced purchase idea.

Throughout this period, Laker was in regular contact with the Department of Trade. He had had discussions with a number of officials there, including Colegate, about ways of controlling charter abuse.

Colegate suggested ABCs as an alternative. But Laker's reaction was luke-warm. He did not think they would work. The same abuses would creep in. Even if both the ABC and Skytrain ideas had sprung from the recognition that not everyone needed the costly, full range of scheduled service, he still felt the markets were distinct. 'There is a short-term booker and a long-term booker', was how he put it.

The chances of ABCs being introduced did not look too bright. In the Skytrain appeal, Sir Dennis Proctor had said that ABCs had a long way to go before they were cleared. Colegate's own ministry, the Department of Trade, had said that the British and the American Civil Aeronautics Board disagreed on at least six fundamental points. At the present rate of progress, it was doubtful whether they would be on sale by 1974.

Why should people have to wait, asked Laker. He certainly couldn't. The Canadian, British and American authorities were now turning down his charter applications so regularly that his 1972 transatlantic charter traffic was going to be about 90 per cent down. Much more of this and there would be no business left.

Laker finds delay galling. Now something had happened to make the endless procrastinations over Skytrain seem infuriating. Right out of the blue had come an unrepeatable opportunity to 'change gauge' as he put it, to go wide-bodied and buy what seemed to him a superb new aircraft for Skytrain – McDonnell Douglas's DC–10.

Laker was enthusiastic, a boy with the best train set in the street. He had long tried to be ahead of the pack, operating new aircraft like the Britannia, 1–11 and VC–10 while his rivals plodded to oblivion with aerial reach-me-downs. He relished the idea of using aircraft to innovate ideas in air travel. Whether it was running decent, comfortable trooping flights or using the 1–11 for package-tour time charters, he liked to be able to put his airmanship to work and draw on his vast experience.

The DC–10 would require all this. But it would put Laker out in front again. Let his rivals use narrow-bodied 707s or DC–8s. The DC–10's economics were unmatchable. Its flying costs across the Atlantic would be higher than those of a 707 but it would carry at least 345 passengers compared to the 707's 158. The aircraft would make Skytrain, lifting it up to a new level of profitability – as he was soon keen to convince Lord Boyd-Carpenter.

BUA's decision to launch into the jet era with the BAC 1–11 had been bold, but the thought of an airline the size of Laker with a long-haul fleet composed of two leased second-hand 707s and modest financial resources buying DC–10s was outrageous. It was not even sure if he would have any traffic for them. How could he possibly afford an investment that would run out at over $60 million? Even his own senior managers were going to take a lot of convincing.

The Laker luck was running strongly again. The big Japanese domestic airline, All Nippon, had decided to buy DC–10s. Out of deference to the state airline, JAL, which had yet to decide between the DC–10 and Lockheed L1011 TriStar, All Nippon agreed to delay its purchase. Mitsui, the massive Japanese conglomerate, agreed to take on the initial contract for six DC–10s, worth nearly $150 million, and transfer it to its subsidiary, All Nippon, later.

With the rival TriStar behind schedule, such an arrangement seemed safe enough but Lockheed was desperately keen to crack the Japanese market. Sales there would influence the choice of other airlines right through the Far East. Yoshie Kodama, an agent with extensive political and industrial influence in Japan, operating secretly on Lockheed's behalf, managed to block still further any decision by All Nippon. Eventually, as one result of the biggest bribery scandals the world has ever known, All Nippon was forced to switch its purchases to Lockheed TriStar jets if it was to keep its airline licences. But work had already begun on the six DC–10s out at McDonnell Douglas's plant in Long Beach, California.

Determined to hold Mitsui to the contract, McDonnell Douglas was willing to help by scouting out possible alternative customers. In 1971 a deal was clinched with Turkish Airlines, who took three, including the aircraft that crashed at Paris in 1974 killing 346 people.

In the same year as the Turkish sale, McDonnell asked Laker if he was interested in buying DC–10s. Laker was thrilled at the possibility of a deal but even apart from financing it, there were problems. Mitsui's aeroplanes were DC10–10s, designed for US transcontinental routes and tailored to the needs of American airlines. They might be too big for Laker's European package tour traffic and lacking in range for the Atlantic charter market or Skytrain. In fact BCAL had already turned them down.

Operating the DC10–10 across the Atlantic was the sort of challenge Laker and his chief pilot, Captain Hellary, relished. By making sure that air traffic control allotted them the best flight levels and airways and aircrews paid attention to fuel conservation, Laker and Hellary had demonstrated that it was possible to operate the 1–11 safely over longer routes than anyone had anticipated. Laker excelled at getting that bit more out of an aircraft than the brochure said he could. Attention to 'good airmanship' was a standing rule in Laker Airways from the start.

There was no question of compromising on safety but if Laker could operate the DC–10 at the limits of its performance, its economics improved markedly. Getting sufficient range for the Atlantic run was no problem. The DC–10 was designed to carry cargo; his would carry extra fuel instead. Planned this way, costs would be much lower than with the 10's more powerful sister ship, the DC10–30, which, if anything has too much, rather than too little, range for the London–New York run.

As Laker began to dig into details, he became more and more impressed with the economics of the DC–10. They were better than he had ever seen in an aircraft before and with 345 seats, it looked hand-made for Skytrain. Where the 707 needed to fill 63 per cent of its seats to break even, this crucial figure fell to 52 per cent for the DC–10. It was a ridiculously low level, Laker thought. The aircraft was perfect.

To some extent, the risks of the deal could be underwritten. Freddie believes that buying the right aircraft new to the market is a sound policy; values always rise. If Skytrain did not materialize, he calculated he could sell or lease the aircraft, or even trade his position in the delivery line for a profit.

The money side was fitting together nicely as well. In all his long experience of the industry, Beckman, who was involved closely in the deal, had never seen anyone strike a better bargain. Even Laker admitted he had been lucky – luckier than he had ever been before. He was buying the DC–10s over ten years with money borrowed at a low fixed interest rate of 6 per cent. That left him with £20 million of capital allowances that would have to be offset before he would have to pay any tax. At the end of ten years, he reckoned he would have aircraft worth £8 million plus.

The real beauty of the deal was that there was hardly any of his own money involved. Through some rugged bargaining, he had come out of the deal with loan-financing of over 90 per cent. Mitsui was carrying most of the risk.

As a precaution, towards the closing stages of the deal, Laker decided to test market the DC–10 around the British travel trade. The industry's response was disappointing. The most commonly used package-tour aircraft had between 120 and 150 seats. The travel operators – the people who put the package tours together – were very distinctly worried by the awesome size of the DC–10, which on shorter runs could carry 380 people. For many of them it was too big a commitment.

Laker reopened talks with Mitsui. Sitting in Beckman's Washington office, facing the company's three negotiators, small, proper Japanese businessmen in neat dark suits, Laker told them they would have to be prepared to help him out if he could not market the DC–10's capacity.

The implications of the change of gauge were enormous, he told them. Overnight his capacity would treble. He wanted Mitsui to agree a formula which effectively meant he was only paying for the planes out of flying revenues. He had not lost confidence in the aircraft, he told them. He merely wanted this extra safeguard just in case he could not fill them.

The trio of negotiators were carefully writing all this down. But the expression 'just in case' clearly puzzled them.

'Let me explain,' said Laker, as the Japanese continued to write. 'I'll give you an example. There was a man selling Rolls-Royces down in Texas and one day this big cowboy came in wearing a big hat and wanted to look over the Rolls-Royces.'

Warming to his story, Laker explained how the Texan noticed that the Rolls had a hole for a starting handle. The Japanese continued writing furiously. 'What's a crank doing in a big, beautiful, modern car like this?' asks the Texan. 'Just in case,' replies the salesman.

'Just in case,' expostulates the Texan. 'Just in case what?'

So the salesman replies, 'You know those things you have here on your chest?' gesturing towards his nipples.

'Yes,' says the Texan.

'Well, you know what they are for?'

'No,' says the Texan.

'Just in case you have a baby.'

Laker grinned broadly at the blank-faced negotiators.

What they eventually made of this back in Japan is not known. But Laker got his pay-as-you-fly deal.

Cautious as ever beneath the show-business surface, Laker held off signing. The Skytrain hearing before the Civil Aviation Authority was due soon. All his soundings of the Department of Trade suggested the prospects were good but on many occasions in the past, Laker had seen official promises turn sour. Just in case . . .

Chapter 19

'The forgotten man'

John Boyd-Carpenter had been a Tory MP for twenty-six years. He served the prosperous constituency of Kingston-upon-Thames to the south-west of London without break since the end of the Second World War, until he was formally appointed the Civil Aviation Authority's first chairman on 1 April 1972. There he succeeded Robin Goodison who had been acting as a caretaker chairman since the CAA's official formation the previous December. Before the war, he had been a successful barrister and his parliamentary career had been a distinguished one. He was acknowledged as a fine speaker and an extremely astute politician. The Conservative Party had had loyal service from him: he had been a respected member of the Cabinet, holding a number of senior posts including the Ministry of Aviation.

The chairmanship of the CAA was an excellent post to crown a distinguished career. It brought with it a life peerage and one of the highest salaries in the state industrial sector. It was also something of a consolation prize for Boyd-Carpenter who had seen the coveted Speakership of the House of Commons go to a Tory colleague, Selwyn Lloyd.

However, the job was more than a reward for loyal political service. Prime Minister Edward Heath had given the job to Boyd-Carpenter because he wanted action. Heath's Government was still wedded to the idea that competition, the free play of market forces and less regulation would bring about the dynamic lift the British economy so badly needed.

What better place to use as a forcing ground for these ideas than aviation? The Edwards Report and the people associated with it had started the currents flowing in the right direction. There were airlines like Laker and British Caledonian, full of enterprise and keen for an opportunity to show what they could do. While Laker was critical of the Edwards Report, which he felt had simply shared out the main business between British Caledonian and British Airways, Edwards had certainly started new ideas flowing. His report had led directly to the creation of the Civil Aviation Authority. Boyd-Carpenter and Heath were astute enough to see that this was a foundation that could be built up and that reducing air fares through competition would be a popular political cause.

The CAA's new chairman, although he had given up a number of important City jobs to take on his new role, was not a professional economist, but those close to him recognized in him a profound belief in the merits of competition; it was an article of faith about which he had no doubt.

He was contemptuous, too, of the way the scheduled airlines operated through IATA which had its headquarters in Geneva, 'that mausoleum of lost causes'. He recognized that IATA as an association did a lot of useful work. Its clearing house, allocating fare revenues to different airlines and permitting travellers to make long complicated journeys with several airlines on one ticket, was indispensible.

Boyd-Carpenter, however, was convinced that IATA had become corrupted into a cartel operating against the public interest. The unanimity rule, first designed to protect the small fry, now gave them too much power. Any emergent nation could set up an airline, however inefficient, and shelter within the rule. Fares were fixed to accommodate them rather than the public. He thought such a regime based on high fares too unstable to last.

The presence of such a strong, outspoken man at the CAA ensured its independence. The CAA had drawn a good number of its key staff from the Department of Trade, though Boyd-Carpenter made sure that the CAA never became entrapped in the Department's apron strings.

In Whitehall parlance, neither its chairman nor its staff could be considered 'safe'. The CAA had a mind of its own with economists and tariff experts to help form policy. Colegate moved to the CAA and four years later Welburn arrived from British Airways on secondment.

The two new arrivals were a powerful addition to Boyd-Carpenter's team. Welburn was a radical in his approach to fare policies and he had an instinctive feeling for people, a belief that the airlines could give them a better deal. Colegate, perhaps less radical, shared similar views, laying more stress on the importance of the consumer than his colleagues at the Department who were preoccupied with the health of the industry, and most particularly of the state airlines, BEA and BOAC.

He was a tireless negotiator who knew the minutiae of the complex world of air transport regulation backwards. But more than anything his long experience in the Civil Service had taught him how to make bureaucracy work to his advantage, how to pick a way through the endless committees and even turn the bumbling machinery of IATA's tariff-fixing to his advantage. Welburn thought him outstanding at this sort of work. He was particularly impressed by his knowledge of when the time was ripe to push an issue, of how, in Welburn's words, he was able to match 'the noises reaching his left ear with those his right ear was picking up'.

Ironically, given how much this group had in common, there was one contradiction between them and Laker. The former were not averse to seeing the IATA airlines jolted by some plain old-fashioned price cutting. Laker, by contrast, was going out of his way to demonstrate that Skytrain would not cause disruption, a euphemism for a price war, or massive traffic diversion from other airlines: he realized he had to convince the more cautious Department of Trade and the US authorities as well as the CAA. He was contemptuous of the IATA set-up but at this point had no interest in declaring war. He believed he had found an untapped market. He wanted quietly to get on with the job of developing it – well, at least as quietly as his outspoken nature would allow. Skytrain had yet to become a crusade.

When the Skytrain hearing opened in that first cool week of August, the CAA put up a strong team. Boyd-Carpenter was chairman. His own deputy, Robin Goodison, a former deputy secretary in the Department's civil aviation division and John Bowley, another former civil servant and an economics and licensing expert, made up the panel.

The contestants were largely unchanged from the first round before the ATLB. Laker had his two lawyers, the British Queen's Counsel, Harvey Crush, and Bob Beckman. Their opponent, British Caledonian, had its own American lawyer, Leonard Bebchick. His offices were only a stroll from Beckman's in Washington.

Like Beckman, Bebchick had a close relationship with his client. He had helped Caledonian win the first charter licence the CAB had awarded a foreign airline. Caledonian had been his first client when he put up his own shingle.

BOAC was still neutral with its solicitor and legal director, Bob Forrest, making representations on its behalf. There was also a handful of expert witnesses: an American airline economics expert for Laker and some of BCAL's management.

The proceedings were held in the CAA's headquarters on London's Kingsway, opposite Holborn tube station. The atmosphere was relaxed and informal. Each side presented its case and was cross-examined by the opposition lawyers and the panel. Sometimes the questioning was fierce; but exchanges were occasionally humorous. If the cast was virtually unchanged from the first ATLB hearing, the main arguments were becoming familiar as well. Would Skytrain have a monopoly? How likely was it to succeed? Was 'the forgotten man' a figment of the imagination?

The hearing abounded with logical traps. Laker had to explain how Skytrain could flourish without diverting large numbers of passengers from existing airlines. BCAL was trying to demonstrate that the venture was a risky one while simultaneously arguing that large numbers of passengers would be poached from existing services.

Boyd-Carpenter set the scene with a few, but important, opening remarks. There were two questions uppermost in his mind. What sort of traffic would Skytrain attract? How could services at such low fares be economically viable? The CAA's terms of reference enjoined it to look to the health of the industry and the well-being of the traveller. Boyd-Carpenter's two questions were the core of the case. Laker had to produce satisfactory answers to them to win.

Crush, for Laker, opened with some strong popular rhetoric which had a distinct echo of his client about it 'The British working man requires to be able to travel without paying for an entrepreneur to take his cut in the charter, without paying for the reservation system, without paying for the middleman's advertising. He wants transportation pure and simple without having to wait two or three months before he could go.'

Then he cited Laker's immense experience – the work with the Tudor, Accountant, Carvair and the development of BUA which had made a profit in every year under Laker as managing director.

Despite Crush's strictures about entrepreneurs, there was no apparent reaction when Laker testified to the immense profit potential he could see in Skytrain. The availability of DC–10s made an enormous difference to the profitability. They also scaled up the size of Skytrain; the estimated average load factor of 70–75 per cent raised Skytrain's traffic to nearly 250,000 people each way, nearly three times the first modest Boeing 707 plan.

After being surprised by the ATLB's fears about crowd control, Laker was ready for challenges about what would happen if Skytrain were an overwhelming success. Characteristically he chose to attack rather than defend. 'I have never known as reason for turning down a service that it was too successful. To say that is rather like the Palladium having Frank Sinatra on and saying, "We are not going to have him tonight, we shall have a queue outside." It is a ridiculous suggestion. What we are going to do is what the fellow at the Palladium does: he opens his doors, allows his passengers to come along, and when he has got his 345 he puts a notice outside, "House full", and all the passengers disappear, or the public go away and find other ways of going.'

Boyd-Carpenter was keenly interested in Laker's claim that in the forgotten man there was a hitherto neglected market. When his opportunity to test the strength of Laker's case arose, this was the topic he turned to first:

'Mr Laker, you said several times you were going for a wholly new market?'

'Yes.'

'Do you mean by that that if you were to be granted a licence in the terms applied for there would be no diversion at all from the existing carriers?'

'I think I said yesterday, sir, it is obviously impossible to say there would be no diversion at all, because one passenger is technically diversion. Obviously it would be ridiculous for me to make a total statement that there will be no diversion, because one is diversion. I am saying that it is my considered opinion that there will be no measurable diversion with Skytrain. We have had examples of this type of business. I have been in the very low fare business many times before; over twenty years ago we were operating very low fares, you will remember they were called colonial coach air services, and with government cooperation in those days we put artificial barriers in the way of passengers. In those days we had to use Imperial aeroplanes, and we used to introduce stops on routes that did not need stops, and yet we achieved tremendous load factors, quite remarkable load factors, 85 per cent to 90 per cent all year round. We made money and the public was happy. The only reason these services stopped was in those days we could only operate to the colonies, and we have none now, and the services were converted as independence came to the colonies into scheduled services – the licences held today by the Eastern, Central and West African services of British Caledonian were all developed from these services. We have a vast experience. We have the position, not our own, but of Loftleidir [the Icelandic airline], and it is carrying in 1971 a quarter of a million passengers. You do not have any screams from BOAC or Pan American about Loftleidir's diversion. This is a different service and it is non-diversionary.'

'The answer to my question is that you say there would be diversion but it would be small?'

'It would be negligible. As I say, I would be stupid if I said none, and you would not believe me.'

'What is the type of person in the new market for whom you propose to cater? Can you identify your forgotten man?'

'Yes, I can. I do not really want to bore you reading from our little blue book but we have assembled a whole lot of research produced by other people and we came out with an average that this low income earner in the United States and this country will be in the age group average of thirty-eight to forty.'

'This is the identikit of Laker man, is it?' asked Boyd-Carpenter.

'Yes,' replied Freddie, 'we refer to him as the forgotten man, as the man not catered for in air transport. He is the chap who gets fourteen or twenty-one days' holiday a year; he has an income of I think $4,000 a year in the United States. It is actually in the book if you would like me to read it.'

'Not at the moment,' said Boyd-Carpenter dryly.

'In the United Kingdom it is something like £1,500 a year,' Freddie continued. 'This is the sort of chap. He is really what I have said, the working man, an ordinary working man with a low income.'

'How many are there in the United Kingdom? What is your potential market – what is the maximum?'

'I would say eight million men plus their families.'

'And in the States?'

'120 million. It is limitless, the bottom of the barrel cannot be reached.'

'Am I right in inferring your eight million in the United Kingdom represent the figure for the paid up membership of unions affiliated to the TUC [Trades Union Congress]?' Boyd-Carpenter asked.

'That is the minimum number,' Laker replied.

After a few more questions, Boyd-Carpenter returned to his main theme.

'You say there is this vast potential market of eight million men and their wives and families in this country, and 120 million in the United States, all of which is going to be opened up by your operating a service to the United States at higher fares than are already open to those who are prepared to join affinity clubs. I find it difficult to follow why they should go with you.'

Freddie was ready for this as well.

'Three million people travelled on charter last year, approximately three million. We are saying in round figures that 200,000 people would travel on Skytrain because they cannot fit into the rules, the existing rules of air transport whatever they may be. They either cannot book up, or are unwilling to book up two months ahead. So there are in our view hundreds of thousands of people who will not be able to book up – let us take six months as it exists today – or are unable to commit their savings to a group that amount of time in advance.'

Boyd-Carpenter's next question was much tougher.

'What you are presenting us with is an immense potential market, which is not travelling at the moment, not because of the fares, but the rigidity of doing business in affinity groups?'

Freddie wriggled. 'I would not say the rigidity of the affinity group system. I would say the rigidity of air transport as it is today.'

Boyd-Carpenter pressed him. 'It is the rigidity that is the central point, it is the rigidity of the rules governing charter operations in the widest term, rather than the level of fares, which in your view is the deterrent to the development of this enormous market?'

'Yes, but I think the level of fares does have a very marked impact on the whole market. I think it would be quite wrong to say that all charter fares are in the £45 bracket. A lot of people pay £75 and £80.

So the fares do happen to have had an impact; and quite frankly we cannot get the fares any lower, substantially lower, than we have them.'

'The more important reason for these people not travelling on the North Atlantic, is it the rigidity or the fares?'

'I do not think there is any one important reason, not one more important than the other. There were three million people in 1971 who were prepared, acting legally, they were prepared to join a group and wait six months before they could travel. That is a substantial market. We have used the illegal group passengers as a market, a pointer to what people will do. We say there is another market that, in terms of the present population, is more substantial than all the others put together, and that will produce a viable operation for us. I am not trying to replace anything, because I believe the man who will book up two or three or even six months in advance, and will cooperate with a travel organizer or organization for a full load, should have and will have a lower price. But it is still not catering for the man who wants to go quickly and who cannot commit himself in advance, at a reasonable fare substantially below anything he could get from an equal type of air transport. This is the quick ticket, no frills, and he will go without food, he will bring sandwiches if he wants to, in order to take advantage of this relatively low fare.'

Boyd-Carpenter finished his examination by asking whether Skytrain's success depended on Laker holding a monopoly.

'No, sir, at no time do we, or have we, done any of our sums on the basis that we have a monopoly of any description but it just happens to be a commercial coincidence that in the short term we could quite easily have a de facto monopoly; but equally as I know, as everyone in this room knows, in a young dynamic industry – relatively young but very dynamic – it is impossible to have even a de facto monopoly for more than a short period of time. Even with competition – and I have no objection to competition – we will obviously have a short time on our own, because your own panel would not license a second operator until we had demonstrated the point, either good, bad or indifferent.'

'The American Government might?' asked Boyd-Carpenter.

'Exactly,' said Freddie. 'We have always assumed the possibility of an American carrier doing it. We cannot base the future, our whole future of Skytrain on the basis that we would have a monopoly.'

The fiercest battle within the hearing was that between British Caledonian and Laker. Crush had opened his testimony by pointing out that there were no competing applicants. In practice British Caledonian saw Skytrain as a head-on competitor for its proposed scheduled service between London's Gatwick airport and New York.

The figures for BCAL's service were in sharp contrast to Skytrain. Laker's rival anticipated that the loss in 1973–4, its first full year of operation, would be £1.3 million – a far larger sum than the £400,000 Laker was prepared to commit and which he certainly did not anticipate losing.

Out of its first year's revenue of around £8 million, BCAL's promotional and advertising budget would amount to £1 million – ten times the revised promotional plan for Skytrain. If Skytrain achieved no more than a 59 per cent load factor, this would still mean Laker carrying two an a half times the number of passengers BCAL forecast for its own first year of operation.

With sums of this order at stake, BCAL was worried. Pugh, by now research and planning director, pointed out that each point his airline lost off its anticipated load factor would amount to 1,440 passengers or £85,000 of revenue. If Laker diverted 5,000 would-be BCAL passengers in the first year, the start-up loss could rise to £2 million.

Pugh's chairman, Adam Thomson, came to the hearing to throw his weight behind BCAL's case. He would be amazed, he said, if they lost none of their traffic to Skytrain. It could place the whole second-force experiment on the north Atlantic in grave jeopardy.

Laker reassured Caledonian that he would try to schedule Skytrain's departure so that passengers would find it impossible to cancel BCAL reservations on the day and switch to Skytrain at the last moment if a seat was available. Pugh pointed out that one Skytrain departure could carry 50 per cent of all the daily average scheduled traffic between New York and London in the months of January and February – and this included first-class passengers.

The rivals were poles apart. The Laker team insisted that BCAL was banging its head against a brick wall asking to launch a conventional scheduled service in the face of massive competition from established airlines like Pan Am, TWA and BOAC.

Not so, BCAL argued. The experience and the marketing contacts the airline had accumulated during the years of transatlantic charter business would help build a market. Still Laker disagreed. His chummy way of giving them fatherly advice to that effect – he had been an objector at Caledonian's licence hearing – grated.

Laker reiterated that his way into the market was to adopt an original approach; to come in on the flank. He rejected ABC's as a possibility to be considered. 'I would just be in the ruck with everybody else. I have spent a lifetime doing something different.

'Frederick Alfred Laker wants to try a new market. I want to be constructive; I want to offer air transport to a lot more people. This is my last minute contribution to British civil aviation.'

As the moment for Crush's closing address arrived, Boyd-Carpenter asked for information in answer to his key question about money. What were the financial resources available in the event of Skytrain being unsuccessful?

Crush's answer was to point out that on accepted accounting methods depreciating the DC-10s over sixteen years with a 10 per cent residual value showed an average projected profit of £1,781,773 per year at the expected load factors with the break-even load factor of only 52 per cent.

As for resources, the CAA, as well as the objectors, had the latest audited accounts. The CAA also had more confidential information about Laker Airways's financial strength and details of how the DC-10 purchase had been arranged. It would find the arrangements to buy the DC-10s 'both remarkable and adequate'.

Before the hearing, Boyd-Carpenter had only known Laker by his reputation. But the airline chief's determined advocacy of the Skytrain case and his claim that the airlines were neglecting a substantial portion of the travelling public made their mark. After the three-day hearing, Boyd-Carpenter rose, impressed.

The licence was granted the following month in September. A CAA courier brought it down to Gatwick by hand. Laker thought it might be misconstrued if a car was sent to the terminal to collect him. So he and the staff had to sit, waiting anxiously, as the messenger set off from the railway station serving Gatwick, walking around the perimeter road, calling first at British Caledonian, and then carrying on to Laker.

'Will I be pleased?' asked Laker when the courier arrived.

'In part,' was the answer.

Puzzled, Laker opened the envelope. Inside was the licence, beginning on the first of January the following year and running for ten years. That was fine, but there were two surprises. If Laker used the DC–10 in the off season, its capacity was to be restricted to the 189 people who could travel on a 707. Nor could Skytrain operate from Gatwick. It would have to be based on Stansted, a wartime bomber airport to the east of London now used for charter flights.

Both variations could cost money but Laker took the surprise laconically. 'Oh, well,' he said, 'I suppose Stansted's ten minutes nearer New York '

The award of the ten-year licence allowed Laker to finalize the contract for the DC–10 purchase. But before he could sign it, there was one last piece of mischief left up his sleeve. On one memorable occasion, Laker's bargaining tactics had so bedazzled the British Aircraft Corporation that they had ended by agreeing to his request for commission. The thought of it was still amusing Laker when he arrived in Tokyo to sign the DC–10 contract. As they were about to walk into the office for the formal contract-signing ceremony with the directors of one of Japan's largest industrial empires, Laker turned to Beckman. 'Is this when I ask them for the commission?'

Chapter 20

'The day I give up Skytrain will be the day I die!'

Even if Skytrain was to be tucked away at Stansted, there was no likelihood of the IATA airlines overlooking the debut of this new low-fare competitor (ironically enough, following the award of a scheduled route licence, Laker was now entitled to join IATA). Deliberately the CAA chose to announce the award of the licence the day after the 108 airline members of IATA had begun their annual general meeting in London for which BOAC and British Caledonian were co-hosts.

The IATA annual general meeting is as much a social affair as one when much serious business is done. Indeed the proceedings often convey the impression that their main purpose is to fix the venue of the next AGM. On this occasion, there were some set-piece speeches. The delegates and their wives attended a special performance of the opera *Tales of Hoffman* followed by a late supper and dance.

A speech the Prime Minister, Edward Heath, made on the opening day, struck the only discordant note. Heath urged delegates 'to strain every nerve' to bring fares down.

'Many voices are saying that changes such as these will mark the end of scheduled services as we know them today. Maybe, but what we must all be concerned with is the shaping of the kind of services the public wants,' he told the meeting.

'Scheduled services will no doubt continue to serve the needs of those who require the facility of "on demand" and flexible booking arrangements. But already there are many who do not require this expensive facility and who do not see why they should have to pay the added cost.'

Some of the delegates thought Heath's remarks a bit distasteful. Rather like talking shop in the mess, but his remarks were a carefully calculated reminder of Government policy. They were a warning to IATA to mend its ways. The CAA had licensed Skytrain and Ray Colegate had written large parts of Heath's speech.

British Caledonian's appeal was inevitable. But it stood little chance. Boyd-Carpenter may have been a supporter of Skytrain but his panel's decision had been a model of propriety. The politician had not forgotten his legal training. He had stuck scrupulously to his terms of reference, carefully examining the important issues. There were no loopholes for a successful appeal.

In February 1973 the British Government formally designated Laker as a carrier under the Bermuda treaty which regulated Anglo-US air transport. Laker was all set. The Americans still had to accept his designation. But that should only be a formality under the treaty. It was just possible, after two hearings and two appeals, that Skytrain would be flying for the 1973 summer season.

With his British base secure, Laker's next move was in America. The first step was a formal, diplomatic one. At the end of February 1973, the British Ambassador wrote from the Embassy in Washington to present his compliments to the US Secretary of State. He had the honour to forward for onward transmission to the Civil Aeronautics Board the originals and six copies of applications by Laker Airways for the issue of a foreign air carrier permit authorizing the operation of scheduled services.

Now, as the Bermuda treaty elegantly phrased it, the next step was one of 'comity and reciprocity'. However flowery such diplomatic language sounded, the meaning was clear enough. The two signatories to the treaty should recognize as far as practicable and in a friendly way each other's laws and usages. The Americans should now reciprocate by accepting Skytrain. There was absolutely nothing the least bit friendly about what happened next.

No stone was left unturned, no obstacle unraised, in an effort to find something, anything, to block Laker's path. The State Department's opening response that the application had been lost was a hint of worse to come. Never before in the history of US aviation regulation that Beckman could recall had the State Department failed to transmit a licence application to the CAB within days. This time it took nearly six months.

From the start, British officials realized that it was not going to be easy. The head of the State Department's Office of Aviation,

Michael Styles (who retired to take a senior job representing IATA in Washington in May 1979) was known as a hard negotiator. The US Government said it wanted consultations about Skytrain. Those were held at the start of February before the formal licence application was made. They got nowhere and the matter was referred back to London where an Anglo-American meeting about the north Atlantic air fares was under way.

The State Department insisted that there were many aspects of Skytrain it could not understand. Officials asked repeatedly for clarification. They lost at least three copies of the application. British officials never managed to pin down quite what the State Department's position was. Perhaps it was simply taking its cue from the CAB.

Eventually the British Government sent a note to the State Department pointing out that the Laker application had already been delayed fifteen weeks. If it were not processed without further 'undue delay', the US would be considered in breach of an international treaty.

In mid-April 1973, after heavy diplomatic pressure from the British Embassy the application finally limped from the State Department to the CAB. As the regulatory body for the world's largest air transport network, the CAB has a staff of over 600 compared to the 150 or so CAA staff working on economic affairs.

The two bodies perform very similar functions but where the CAA employs economists, the CAB until recently staffed its bureau of economics entirely with lawyers – a practice which seemed to encourage a certain innate conservatism. There was also a conviction that America usually led in air transport innovation – a point which Laker had touched on at the CAA hearing. Whatever the cause, the CAB's senior staff found this strange creature that had winged in from the other side of the Atlantic difficult to come to terms with.

Skytrain was seen as a threat to US carriers. It was a hybrid, something that did not fit preconceived ideas about air transport in the States, and therefore worrying. Secor Browne, chairman of the CAB until 1973, was anxious to try to clear up the affinity mess but was fearful of Skytrain's impact on the scheduled airlines.

Air transport is America's main mode of travel and Browne saw a threat to what was an essential public utility. Scheduled airlines, he felt, had to take the rough with the smooth, operating some poor routes in the public interest as well as profitable ones. There was no such thing as a free lunch. If airlines like Laker could move in, skimming the cream off major routes like the north Atlantic, the system would gradually erode until governments were paying airlines to operate indifferent routes.

He respected Laker's acumen but felt that his charter was not to maintain a far-flung communications network. Nor could he see an obvious gap in the market. The US supplementals, the charter airlines, were capable of catering for tourist traffic if the rules could be sorted out.

Browne's concern for the well-being of the scheduled airlines had good cause. America's major international airline, Pan Am, was losing money heavily and was in a bad way, forecasting even bigger losses to come. Najeeb Halaby had resigned as chairman in 1971 and now quit altogether. Within a few months, Browne's successor, the still more conservative Robert Timm, who argued even more vigorously that his job was to support US airlines, had Pan Am on his doorstep seeking a subsidy – a humiliating situation for an airline that, until very recently, had enjoyed worldwide respect for its technical leadership and commercial sense. Within Washington, Pan Am had considerable influence. Not for nothing had rivals dubbed it 'the flying arm of the State Department

There had been times when British officials had interpreted Browne's open-mindedness about charter reforms as a hopeful pointer to Skytrain's chances. But after Timm had taken over as chairman in 1973, they found him far harder to deal with, a much more unimaginative man.

Before Laker could even begin to convince the CAB that he had a case, there was a dispute with the CAB's Bureau of Enforcement director, Richard O'Melia, to be resolved.

The British Department of Trade believed the business of affinity so asinine that they were sympathetic towards the airlines who were inescapably becoming caught up in it. Officials like Colegate felt that the rules, lacking in logical foundation, were unenforceable. When one official was asked what proportion of charters were 'bent', he replied that offhand he could not think of any that were sound. It was not just the travelling public who had come to believe the law was an ass either. Colegate thought this the first industry he had seen where people got fined for cutting prices.

O'Melia, however, still believed that, properly disciplined, affinity could be the backbone of the charter business. He was greatly respected for his honesty and integrity. He pursued charter violators with the zeal of an inquisitor and Laker, as far as his bureau was concerned, was one of the worst offenders of all.

There was no personal animosity. The enforcer was deeply touched at the end of 1973 by a gesture on Laker's part. Despite their battle, Laker wrote to the Senate committee assessing O'Melia's fitness to become a CAB board member to say he was a man of great fairness and professionalism.

Earlier in the year, the relationship between the two had looked very different. Laker had vexed the CAB intensely by not answering their inquiries. The board were convinced that he had 'fired' one employee so that he would not be able to appear as a witness about charter violations. Laker was equally angry. He saw it as a witch-hunt against his airline.

The truth of it was that the CAB was getting tough. In the previous year Japan Air Lines, World and Pan Am had been fined for selling tickets off cheaply while Alitalia, after an offer of $30,000 had been turned down, finally paid up $50,000 for breaking the regulations on charters and the sale of youth fares. The CAB had also asked a Federal judge to stop Donaldson, a British airline, from making charter flights without approval. That summer there was a spot check at Kennedy which led to the suspicion that more than one in ten of travellers was on an illegal ticket.

In January 1974, it was Laker's turn. The enforcement bureau issued a petition calling on the CAB to suspend Laker's foreign air-carrier permit because of charter violations in the period 1970–2. Some months earlier O'Melia had told Laker that he was prepared to 'wipe the slate clean' in return for him handing over $90,000 to the bureau although Laker claimed no specific charges or details of alleged misdemeanours had even been presented.

When Laker tried to obtain more details, the CAB refused to divulge them. It took months to persuade them to reveal a partial list of the witnesses they planned to call. Angrily he pointed out that he was being given no chance to plead guilty or not guilty. He felt he had tried as hard as anyone to keep within the rules. He held 18,000 sworn affidavits, stacked in boxes in Beckman's office, from US passengers that they had not broken the rules. British passengers signed similar statements on Laker tickets before they got on the plane.

Since March 1972, he had not operated a single charter to or from the US without CAB approval. Furthermore some of the flights listed in the CAB complaint were for bodies as respectable as the Ministry of Defence and Ministry of Technology staff associations.

Laker was furious but it was fruitless. Several sources within the US State Department made it flatly clear that his Skytrain permit application would not be processed until the charter violation proceedings, which could in some cases take as long as two years, had been settled. It was only too clear that without a 'confession', there would be no progress on the licence.

Beckman tried arguing with O'Melia, pointing out that never before had there been a case of an application being held up pending the resolution of an investigation. But O'Melia was determined to sustain the authority of his bureau and remained unmoved. Finally Laker told Beckman to find out what fine had to be paid to get the Skytrain licence application moving.

'What do you want?' Beckman demanded of the bureau.

'The highest fine any airline has ever paid,' was the reply. 'The last one was $75,000, we want $101,000 this time.'

Beckman called Laker from his home – on the kitchen phone – and told him.

'Pay it,' replied Laker. 'Do you know how much those DC-10s are costing me?'

Beckman wrote out a cheque and handed it over to the CAB in July.

Laker insisted that the fine was paid under duress. 'I was faced with the question of do I sell my pride for that figure or do I fight and put my whole business in jeopardy? I said I would capitulate. We agreed a confession but it was watered down because I have never been accused of cheating, lying or falsifying documents. Being in front of the game, and trying to outsmart my competitors, yes; but cheating, no.

'I said I would never give in, but in the end, like everyone else, I had my price.'

The first of the CAB's pre-hearing conferences on Skytrain took place at the end of the month.

American airlines were either opposed to Skytrain or curious about how it would operate and several of them appeared at the main hearing before the CAB's administrative law judge, Greer M. Murphy, in December 1973.

His inquiry was every bit as thorough as the CAA's hearing, though the American system requires more of the evidence in writing, cutting down the hearing. When he had appeared seeking a charter licence in 1969, Laker had been startled by the brevity of the CAB's hearings and this time Beckman coached him. He was to curb his normal eloquence that usually turned the answer to questions into a speech and cut it short. Beckman awarded him points for brevity and within Laker Airways, it was promptly christened 'The yes, no, don't know hearing'. When it was finished, Laker cheerily asked: 'How did I do, Bob?'

In the written evidence, Laker had to forecast operating revenues and expenses by aircraft type for the year beginning 1 April 1974 covering charter and scheduled operations separately between London and New York. These were to take account of four assumptions about the competition. They ranged from a situation where Skytrain was alone in the market to a complete free-for-all where Laker would be competing against TWA, Pan Am, National, BOAC, British Caledonian and the five US supplementals, or charter airlines – Capital, ONA, TIA, World and Saturn.

In March 1974, after digesting the evidence, Murphy, who was thought 'a super man' by Laker people who met him, recommended in favour of Laker being given a permit. The question of the charter violations had been raised again, although O'Melia himself had made it clear that as far as he was concerned payment of the fine had closed the matter. Murphy said they were not a 'rational reason' for denying permission to start a scheduled service. The judge's main criticism was that the fares were too low. As the summer level of £37.50 had been set in 1971, before the 1973–4 fuel crisis, Laker was already recalculating it.

Laker's elated reaction was that 'this is what we have been working and waiting for through the past three years'. But he was premature. However angry the British authorities were becoming, the Americans were not prepared to give way. Comity and reciprocity were conspicuously absent.

The board of the CAB, under its new chairman, Timm, still had to review the judge's decision. They were quite brazen about it. Beckman could only fume as the board did everything to stall, hearing further oral arguments and requesting briefs.

They could not hold the case, they told Beckman, the chairman was out of the country. Hold it without him, Beckman snapped back.

By spring, the Watergate crisis was building up fast. Hopes sagged in the Laker camp as Beckman reported that Washington was paralysed. The canker in the White House was spreading through the administration. Airlines had been among the big contributors to Nixon campaign funds. Cynically Beckman saw the delay as the White House giving them value for money. Then very suddenly on 6 June the CAB's decision was passed to the White House in the greatest secrecy.

In the normal pattern of events, this would have been for the formality of the President's signature. Beckman, however, strongly suspected that the CAB, irrespective of the US's treaty obligations, had done the unthinkable and passed a negative decision to Nixon. It was the only conceivable explanation for the secrecy and speed with which the CAB had acted.

The first leaks in August confirmed the suspicions. Officials let it be known off the record that they had turned down Laker. Despite the fine, despite O'Melia's closing of the case, depite Murphy's decision, the board had fallen back on a plea that Laker was 'unfit' because of what they now described as his charter conviction.

No one seriously believed this was anything more than an excuse. The fuel crisis was taking its toll of the US airline industry. Pan Am was now teetering on the edge of bankruptcy. The whole episode showed how partial America's supposed love of competition could be. When it helped Uncle Sam's boys, fine; when the boot was on the other foot, kicking the loser was a foul.

Whatever the CAB thought, the Laker strategy was to get his application into the White House where British diplomatic pressure could be brought to bear more effectively. In mid-August British officials met representatives of the State Department and the CAB to let them know how seriously they viewed America's failure to comply with its legal obligations under the bilateral treaty.

The Embassy in Washington threw its weight into the fray. With overcapacity in the UK package tour market, and three wide-body DC–10s to keep busy in addition to his existing fleet, life was by no means easy for Freddie. Profit margins were not much better than fifteen pence a passenger. But his resolve only stiffened. 'The day I give up Skytrain will be the day I die.'

Chapter 21

'The writing on the wall'

At the end of 1972 Freddie's businesses were poised on a knife edge. If he had known then that Skytrain was going to take six years to put into operation even his steel nerves might have cracked. He might easily have had second thoughts about going through with his deal to buy his first two DC–10s, favourable as the terms were.

He had already stalled signing the contract for nearly nine months. Although he had announced that he was to buy the two jumbos at the end of February for a cost of $47 million, he did not finally sign the contract until October after the CAA had granted him a licence for Skytrain. Delivery of the first DC–10 had been put back from June and the second from September, but the two finally arrived at Gatwick in November.

By then Freddie knew that his transatlantic charter business was in shreds due to the combined efforts of the DoT, the CAB and the Canadian aviation authorities, which were also tightening up their control over charter flights. At the same time he was uncomfortably aware that the mainstay of his group, the Mediterranean inclusive-tour market, was under intense pressure. Yet he had just taken delivery of two of the biggest passenger aircraft in the world, virtually tripling his seating capacity and burdening Laker Airways with a massive new debt, however favourable the terms might be.

The next two years were to be as testing a period as he had ever experienced. The writing was on the wall. Price warfare in the inclusive tour market since 1970 had reached ridiculous levels. In April 1971 Lord Brothers had been offering three-day package tours to Majorca for £9.99 including a room with a private bath as well as air travel. It was the lowest deal yet in the struggle to keep hotels and seats full. The price war had been sparked off in 1970 by

Thomson Skytours, which offered Mediterranean four-day winter breaks at only £18. In the year to 31 March 1972 Laker Airways had only made a profit of £276,000 and for the past two years had been carrying less passengers than in 1969, at a capacity rate of 78.3 per cent the lowest of all the big inclusive tour carriers.

Compared to the major operators, though, Laker's holiday companies were doing remarkably well. In 1972 Lord Brothers made £40,000 profit and Arrowsmith £100,000. Thomson lost £1.6 million, Horizon Holidays £388,000 and Clarksons a massive £4.8 million. The race for the volume market, initiated by Gullick and joined by Thomson and Vladimir Raitz in particular, was taking its toll.

Fortunately for Laker, just at this critical time he recruited a replacement for the managing director of Lord Brothers, Bob Lewis, who was dying of cancer. It was not the most auspicious way for George Carroll to take a job with Freddie, but it could not have proved more valuable to Laker.

Carroll had been Freddie's PA at BUA and had then been promoted to head the group's growing travel business. When Freddie left BUA he asked Carroll if he would like to join him, but did not have a job to offer that matched Carroll's existing responsibilities or pay. Carroll apologized but Freddie said, 'Never mind, you stay where you are.'

Carroll did stay, to turn BUA's travel interests into a major holiday group under the name of Castle Holidays which by 1972 had a turnover of £7.5 million. But in 1972 Castle became a wholly-owned subsidiary of the Cayzer interests in the aftermath of the BUA takeover and was subjected to radical reorganization by Sir Nicholas. Carroll found himself demoted to just one of a number of directors answerable to the Hon. Anthony Cayzer. He found it a bit too much to take, especially as he was by then one of the most important figures in the travel industry. He was chairman of the Tour Operators Council and also of the vital Tour Operators Study Group Trust Fund, which had been set up to administer the bonds that travel companies put up to underwrite the risk of any of their customers being stranded.

It was at that moment that Freddie turned up to offer Carroll a job. He matched everything that Carroll was being paid by Castle and then squeezed £5,000 out of the Cayzers in compensation for loss of office, a typical piece of Laker cheek. Officially Carroll left his old job at the end of June, but he was already working for Freddie in May.

He could not have arrived at a more crucial time. The previous autumn the package-tour operators had met at the Association of British Travel Agents' annual conference, held in Cannes. Two of the top five, Horizon and Global, had pleaded for higher margins, but Clarksons had refused to concede that low prices were to blame for the industry's problems. Thomson, in spite of being pasted by Clarksons, went along with the industry leader in maintaining that volume was the answer. Margins, though, were frighteningly thin, with the break-even load factor on charter planes up to 85 per cent and most Spanish hotels demanding advanced payments, or 'bed deposits', of up to £300 a room.

What the rest of the industry did not realize was that Clarksons was losing money. 'The secret is carrying volume at a profit which we have done,' it said. In 1971, in spite of increasing turnover by £9 million to £31 million, Clarksons had in reality lost £2.6 million. No wonder even the biggest of its competitors were baffled.

Under George Carroll's management Laker's holiday companies pulled in their horns. Carroll and Harry Bowden Smith could see no point in carrying hundreds of thousands of people at a loss of £4 a head, which was the estimate put on Clarksons's plight. Even so, no one anticipated the disasters ahead. During 1973, the inclusive-tour industry struggled on without the public being aware of the tensions threatening it.

Freddie's first DC-10, christened *Eastern Belle*, was delivered to Gatwick on 17 November. Captain Hellary flew it across the Atlantic and Freddie was there to meet it. It was followed ten days later by *Western Belle*. The planes were fitted with seats and cinema and then took off on a barnstorming tour round Britain, landing at virtually every airport in the country capable of taking them. These included Birmingham, Bournemouth, Bristol, Glasgow, Liverpool, Manchester, Newcastle, Prestwick and Teesside. Freddie even flew *Eastern Belle* to the seaside airport of Hurn and took his old mother up for a flight. The giant planes flew schoolchildren on day trips to the Continent as part of the programme to get the British public used to the idea of flying in them. There was still considerable public doubt about the safety of jumbos, based on nothing as yet but the psychological feeling that the more people are at risk together, the bigger the risk must be.

Then on 21 November *Eastern Belle* flew its first 'paying' flight to Majorca, loosely packed with 331 passengers on an *ad hoc* charter, including a large contingent of travel agents. In the New Year, a DC–10 joined one of Freddie's 707s on a four-week contract flying daily drafts of pilgrims from Jeddah to Mecca in Saudi Arabia for the Hadj.

With Skytrain still not approved, it was only too obvious that the DC–10s had to be found some regular paying business. With the encouragement of Bowden Smith, Freddie swallowed his pride and ate his public criticism of advance-booking charters, just agreed by the Europeans, Canada and America. He announced that Arrowsmith was to use one of the DC–10s on a weekly charter from the North of England to Toronto. Soon this expanded with other ABC services from Scotland to Canada.

The first Arrowsmith charter flight took off from Manchester on 2 April with its seats filled by passengers eagerly taking advantage of the remarkably low early-season return fare of £45 to Toronto. Similarly priced charters began at the same time from Gatwick on a three-times weekly schedule.

Laker Airways passenger loading received a fillip in the middle of the year, when Donaldson International Airways had its application to fly between Gatwick and Prestwick in the UK and Toronto abruptly refused by the CAA and went into liquidation. The report said the airline had shown an unacceptable degree of unconcern for the convenience and peace of mind of the travelling public. The CAA also denounced the airline's weak management and financial viability.

Donaldson had committed itself to fly 5,000 ABC passengers, some of them the following weekend. It sold the business to Laker Airways, which obtained permission from the Canadian Transport Commission to carry them. To fulfil its obligations, Donaldson also had to charter three round trips in DC–10s, and two in a 707 from Freddie.

Although the DC–10s had not been working anything like near capacity, they had done well enough to keep Laker Airways solvent. If only Skytrain could win American approval, everything should be well.

They say it never rains but it pours. October 1973 was when the OPEC countries tripled the price of oil and in 1974 the inclusive-tour bubble finally burst.

It is hard to tell whether the one sparked off the other. At the end of October Freddie forecast that the average fuel cost to the airlines would rise by between 60 per cent and 70 per cent and estimated that on the London–Barbados route flown by International Caribbean Airways the price of the fuel used by the relatively thirsty 707s would double. The DC–10s, on the other hand, had already proved their economy in terms of passenger miles and the fuel crisis would only widen the gap. At the beginning of 1974 Britain plunged into the three-day week. Package-holiday bookings were down by 30 per cent and the operators trembled before the prediction that short-time working would lead millions of potential customers to do without their annual flights to the flesh-pots of the Costa del Sol.

Freddie was the first to grasp the nettle. Lord Brothers began collecting fuel surcharges on its Canadian ABCs, beginning at £5 and rising to £8 by the third week in January. Other airlines reacted in different ways. Most approved a formula for surcharges worked out by the Tour Operators Study Group. BOAC slashed its holiday flight programme by 20 per cent.

In the midst of these troubles, Vladimir Raitz's company Horizon Holidays went under, the first major casualty.

Raitz approached British Airways, Thomson, Thomas Cook & Sons and others, but could not find anyone interested in rescuing Horizon Holidays. With one exception. An urgent meeting with National Westminster Bank, Horizon's biggest creditor, and Court Line, which began at 12.30pm on 31 January resulted in Court Line agreeing to buy the goodwill of the bankrupt company on the basis of paying £1 for every Horizon passenger flown by Court Line Aviation over the next three years.

On the surface, Horizon's 100,000 potential holidays had been saved. But in reality Court Line had only agreed to the deal to fill the empty seats yawning on its fleet of BAC 1–11s, due to the barely hidden crisis that was afflicting Clarksons.

Court Line and Clarksons had become increasingly interdependent since 1970, when the shipping group had ditched its scheduled flying operations which it ran as Autair and bought a fleet of 1–11s exclusively for charter business with Clarksons as its major customer. In 1973, Court Line had been compelled to buy control of Clarksons to protect its air traffic volume in spite of the holiday company's appalling financial state.

The purchase of Horizon did little to help. To begin with Court Line ran straight into violent objections from British Caledonian when it began diverting Horizon's holidaymakers onto its own planes. BCAL, which had already threatened to have Horizon compulsorily wound up if it was not paid over £100,000 owing to it, forced Court Line to compensate it for its loss of Horizon business by hiring one of its jets, fully crewed, as well as providing it with other business. At the same time the number of Horizon passengers fell far below expectations, partly due to the money-back guarantees that Thomson had introduced and which had been copied by its competitors. Laker alone picked up 8,000 Horizon customers.

In August, burdened beyond hope by its debts, Court Line itself went into liquidation, creating havoc in the holiday industry and panic among thousands of ordinary people threatened with the loss of their holidays.

As with Horizon, Court Line's collapse provided new business for Laker Airways. Freddie picked up much of Clarksons's advance-booking charters, which had grown into a large business with separate offices in Southall. This part of the Court Line empire was ironically poised to succeed, and could have proved a major threat to other ABC operators including Laker in the very near future. Laker Airways also secured its share of the inclusive-tour market that was suddenly up for grabs. Freddie was helped by having the DC-10s which were still relatively under-used. The big planes began dropping down from the skies on runways all over the Mediterranean.

Nineteen-seventy-four was the most successful year ever for Freddie Laker's little empire. The collapse of Horizon and Court Line had provided a bonus of unexpected business, as well as clearing the way for the inclusive tour industry to return to more rational pricing policies. George Carroll's TOSG (Tour Operators' Study Group) air travel reserve fund gradually coped with the liabilities thrown up by the Court Line disaster and had grown into a £15 million fund. In between his official duties, Carroll had begun to rationalize Laker's various holiday companies, changing the name of Lord Brothers to Laker Holidays and laying down a sound business organization to handle the rapidly growing ABC business to Canada and the United States. In the next five years Laker Holidays increased its turnover from £3 million to £30 million and underpinned the continuing struggle to start Skytrain – and to operate it at a profit.

Just how well Laker had survived in 1974 was revealed at a CAA hearing on 7 February 1975 when British Airways tried to have Laker's Skytrain licence revoked. Although Freddie calculated that if his Skytrain licence was withdrawn and the worst happened, he had to return his DC-10s, now numbering three, to Mitsui – he would lose nearly £7 million – he said that this had already been written off and that he had managed to pay his way with the planes, which had brought in $25 million in revenue in two years.

Chapter 22

'Bums and gangsters'

In autumn 1974 Laker's patience appeared to snap. At a travel-trade conference in Majorca, he delivered a wildly intemperate speech. Civil servants at the Department of Trade, he trumpeted, were 'bums and gangsters'. Underlining his bitter contempt for them, a furious Laker added: 'If any of them want to victimize me I will die for England with the Union Jack in my hand. I don't want any hammer and sickle in my back.'

It was an extraordinary outburst, exceeding by far Laker's usually good-humoured contempt for red tape and bureaucracy. The civil servants themselves were furious. One rang the CAA and asked what they were going to do about it? The CAA's irreverent laughter did not help. As one of its senior staff pointed out, Laker could not be talking about him or it would have been 'bums, gangsters and bastards'.

Laker believed his anger justified. He had discovered that the Department, or at least some of its staff, was not such an enthusiastic supporter of Skytrain as the Government's public position might suggest. There had always been a feeling within the Laker camp, one that they drew from their official contacts in Washington, that the Department's support was not entirely wholehearted. At the very least, some Washington officials seemed to believe that if they could stonewall Skytrain for long enough, an election and a change of government might just make it go away.

This time, however, the endemic overcapacity on flights between Europe and America was getting out of hand. In the first ten months, the twenty airlines flying the route had sold only 8.3 million of the 14 million seats they had on offer. Collectively they appeared to be heading for a £100 million loss as the fuel crisis began to bite.

BOAC, by this time part of British Airways, was doing better than average. Traffic had actually improved and the airline claimed to have pulled ahead of TWA and Pan Am to become number one between Britain and America with 40 per cent of the market. Its London–New York route was still profitable, if only just.

Pan Am, however, was on the verge of collapse. In August 1974, its management had pleaded with the US Government for emergency financial aid of $50 million with a continuing $10 million a month subsidy. Without this, the airline would not be able to continue to pay its bills from October. It was also highly likely that the banks would start to call in Pan Am's loans which had reached nearly $400 million.

Throughout most of 1974, Pan Am had been holding talks with its rival TWA about the possibility of sharing their transatlantic routes or even merging. In principle the two airlines were breaching US anti-trust laws by even holding such talks but the Nixon Administration gave the talks clearance, invoking the emergency conditions generated by the fuel crisis which looked like adding $200 million to Pan Am's 1974 fuel bill.

While this crisis was building, Laker was patiently pressing his case. Twice during August, he wrote to the British Secretary of State for Trade, Peter Shore, to give him reassuring details about Laker Airways' financial health. In the first letter, Laker suggested that if he got the go-ahead, he might be able to employ some of the people made redundant in the Court Line crash. 'I'm still convinced that in the final event one of our British Ministers will have to contact Dr Henry Kissinger [then US Secretary of State] himself to win Skytrain approval,' his letter added.

On the second occasion, he told Shore he was sure he would agree, 'that with the Skytrain licence Laker Airways will be without a doubt the most successful and most financially sound company in the UK.'

Just over a fortnight later, Laker got a reply from Shore's junior Minister, Stanley Clinton Davis. He said he welcomed anything that strengthened the air transport industry and added: 'On Skytrain, I understand you will have been keeping in close touch with officials here, and will therefore know that both formal and informal representations were recently made to the US authorities on this matter. These should have left them in no doubt that we expect full compliance with the terms of the UK–US air services agreement as regards the designation of Skytrain.'

Even if the Americans, preoccupied with the imminent collapse of

Pan Am, the 'flying arm of the State Department', were not listening very hard, it was at least some encouragement to Laker to know that his own Government was still pitching on his behalf.

Then the transatlantic airline crisis took a new twist. The American authorities, from the State Department through the Department of Transportation to the Civil Aeronautics Board, began to focus on cutting capacity on the north Atlantic and raising fares as an answer to the problems of Pan Am and avoiding paying it a subsidy. Discussions were soon underway with the approval of the US and British Governments between the main carriers flying the north Atlantic – Pan Am, TWA, British Airways and British Caledonian.

Laker was immediately suspicious. Although Skytrain had yet to fly, his airline was a designated transatlantic scheduled carrier and he felt he should have been involved in the discussions, yet he knew next to nothing of what was going on. The interests of Laker Airways, he realized only too clearly, were the last thing the other airlines would concern themselves with. He suspected that the other airlines would be only too willing to see his plans killed off if it suited them.

On 12 September he wrote an angry and bitter letter to George Rogers, the Department of Trade official responsible for negotiating international rights for British airlines.

In it he complained violently about his exclusion from discussions on north Atlantic scheduled air fares and capacity agreements, claiming that Skytrain gave him equal rights to British Airways and BCAL.

He also objected to the Government's ideas about minimum charter floor prices. As the acknowledged number one ABC operator in the United Kingdom, he claimed, it was quite unreasonable that his views should not be sought in detail.

His impression, he wrote, was that the Government's visit to Washington was to agree to a further contraction of the British share of the north Atlantic air transport cake and to charge the consumer more. The view that British Airways and BCAL should enter capacity limitation agreements was in Laker's view wrong. If British Airways and BCAL continued to contract their business and raise fares at the same time, they would be on the road to economic suicide.

Freddie pointed scornfully to the fact that scheduled carryings in the past year had fallen while those of his and other ABC carriers had doubled across the Atlantic. The scheduled carriers, he argued, had diverted their passengers to the ABC flights by charging excessively high fares. If Britain was to survive it had to stop being negative. It needed to go forward and fight, increase its frequencies and capacity and lower its basic air fares. Additionally it should tell the Americans forthwith (printed in angry capitals) that the Bermuda agreement must be adhered to and that fair and equal opportunity meant exactly that.

His bold, impatient signature terminated a 1,750 word diatribe contrasting implacably with the views of the anti-capitalist Labour Government and the institutionalized Civil Service.

Eight days later Rogers replied. He had received Laker's letter just as he was on his way to Washington for discussions with the US authorities. This meant, he said, that he had an opportunity to study Laker's views with care before the talks started.

He expressed surprise at Laker's complaint that he felt he had not been consulted. His letter went on: 'During the past two years or so, there have been numerous and lengthy consultations with you on all aspects of your Company's problems; and the Parliamentary Under-Secretary of State for Companies, Aviation and Shipping wrote to you as recently as 11 September. It was only natural that you were not involved in the recent discussions about rationalisation of capacity on the North Atlantic, since those discussions were confined to the winter season 1974/5 when it seems unlikely that you will be operating a scheduled service.'

The airlines held their capacity talks in Washington on 18 September. On the 23rd, the Department of Trade announced the results. 'Aviation delegations representing the United Kingdom and United States Governments have reached agreement this week on the need for vigorous action to restore profitable airline operations in the north Atlantic market by eliminating excess capacity and establishing a cost-related fare structure . . . in accordance with the objective agreed by the two Governments, US and British airlines providing scheduled services between the two countries have agreed to capacity reductions for the winter season (November 1974 to April 1975) of some 20 per cent compared with the equivalent period of last year.'

On the face of it, the two Governments were taking sensible action to contain the airlines' problems on the north Atlantic. The agreement covered only the winter and Laker's Skytrain was still not flying. But an angry and still deeply suspicious Laker continued to hammer away at Rogers. On 26 September, he wrote yet again.

In five crisp paragraphs he challenged everything Rogers had done. 'I object most strongly to being treated as a child,' he wrote. As far as he understood the law of the land, the civil service was there to translate the will of Parliament. Her Majesty's Government had designated Laker Airways to operate the London to New York route without hindrance from Rogers or anyone else. It was Rogers's responsibility to obtain Laker his traffic rights without delay, but in the face of his solemn obligations the civil servant had gone to the Americans and made a deal which negated Freddie's Skytrain licence and was tantamount to destroying his business.

Freddie added that he was sure Rogers had acted without Ministerial authority. The Secretary of State, Peter Shore, had made the position clear to Laker in his letter of 24 July and Clinton Davis had confirmed it on 11 September. No responsible minister would write such letters and then do the opposite. That, claimed Freddie, would be plain dishonesty.

He told Rogers that he would be taking the matter up at the highest level and he finished his letter by demanding what right the luckless civil servant had to decide whether Laker Airways operated that winter.

This time Laker received a placatory reply from the Minister himself, Peter Shore. But the letter revealed that, even if indirectly, Laker's interests had been at stake in the Washington talks. Indeed the agreement would have to be amended should Laker get a chance to fly on the north Atlantic that winter: '. . . I attach a copy of the press statement which announced the conclusion of this agreement and which was issued by this Department on 23 September. As you will see, the statement is clear that the agreement between airlines covers only the winter season of 1974/75. The problem of excess capacity that would have resulted from the plans of the existing carriers on the North Atlantic was urgent and I am sure that it was necessary and in the national interest that the agreement should have been reached and governmental approval given.

'We have continued to take the opportunity whenever possible of reminding the US Government of the strong representations we have made about your permit. Our Embassy in Washington did so again only yesterday. We are continuing to press the US Government for an early and favourable decision. If however the US authorities grant a permit subject to various conditions about the way in which the service is to operate, such as those contained in your CAA licence but more restrictive in some respects, we shall want to discuss them with the US Government so as to make sure they are acceptable. Such conditions might include the timing of the start of the service.

'It is impossible to forecast now how soon you would be able to start operations after the grant of a permit. The Capacity agreement for the winter does not therefore include provision for Skytrain.

'If we are able to make quicker progress with the US Government so that Skytrain can start in the course of the winter, we will naturally consider negotiating an amendment to the agreement.'

At this point, Shore's letter might easily have ended the matter. But in Washington, Beckman used the Freedom of Information Act to obtain a transcript of the capacity meeting between the airlines held in room 726 at the CAB on 18 September.

Present at the meeting were W.H. Waltrip from Pan Am, William Slattery and K.L. Briggs from TWA, O.C. Cochrane from British Airways, Charles Powell and Peter Jack from British Caledonian, Richard Dreisen a CAB official, and Alexander Gordon-Cumming, formerly with the Department of Trade and then aviation counsellor at the British Embassy in Washington. The meeting was held in the morning to finalize details of the agreement before reporting back that afternoon to British and American officials at the CAB.

It was unlikely, as Rogers had pointed out in his letter, that Laker would be operating a scheduled service that winter. His airline, nevertheless, was the main talking point of that morning's meeting.

Slattery of TWA touched on the question first. 'What do we want to say regarding the possibility of a fifth carrier in the New York line? How do you want to phrase how that will affect what we've accomplished today?'

Waltrip made Pan Am's attitude clear. 'My recommendation would be that it automatically would terminate the New York–London agreement.'

Charles Powell for BCAL cut through the generalities that followed. 'In other words, if Laker would receive Skytrain tomorrow, this agreement would be null and void immediately, even if they don't pick it up until next June or something?'

'Right,' said Waltrip.

Powell wanted to know what would be the purpose of cancelling the agreement. Waltrip told him that Pan Am might operate a skytrain service itself. TWA's representative Slattery also felt that the agreement would have to be terminated.

'The advent of another carrier on the route just doesn't make any efforts that we've gone through in the past five days worthwhile. We've been discussing a rational situation here and trying to rationalize capacity. The advent of a fifth carrier makes this a kind of nonsense.'

It took a little time before Cochrane of British Airways interceded.

'I would deplore any precipitate action in breaking an agreement that has taken so long to reach,' he said.

'Are we saying that the total agreement is off, or the New York–London part is off?'

'New York–London terminated immediately,' Slattery said crisply.

'Right,' added Waltrip, 'and we would have the right of review of the rest of the agreements – you as well as us. I mean, you might want to cancel.'

Laker was shocked by the transcript. All his suspicions were justified. The British delegates were unhappy about the Americans' insistence on a cancellation clause. But the carriers clearly saw his presence as being incompatible with the capacity limitation agreement. Its continuance depended on his absence. Equally it was explicit that they hoped to mount a similar agreement for summer of 1975.

What made him still more angry was that both Governments, and especially Rogers and other civil servants at the Department of Trade, were prepared to support such agreements. Yet both before and after the winter capacity meeting in Washington, Shore, Clinton Davis and an aide of James Callaghan, who was then Foreign Secretary, had written to Laker assuring him they were doing everything they could to get the Americans to designate him.

Beckman swiftly intervened, bringing a suit on behalf of Laker under the US anti-trust laws against TWA, Pan Am, British Airways and British Caledonian for conspiring to exclude Laker from competition. Beckman's suit stated that the CAB's authority, which had immunized the defendants' discussions from anti-trust laws, was a narrow one. 'The defendants were expressly confined to discussions of capacity agreements for the purpose of alleviating the fuel crisis and coping with the high costs of aviation fuel. The authority to hold discussions did not include authority to discuss means to exclude Laker's service from the New York–London route,' said the petition.

The suit's contention was that earlier capacity meetings had failed to reach agreement and that the airlines had been told by their Governments to try again. Their response had been to negotiate an agreement dependent on Skytrain not operating 'for the specific and primary purpose of threatening, intimidating and improperly coercing the US Government to delay Laker's authorization.'

Beckman thought his case a cast-iron one and sought damages of $40,000 a day for each day that the institution of the Skytrain service was deferred. As soon as the accused airlines turned the matter over to their outside lawyers, Beckman received a call. Would he agree to settle if they took a consent judgement?

His answer was yes. Freddie wanted the licence, not the money, Beckman told them. He negotiated to file the consent judgement; the carriers agreed to withdraw their original agreement and make one that did not exclude Laker.

Freddie was convinced that the British delegation at Washington had acted without ministerial or top Civil Aviation Authority approval. It was inconceivable, he felt, that men like Shore, Clinton Davis, or Lord Boyd-Carpenter could have given him so much support and then allowed the delegation to go to Washington and agree to something which was so damaging to Skytrain.

He was right at least about the CAA. One of its most senior officials, Ray Colegate, had travelled with the delegation but his prime objective was to negotiate new charter rules. Not until he returned to London did he become aware that while he was preoccupied with the charter talks, the winter capacity meeting had negotiated an agreement conditional on Skytrain not starting. His chairman, Lord Boyd-Carpenter, was furious when the full story began to emerge. But this was nothing compared to Freddie's explosive reaction.

He finally learned the full details of what had gone on in Washington just as he was about to fly a group of travel agents down to Palma in Majorca to tell them about the future of Lord Brothers, now to be renamed Laker Travel. There he exploded into the 'bums and gangsters' outburst, aimed, not, as he said later, at thousands of civil servants up and down the country, but at 'a handful at the top of the air industry side that have popped up here, there and everywhere for the last twenty-five years, I call them the "same old gang" of restrictionists.'

The speech was satisfying at the time but even Laker came to realize that he had been undiplomatic. But there was no living it down. A BBC TV crew had travelled with him to Palma. The speech made the news and reared its head yet again when a documentary on Laker Airways was broadcast the following year. Shore himself reproved Laker for publishing correspondence with the civil servants who, he said, could not answer back. The gulf between Laker and the Department was now very wide.

Chapter 23

'The twenty-ninth chapter of Magna Carta'

David (later Sir David) Nicolson, chairman of newly formed British Airways, was convinced that controlling capacity was the answer to the north Atlantic problem. The evidence was there for anyone to see. On the routes to Canada, where British Airways and Air Canada pooled their revenue and shared it out according to an agreed formula, the number of seats in the market could be regulated, aircraft flew nearly full and profits were high.

To America there was no such permanent agreement. The run to New York was a prestige one and airlines like Iran Air and Air India were keen to fly it even if they made no money. Nor could the airlines compete on price. They flew the same kind of aircraft and the only way they could compete for more of the market was by putting on more departures. With no pooling agreements and no capacity regulation it was a tough, unruly market. Where British Airways' flights to Canada made money they only just broke even on the American route.

Nicolson felt it ridiculous that Laker should be allowed to dump another half million seats on a route where the airlines had seven and a half million empty seats a year. He believed the only result of Skytrain would be to make British Airways' flights to New York less profitable. He wanted Laker stopped and the withdrawal of the transatlantic permit awarded to British Caledonian – which had suspended its New York service in autumn 1974 because of the post-oil crisis slump.

Such thinking reflected a major reversal of policy within the airline. Only two years earlier at the CAA Skytrain hearing, BOAC's solicitor, Bob Forrest, had told the panel that 'BOAC has no basic objection to the operation by independent airlines of scheduled services for the carriage of very low-fare traffic instead of and in lieu of the operation of affinity charters.'

Indeed, he added that BOAC did not seek protection from competition or oppose innovation. 'We are converted to the idea of competition rather than protection.'

Overcapacity had been accentuated because the downturn in the market had coincided with the introduction of large numbers of Boeing's new jumbo, the 747, which had over 400 seats compared to the 707's 150 or so. It was having a devastating effect on airline profits. BA had hoped to make £80 million in 1974 but in the end counted itself lucky to scrape together £63 million.

What made its impact still worse on BA was the policy of no forced redundancies that the unions had compelled Nicolson to adopt to smooth the merger of BEA and BOAC into British Airways. The hope, largely dashed by the oil crisis, was that continued traffic growth would mop up excess manpower.

During the early Skytrain hearings, BOAC's position of neutrality had cloaked the traditional rivalry between public and privately-owned airlines. Now BA's particular problems were reason afresh to resuscitate the traditional battle between state and independent airlines.

There was no personal animosity to Laker. Nicolson was a staunch supporter of free enterprise himself but felt as chairman of the state corporation that he should press its best commercial interests. And he knew the Americans did not want Laker from the talks BA had had with them in September 1974. Nevertheless he was effectively seeking to cancel the guiding principle to emerge from the Edwards Report that where traffic was sufficient, two British airlines might be designated to serve the route. It was an attempt to reverse this three-year-old policy of more competition, replace it with capacity agreements, which to many were a euphemism for a cartel, and restore BOAC's traditional monopoly of long-haul international routes. Whatever personal feelings Nicolson harboured about private enterprise, it was a declaration of war on Laker.

The first shots were fired in January 1975 when the CAA heard an application from British Airways to revoke Laker's Skytrain licence: 'a stab in the back,' Freddie called it. The hearing was taken by two members of the original Skytrain panel – Boyd-Carpenter and Robin Goodison – with a third and new member, Ray Colegate.

British Airways threw everything into the battle. The airline was not opposed to lower fares but reiterated its doubt about the existence of large enough numbers of 'forgotten men' to constitute an adequate market. ABC charters were now available (although the APEX struggle was still going within IATA). More damage would be done to scheduled services by Skytrain than British Airways had previously estimated. Its principal witness was O.C. Cochrane, the western routes manager, who had been at the Washington capacity meeting. He thought 40 per cent of the diversion to Skytrain would be from British Airways, costing the corporation £3 million in revenue a year.

The panel was also urged to consider the review of policy now being mounted by the Department of Trade – with, they were reminded, CAA help – and that Laker Airways still had many obstacles to clear before they could begin operating Skytrain. It was also relevant that the north Atlantic operators had recently concluded agreements governing capacity.

Beckman's swift legal action had 'bounced' the north Atlantic carriers out of one attempt to squash Skytrain. This was the comeback.

Laker defended himself stoutly. Traffic on the north Atlantic would soon recover as it had in the past. He had made a massive investment in Skytrain – over £31 million, he claimed. Taking away his licence would be conceding victory to the Americans who had so far acted illegally. There was the plain question of natural justice. 'There's no case on record where a licence has been taken away from an operator who has done no wrong,' he argued.

'Are you sure?' demanded British Airways' secretary and solicitor, Bernard Wood.

'This is the twenty-ninth chapter of the Magna Carta,' Laker snapped back.

'We are not talking about the Magna Carta,' said Wood.

'This is what the Magna Carta is all about – you do not deprive a man of his life and goods,' retorted Laker.

Freddie was becoming irritated. Skytrain's score was now an incredible tally of four hearings and three appeals. But his impish sense of humour was soon back. He and an assistant unravelled a roll of paper containing the names of 4,000 people who had written to him supporting Skytrain. Wood inquired if they had all been complimentary. All but one, Freddie replied, and paused. Wood fell into the trap.

'What did that one say?' he asked.

Laker grinned unkindly – 'Knickers to you,' he said.

Beckman had worked hard preparing his peroration of which he was rather proud. Looking towards Boyd-Carpenter who had already defused the Magna Carta argument by doubting whether King John's barons had given much thought to aviation, he began. It was inconceivable, he said, that the country which gave the world the inventors of the railway, TV, the microphone, cathode ray tubes and jet engines should turn down, take away, deny and destroy the Skytrain idea.

As his speech moved towards a climax, a voice at the back of the room muttered: 'I didn't know Laker invented all those things.' To the chagrin of Beckman, whom Laker now referred to as his 'expensive American lawyer', the room dissolved into laughter. Laker, grinning widely, tried to comfort him. 'It must have been a British Airways' employee,' he said.

For just over a fortnight, Skytrain's future hung in the balance. Finally the CAA's decision, its anxiety visible, was published. The panel accepted British Airways' arguments that traffic had declined in 1974 – for the first time since the war – and was bearish about the future. Still Boyd-Carpenter and his colleagues rejected one possible solution. Placing even stricter curbs on Skytrain's capacity or demanding further fare increases to restrict diversion would be unjust.

The panel thought the experiment was still a worthwhile one and bitterly criticized the Americans for 'unconscionable procrastination'. If they had acted diligently, Skytrain would have been in operation before the market growth broke. It was also aware that Laker had entered into the DC–10 contract on the strength of the authority's licence. If he had to return them to Mitsui, as was conceivable, the net loss to Laker would be between £6 million to £7 million. While this money had been spent and would require no further write-off, the panel felt it would be wrong to bring about this situation without compelling reason – not least because the Americans had evaded solemn treaty obligations.

The revocation was denied. But the panel felt Laker should wait until the market recovered. This would probably be at least a year, leaving time to secure American approval. British Airways did not appeal. Instead, just over a month after the CAA's decision, Shore decided to include Skytrain in his Department's civil aviation review which had been underway for nearly four months.

Shore had announced the review less than a month after Labour had won the election in 1974, even before Nicolson had made public his demand for curbs on the independents. Initially the review mainly concerned British Caledonian's relationship with British Airways but it had seemed inevitable that it would extend to Skytrain.

The independents, and most particularly British Caledonian as the second force, had been given more opportunity since the Edwards inquiry which had been carried out under an earlier Labour Government, but there was more than a hint of the direction this new review was likely to take in the exchanges in the House of Commons when Shore announced it.

'This is the third time in the history of British civil aviation that a privately-owned second force has artificially been created for doctrinaire reasons to compete with the publicly-owned flag carrier,' claimed Ian Mikardo, MP for the constituency bordering Shore's. 'Each time it has done damage to the flag carrier without doing any good for itself and then it has had to be baled out. No country in the world, not even the United States, can now afford two flag carriers. Is it not about time the Labour Government carried out Labour Party policy [of nationalization] in this sphere if in no other?'

Mikardo's fiery call for nationalization overlooked the fact that British Caledonian and Laker had built their plans on the foundation of the previous Labour Government's adoption of the Edwards Report. But Labour's left-wingers had always thought Crosland too far to the right for their tastes. They had consistently opposed the creation of the second force – indeed anything that smacked of independent enterprise in aviation.

Caledonian's chairman Adam Thomson was already battling fiercely for the future of his airline. He and his colleagues had implemented their 'S' (for survival) plan which with its redundancies and route cutbacks, had saved Caledonian from being dragged under during the industry-wide crisis of 1974.

Since then Thomson had talked with senior officials at the Department of Trade about the future and had received the first intimation of a possible shift in policy. Instead of having 'double designation' with an independent and state airline flying the same route, would it not be preferable to confine the second force and British Airways to mutual 'spheres of interest'?

Caledonian had hoped to devise some working arrangement with British Airways. But as the review progressed, Shore was coming under intense pressure from British Airways, which was lobbying the Department as hard as it knew how, and from his own anti-private-enterprise left-wingers. Both of them wanted to see the second force's wings clipped.

Shore was trying to be as fair as possible but while Thomson thought Caledonian would get enough out of the review to survive, he feared that the longer-term outlook would be less promising. His only real negotiating card was that no one actually wanted to see the second force go under. The left-wing-union alliance sought to strengthen the state airline but not at the sacrifice of the thousands of jobs at Caledonian. British Airways, already heavily overmanned, did not want to find itself in the position of mounting a rescue operation. The argument began to focus on how big BCAL's sphere of interest might be.

Despite the contacts between Caledonian and the Department, there was considerable disquiet generally within the independent sector about what was going on. Years earlier Shore had written a book, *Entitled to Know*, about 'open government'. But so secret were the review's deliberations that airline managers began to joke about practising what you preach.

Laker Airways seemed to be coming off a distinct third best. The main battleground was between BCAL and British Airways and Laker was only included in the review late in the day. There was a deep personal gulf between Freddie and key officials in the Department. In April 1975 Laker submitted a Skytrain supplement to the review board but what consultation there was was limited.

To try to convince Shore, Freddie submitted the results of public attitude surveys carried out by Market Opinion Research International. The choice of MORI was a shrewd one. The Labour Party itself had used its services in the previous year's election campaign. The results overwhelmingly supported Laker's arguments. There was no question of the finding being rigged. MORI chose thirty sampling points in the London area, including the constituencies of Shore and his junior Minister, Clinton Davis. The majority of opinion in favour of Skytrain was so great that there was no doubt about the margin of error.

Any politician choosing to back Skytrain, the survey implied, was onto an enormously popular policy. Many of the respondents – in the lower-income groups and highly likely to be Labour voters – would love to travel to America but could not afford it because of high fares If they came down to Skytrain's level, feelings changed dramatically. Scaling up the results suggested something like an extra quarter of the population felt they could visit America at Laker-level fares.

During the course of much of the review, Pan Am, TWA and British Airways had continued to discuss ways of cutting out some of the excess capacity on the north Atlantic. While it was never made explicit, the Department and Ministers sensed that Skytrain was an obstacle in the path of developing an agreement to control capacity.

Freddie's home base was now beginning to look far from secure. He had drawn plenty of support from the defeated Tory Government and its leader, Edward Heath. But with Labour in power, it was different. While Lord Boyd-Carpenter was still at the CAA, Shore, the new Minister at the Department, could hardly have been more different. Boyd-Carpenter was all for individual initiative, enterprise and competition. Shore was on the left of the Labour Party, a believer in state control; his views about the balance between public and private enterprise were diametrically opposed to Boyd-Carpenter's.

With his adversaries at the Department of Trade controlling the review, Freddie's position suddenly seemed very exposed. Only a moment's reflection was needed to show that the new scheme of things was unlikely to have much room in it for Laker Airways.

Chapter 24

'We've won, we've won!'

Freddie was on his eighty-five-ton yacht *Tutinella* in the Mediterranean in summer 1975 when he received a call saying that Shore would like to see him in London. Breaking off his holiday, he flew back from Alicante. Soon after lunch, on Tuesday, 29 July, he presented himself together with his deputy Cliff Nunn at the Department of Trade, a few yards from Westminster Abbey.

Waiting for them was Shore, his junior Minister, Stanley Clinton Davis, and the civil servants involved with aviation, George Rogers and David Hubback. Shore was to the point. In a few minutes, he would be making a statement to the House of Commons about the review's outcome. British Caledonian was to survive with a tolerable sphere of interest but he wanted Freddie to know that because of the collapse of the north Atlantic market, Skytrain would not be allowed to go ahead.

Laker must have sensed what was coming. It was a fearful blow, nevertheless. He tried reasoning with Shore. He pleaded for a chance to be allowed a two-year experiment, calling it off after a year if it did not work. Shore put this to his officials who indicated that this was no time for back-sliding. The new policy must stand.

Laker's calm broke. He told Shore it was immoral and illegal. Shore, who privately thought it was Freddie Laker behaving like Freddie Laker, said nonsense. Freddie was very disturbed. Shore sympathized but pointed out that new charter rules and the larger problems of the whole industry had left no room for Skytrain.

Shore went straight to the Commons to announce the broad outline of his review. Above him, Laker sat in the Strangers' Gallery; just in front of him was Lord Boyd-Carpenter. Both men listened as Shore drew the CAA's teeth.

At first, Shore's statement caused some confusion. Labour MPs congratulated him on postponing Skytrain for at least twelve months, then complained that BCAL should have been absorbed into British Airways.

More quickly, Tory MPs grasped that a death blow, rather than a stay of execution, had been dealt to Skytrain. Former BOAC pilot Norman Tebbitt (subsequently a Minister in Mrs Thatcher's Government) moved swiftly into the attack. Did Shore 'think that Freddie Laker, with three DC-10s and his handful of employees, is such a menace to British Airways with its scores of aircraft and its 60,000 employees that he must be put down in this ruthless manner in order to protect British Airways?'

Then, although at that time he could not have realized how crucial this point was to become, Tebbitt's misericorde found the chink in Shore's armour. 'Does he feel,' asked Tebbitt, 'that he has now changed the relationship between himself and the CAA to such an extent that there should be legislation to emphasize the fact that the CAA is now nothing more than an office boy and that the Secretary of State has taken over personal management of the policy which the CAA was given to administer?'

Shore disagreed with this. 'I am sure that none of us thinks anything of the kind about the CAA and would not dream of describing in those terms the relationships which exist . . . I regret the necessity of doing what I have done with regard to Laker Airways but I do not think we acted ruthlessly. We had already had to rule out the possibility of Skytrain operating for at least a year and I think it is only fair for me not to play Mr Laker along. That is why I have said openly that, for as far ahead as I can see, I do not see how we can let him proceed without damaging the others and still bring benefit to the nation as a whole.'

Moments later, a new ally joined Laker. The leader of the opposition, Mrs Margaret Thatcher, asked: 'Is it not the nub of what the Secretary of State is saying that the private carrier is so efficient and so good for the consumer that the nationalized industry cannot compete?'

Shore bristled and tried to brush her aside. 'I honestly do not think that that kind of over-simple free-enterprise rhetoric is the right way to approach the future of the civil aviation industry. All who have had to deal with the civil aviation industry know that to begin with we are dealing with a highly regulated industry in which there is massive international competition. Further, anyone who knows anything at all about it knows that the great problem in relation to the whole of the north Atlantic is massive overcapacity.'

This was only a brief parliamentary work-out. After another minute or so, MPs switched to another topic.

Five days later, *The Sunday Times Business News* added to Laker's misery by reporting that the Americans were close to approving Skytrain. Informed sources there said that President Ford was on the verge of returning the CAB's letter, which was still believed to say no, with instructions that they were to approve it.

By this time Freddie was back aboard *Tutinella* thinking. The position was now a puzzling one. Largely thanks to pressure from Skytrain supporters, Shore had merely said that the service could not start. He had not withdrawn the Government's formal designation of Laker Airways as a British scheduled carrier. The CAA's licence had not been cancelled. Nor had British Airways appealed against the CAA's decision to uphold the Skytrain licence. The final details of the review would only appear that autumn in a White Paper.

With the tireless Beckman's help, Freddie realized that all was not yet lost. The law laid down that the licence could only be revoked by the CAA. The Minister had not used his own particular discretion, where he could claim foreign policy grounds were involved, to revoke the licence. Beckman argued that Shore was simply saying that with all the authority invested in him by the Crown, the service will not be allowed to start. Laker's lawyer found the case fascinating. He could see antecedents as far back as the reign of James I when Lord Coke claimed he was subject to the law while the angry King countered by maintaining the royal prerogative.

Within the Department, Shore had been advised that he had the power under the existing law simply to make an Order: there was no need for new legislation – despite what Tebbitt had thought – which would mean the irritation of competing for parliamentary time as well as getting a Bill drafted.

If necessary, Shore felt he could have carried the House with a Bill but it was a matter of expediency. He had no intention of trying to 'bounce' Parliament. There was to be a White Paper detailing the new policy and this would provide an opportunity for a vote, even if it was only a vote to approve an Order rather than legislation.

Shortly after this first clash in the Commons, Laker visited Mrs Thatcher in her office at the Commons. He had got to know her husband Denis Thatcher well. They had both been on the board of Castrol, the oil company, whose managing director had been 'Molotov' Watson, Laker's pilot in the days of the Air Transport Auxiliary. Freddie stood for almost everything Mrs Thatcher, who had also worked her way up from a modest background, believed in. She was prepared to give him what assistance she could and was helpful in arranging a longer parliamentary debate two days later.

Until this point Laker had never been particularly involved in politics. From the moment when Sir Dennis Proctor had ruled that Skytrain had merits, Laker and his management had been lulled into believing that it was only a matter of time before their case was vindicated. They had never thought to bother with any political lobbying. When Shore slammed the door shut in their face, one of Laker's staff likened it to a baby falling over a cliff edge.

Now, while Freddie thought there might be legal grounds for counter-attacking Shore, he wanted to see if victory could be achieved more simply by getting the Order defeated in Parliament. Any guidance issued to the CAA which would be presented in the White Paper had to be approved by both the House of Lords and the Commons. With so much opposition from unions and left-wing MPs, Laker's chances of winning in the Commons were none too high. The obvious place to try was the House of Lords. There, with the help of the late Lord Lyons, a shrewd public relations man, Labour supporter and friend, Lord George-Brown and some other sympathizers, Freddie set about trying to enlist support among the peers.

The wait for the crucial vote was longer than anticipated. The publication of the White Paper was delayed as British Airways and British Caledonian fought for their spheres of interest. BA was determined to give as little as possible and the argument came within a hair's breadth of Thomson's absolute sticking-point. Reluctantly he was prepared to concede Caledonian's licences to serve New York, Los Angeles, Boston, Toronto and Singapore via Bahrain. In return, his airline would get South America as its 'sphere of interest' – a lineal descendant of the BUA route to Brazil. But Thomson would not surrender the right to fly to Atlanta, capital of America's booming Sunbelt, and Houston in Texas. With the talks near breakdown, he won his point. His opponents were prepared to see BCAL emasculated but not wiped out.

The White Paper finally emerged, months late, in February 1976. The Government won the vote in the Commons and in the Lords. To oppose the Government and approve Skytrain would have also meant rejecting the spheres of interest policy affecting British Airways and British Caledonian and MPs were reluctant to do this. The Lords passed a separate motion in favour of Skytrain, giving a hint of what sort of result a straight vote on Skytrain might have produced.

Four and a half years – and hundreds of thousands of pounds in legal fees – after that very first hearing before the ATLB, Skytrain seemed as elusive a dream as ever.

If ministers had wanted to stiffen Freddie's resistance, they could not have made a better fist of it. The CAA had accepted that Laker had bought the DC–10s as a consequence of the licence having been awarded. Shore's junior, Stanley Clinton Davis, would not accept this. He told the Commons that Laker had taken a calculated risk in buying them. He had failed to recognize that there might be problems with the US authorities. And Skytrain would need one rather than the three DC–10s which Laker now had. It was, of course, Clinton Davis who had written to Laker in September 1974 to tell him about the vigorous representations they were making to the US authorities.

Clinton Davis also made it explicit that Skytrain was being sacrificed to help not just British Airways, but the two big American carriers, TWA and Pan Am. The loss of £10 million that British Airways was expected to make in the early part of 1975 was not simply north Atlantic travel, he said, and was not to be compared with the substantial losses being suffered by the American airlines. In one of the most revealing remarks made by any Minister in the whole affair, he told MPs: 'What I say about Skytrain in this respect is that its introduction would make it very difficult to persuade the United States airlines to continue to restrict their capacity.'

This was exactly what Laker had suspected about the winter capacity meeting in Washington. Pan Am had insisted on the agreement containing a provision for terminating it if Laker was allowed to start Skytrain, and British officials were prepared to accept this.

Whether they realized it or not, it is hard to avoid the conclusion that the Government's policy was as likely to help the American airlines as it was the British aviation industry as a whole. 'The Pan Am canker' was Laker's harsh phrase for it.

The Tories were opposed to any efforts to limit capacity or dilute the competition. They were solidly for individualistic entrepreneurs like Laker. He had his own answer to the recession. 'Nobody has ever fought inflation or depression by contraction,' he said. 'If they had anything but rocks in their heads they would know that only vision and expansion is going to save this country's bacon.'

The Tories loved it.

Labour still stuck to its belief in regulated competition (which in practice often added up to a monopoly if there happened to be a state corporation in that particular industry); paid little attention to the consumer as an individual; and in this particular instance were circumscribed by the influence of the left. The unions might grudgingly have been forced to accept the continued existence of privately-owned British Caledonian but they had fought hard behind the scenes to stop Laker. They remembered their struggles with him at BUA and his continuing reluctance to recognize them; Laker employees still had individual contracts.

Freddie's notions of enterprise were equally an anathema. With his usual instinct for candour rather than diplomacy, he told radio listeners: 'I will continue to be a buccaneer, and I can tell Mr Shore and all the people that think like him, that Skytrain will remain on the DC-10s until I die.'

Clinton Davis hit back at him. He doubted whether the scheduled air services of the world were necessarily areas for buccaneering.

Burying Skytrain was not enough. The White Paper hammered the nails in the coffin. A year earlier when it attempted to revoke Laker's licence, British Airways had estimated the potential damage to it from Skytrain as £3 million. Now the Government estimated the loss to BA as £6 million if Skytrain and one corresponding US service were operated. Laker's people could not help thinking statistics could be made to do all sorts of things. If BA was so keen to see Skytrain stopped why had it underplayed the potential damage at the revocation hearing by using only the £3 million figure?

The actual means of execution was simple. The new 'guidance' confirmed BCAL's sphere of interest as South America, West and Central Africa and the south of the United States. To tidy up the spheres, the two airlines swapped routes with BCAL trading the Seychelles and East Africa for mid-Atlantic routes.

Laker had been pondering the possibility of legal action even before the appearance of the White Paper. He felt strongly that he had been wronged. He told colleagues that it was like letting a man build a hotel and then taking away his planning permission. His first contacts with lawyers were disheartening, however. They were unenthusiastic about taking the case on. Lord Boyd-Carpenter, himself a former barrister, told Laker not to waste his money. You can't beat City Hall was the general view. But in the end he had found a barrister, Andrew Bateson, bold enough to tackle it. The writ was issued.

Magna Carta and the stubborn resistance of John Hampden to King Charles I's efforts to raise money are landmarks in the development of the English constitution and its central notion of the rule of law sanctioned by Parliament.

King John's barons, as Lord Boyd-Carpenter had dryly pointed out, knew little of aviation but stood out vigorously against what they argued was the King's arbitrary exercise of power. Hampden went even further. His insistence that Charles could not raise taxes without parliamentary approval landed him first in prison and then contributed to the outbreak of civil war.

Whether Laker at his most militant ever contemplated quite such a draconian solution is improbable. He was a reluctant Hampden but he had all his zeal. Throughout the battle for Skytrain, he was sustained by a profound sense of righteousness. His low-fare, no-frills service made honest, down-to-earth sense. Nor had he done any wrong. He had tried to champion the forgotten man but had become a victim of the confusion of bureaucracy and arbitrary shifts in government policy. His attempt to challenge the efforts of the scheduled airlines to maintain their monopoly had been a brave one.

When he decided to go to court, he was walking that same path that made Hampden a folk hero. The comparison between the two men is not fanciful. Hampden's ship money case was cited as a precedent during Laker's courtroom struggle and both men were pleading the same arguments. In 1637, the Attorney General insisted that the King had 'absolute power' and that there was no 'King-yoking' policy requiring parliamentary consent. Three hundred and forty years later, Attorney General Sam Silkin still claimed that the prerogative of a Minister of the Crown could not be fettered. Shore, he argued, had the right to direct the CAA to take away Laker's licence.

The hearing was in Queen's Bench Court number seven where much of Leon Uris's novel *QB VII* is set and Robin Flood, Laker's publicity manager, was quietly impressed that their case was being heard in such a famous court. It was certainly a fortunate one. Unlike Hampden who lost his first court case, and despite the pessimists, Laker scored a notable victory over the Department.

Mr Justice Mocatta, regarded as a middle-of-the-road, establishment judge by the legal profession, ruled that Shore had acted *ultra vires*. He had exceeded his authority or the powers given to him.

His judgement noted that the 1971 Civil Aviation Act had conferred certain duties on the CAA of:

- making sure that British airlines provided air transport to satisfy all substantial categories at the lowest charges consistent with the highest standard of safety and efficient operators making an economic return.
- ensuring that at least one major airline not controlled by British Airways had a chance to participate in achieving the above.
- encouraging airlines to increase their contribution to improving the balance of payments.
- subject to the above, furthering the reasonable interests of air transport users.

Shore's new guidance proposed two major changes to this. Future policy would be not to allow competition or the licensing of more than one British airline on a long-haul route. It spelled the end of the competition envisaged in the 1971 Act. The guidance confirmed that the two main airlines would have an effective monopoly in their own spheres.

In court the Department of Trade claimed that Laker's initial designation was an exercise by the Crown of its prerogative powers. The intended de-designation was a further exercise of its prerogative powers; this was a matter of executive discretion and not something that had to be justified in the courts. Furthermore the exercise of this prerogative could not be waived or fettered.

Freddie's lawyers argued that such a dramatic change was beyond the power of the Minister.

Much of the material before the court concerned the familiar arguments about whether Skytrain could succeed commercially and how much traffic would be diverted from the scheduled airlines.

Mr Justice Mocatta said it was not his concern to decide such issues. Cutting through the hours of argument and cross-examination that had trampled this ground so thoroughly, he introduced some magisterial common sense. Echoing the sceptical feelings many must by now have harboured about the protracted Skytrain debate, he said that those arguments could not be resolved with certainty without either the gift of prophecy or putting the matter to the test by allowing Skytrain to operate.

He agreed wholeheartedly with Freddie's argument that such dramatic changes as the Minister proposed to the CAA were beyond his power. It was not a guidance but a direction which drastically altered the duty conferred on the authority. There would be judgement for Laker.

The court would have been powerless if Shore had taken his cue from Norman Tebbitt's hint and legislated to change the CAA's guidelines. Now bad advice from his officials had left him in the same dilemma as Charles I, who had tried to finance his naval fleet without recourse to Parliament. Mr Justice Mocatta described Shore's actions as 'unrealistic and bizarre'. It was a humiliating defeat for a politician who has aspirations of leading his party.

By now it was becoming questionable whether there was even any need to change aviation policy and drop dual designation. IATA's own traffic figures showed that all categories of north Atlantic passenger traffic, both chartered and scheduled as Freddie had forecast, were recovering strongly. Moreover the upturn had been under way from 1975 onwards.

The constitutional issues raised by Mr Justice Mocatta's judgement were so important that the Government was bound to appeal. The case, touching so closely on the liberty of the individual, was the sort that Lord Denning, as Master of the Rolls, the senior civil judge in the country, takes a particular interest in and selects for hearing in his appeal court.

A brilliant man who had been a Wrangler at Cambridge, Denning believes in the model of the great judges of the eighteenth and nineteenth centuries who had been prepared, by establishing precedent, to develop the law. At the same time he is a man of immense compassion: Tom Denning who, given the chance, broadened still further his kindly Hampshire accent for litigants, such as Freddie Laker, who chose to appear in person.

Some of his most famous cases had centred round the wife's equity in the matrimonial home. On more than one occasion, Denning ruled that the divorced wife was entitled to half the home. He continued to do so as often as the Lords overruled him until finally it became only too obvious that Denning's justice was right and the law was changed. The Lords might find his stance on occasions irritating but for those seeking justice his heart was certainly in the right place.

Denning, sitting with Lords Justice Roskill and Lawton, dismissed the Government's argument that Shore's policy had been approved by a vote of both Houses of Parliament. A vote was not the equivalent of an Act of Parliament; it could not override the law of the land. He emphasized the strength of the case for Skytrain by pointing out that the CAA had applied itself most conscientiously and sensibly to the task of fulfilling its original objectives. After both Skytrain hearings, its decisions had been well reasoned.

Eloquently, he argued:

'Seeing then that those statutory means were available for stopping Skytrain if there was a proper case for it, the question is whether the Secretary of State can stop it by other means. Can he do it by withdrawing the designation? Can he do indirectly that which he cannot do directly? Can he displace the statute by invoking a prerogative? If he could do this, it would mean that, by a side wind, Laker Airways Ltd would be deprived of the protection which the statute affords them. There would be no inquiry, no hearing, no safeguard against injustice. The Secretary of State could do it of his own head – by withdrawing the designation without a word to anyone. To my mind such a procedure was never contemplated by the statute. The Secretary of State was mistaken in thinking that he could do it. No doubt he did it with the best of motives. He felt that it was for the public good that Skytrain should not be allowed to start. Nevertheless, he went about it, I think, in the wrong way. He misdirected himself as to his powers. And it is well-established law that, if a discretionary power is exercised under the influence of a misdirection, it is not properly exercised, and the court can say so.

'It is a serious matter for the courts to declare that a Minister of the Crown has exceeded his powers,' concluded Lord Denning. 'But there comes a point when it has to be done.' Lords Justice Roskill and Lawton agreed.

Laker could not have put it better himself. When he heard the news, he whooped his way up and down *Tutinella*'s deck: 'We've won, we've won.'

But it was not over. The Attorney General, Sam Silkin, immediately sought leave to appeal to the House of Lords, undeterred by Lord Justice Roskill's dry remark that 'at the end of the second half, Mr Attorney, you are four nil.'

A massive row now broke out in Whitehall. By now Shore had left the Department of Trade to move to the Department of the Environment and the appeal had ostensibly been launched in the name of his successor, Edmund Dell. In fact the process of appeal to the higher court had begun before Dell's arrivai and was in practice irreversible. Now Dell dug in his heels. To general dismay, he refused to go to the Lords.

During his early period at the Department, Dell had not been involved with Skytrain. Finally it came to him as an issue arriving out of the court's decision. Dell, a right-winger, was at the opposite end of the Labour Party spectrum to Shore. He was less committed to unswerving support of the nationalized sector of the industry and less prepared to follow the unions' every bidding. His reaction was instinctive. Why on earth should the Government oppose Skytrain?

For the government lawyers, Skytrain had become an irrelevancy. They were preoccupied with the need to reaffirm the Crown's prerogative. Whatever Denning had said – and they claimed there were some factual errors in that – they argued that the judgement would be reversed by the Lords who in their opinion would take a sceptical view of his decision anyway. They urged Dell to appeal. If necessary, they could do it with a hastened procedure that would fit his aviation policy timetable, now complicated by the decision to renegotiate the Bermuda treaty.

Within the Department, Dell was also advised he could try using section four of the 1971 Act, instead of three which Shore had used. Section four gave the Minister absolute right to take a decision affecting civil aviation if international relations were involved. The civil servants, worried that Dell's attitude was inconsistent with the policy Shore had laid down, were keen that he should try this.

The new Minister held his ground. He felt that switching to section four would make the Government look particularly bad after the defeat in court. He needed no MORI polls to convince him. By now the public appeal of Skytrain was only too obvious. Arguments became so fierce that at one point Dell thumped the table. It was his neck on the political block, he told his officials.

The main battle switched to the Cabinet Committee. There it was clear that Skytrain's allies in the Labour Government were few and far between. Laker's opponents emphasized the impact Skytrain would have on British Airways and pointed out how much the unions disliked him. It was not just that Laker was a competitor of the state sector, he was a known opponent of unions.

Colleagues told Dell he lacked political judgement, a veiled way of reminding him how powerful an influence the unions were in Labour politics. At no point does anyone seem to have suggested that promoting cheaper air transport might prove a popular public issue. Only grudgingly did the united opposition give way. But they had little choice. There had been yet another shift in policy. Dell, or at least his officials, had decided to revoke the Bermuda treaty, the agreement covering air services between Britain and America. Far from being a nuisance, Laker had an important role to play.

Chapter 25

'PanAmania'

Laker was still 'a flying spanner' with the Air Transport Auxiliary when the Bermuda treaty, which had come to figure so largely in his business life, emerged out of the complex aviation politics of the post-war period.

Under the Bermuda agreement the routes to be operated by the two countries' airlines were to be negotiated. There were to be no restrictions on service frequency or capacity. If one country felt concerned by what was happening, capacity on the route could be reviewed. Fares were to be fixed by governments agreeing rates that had been thrashed out within IATA.

The Anglo-American agreement set a precedent for a series of bilaterals between other countries and the fixing of air fares.

Thirty years later, a month before Mr Justice Mocatta ruled that Shore could not bar the operation of Skytrain's licence, the Labour Government announced that it wanted to renegotiate the Bermuda treaty. Its goal was to ensure Britain got a more equal share of the benefits from UK–US air transport market.

Once again the DoT's aim was to try to strengthen British Airways' position. The scheme was that a new treaty would reduce 'wasteful' competition and increase British aviation's share of the market by bringing in capacity controls and enshrining in the treaty the principle of single designation which would mean only one US airline and UK airline on the same route.

The thinking behind this was clearly related to the new aviation policy promulgated by Shore. The 'spheres of interest' policy which ended competition by UK airlines on a single long-haul route dovetailed neatly with a 'Bermuda Two' built around single designation. The only snag was that this left no room for Laker.

Skytrain was an irritating knot in the neat and tidy grain of policy. It was an approach strongly opposed by the CAA.

As Bermuda Two negotiations began to pick up steam in spring 1977, the defeat in the courts meant that the Department once again had to promote Skytrain. How, wondered observers, would the Department manage to accommodate Skytrain and single designation?

The talks, held in London, were soon floundering. The Americans rapidly scotched the British plan to preserve single designation. They refused point blank to include a clause accepting Skytrain as an isolated and special kind of low-fare competition ranking somewhere between scheduled and charter services. Their opposition only vindicated the CAA's view from the start that insisting on single designation was an untenable position: it was wishful thinking to believe the Americans would take either Pan Am or TWA off the London–New York route just to humour the British.

The Americans were becoming increasingly irritated by the abrasive style of George Rogers, the senior British negotiator. His job entails frequent overseas travel and long absences from home and is not one of the most popular in the civil service. But when the opportunity arose, it allowed Rogers, who had been in the Ministry of Supply, a chance to make the crucial promotion to Under-Secretary.

He threw himself in the role of the Department's 'hard man' negotiator with zeal. Dell was quite pleased to have such a tough operator at his disposal. Not everyone shared this view, however. Within government circles there was a feeling that Rogers's 'macho' approach, his tendency to regard the negotiations as an end in themselves, was counter-productive.

The Americans shared this view wholeheartedly. They reached the point where they were unwilling to continue negotiation with Rogers. To force the issue, they raised the status of their senior negotiator to ambassadorial level by bringing in Alan Boyd, a former Secretary for Transportation. The British responded by calling in Patrick Shovelton, who as deputy-secretary ranked above Rogers in the Whitehall hierarchy.

The Americans had also been startled to discover the extent of the British negotiators' unpreparedness when the talks opened. As the British had revoked the treaty on the grounds that they were not getting their fair share of the market, the Americans asked to see the economic analysis underpinning this argument.

One had not been prepared, Rogers confessed. There then followed an extremely embarrassing day when Rogers had to eat humble pie and seek the aid of the CAA. To a large extent, the whole Skytrain battle had become a trial of strength between the Department and the CAA. Now Laker's consistent ally realized this was an opportunity to restore the ground the CAA had lost since 1973 and to consolidate the authority's standing as originally intended by the Edwards Committee and Parliament. Senior CAA officials agreed to help Rogers – but only on the proviso that there would be no question of the Department using the figures to suit its own purpose.

Rogers was left on the sidelines as Shovelton and the CAA's officials, who included Ray Colegate, buckled down to it. His near-total exclusion from the talks got them moving ahead once again. Occasionally, if he felt the Americans were getting too difficult, Shovelton used to admonish them, 'Be careful or I will get George back.'

Dell, like the CAA, had never believed that the Americans could be persuaded to accept single designation given the volume of traffic between London and New York. It was why Skytrain was needed, he explained to his ministerial colleagues. If the Americans were to designate two airlines on the New York run, and almost certainly the route to Los Angeles, Britain would need another scheduled carrier. And, as the Lords of Appeal had made it clear by now, it had one in the guise of Laker's Skytrain. Laker was back in business.

On 18 February 1977, the British Embassy in Washington asked the State Department to resume processing Laker's application for a foreign air-carrier permit. Almost to the day, Laker was poised where he had been three years earlier.

In the United States, however, the climate of opinion had swung heavily towards protecting the interests of the consumer. No less a person than Senator Edward Kennedy had taken up the banner. Kennedy had become chairman of the Senate committee dealing with administrative practices and procedures. Not surprisingly for a politician of his stature, Kennedy wanted to raise larger issues than whether the proceedings of government agencies were too complicated – an important but scarcely highly visible topic. Instead he chose to tackle the work of one particular agency and what it was actually doing. Michael Levine, a tubby young Californian economics and law professor, had made a study of the extremely competitive Californian air market in the years up to 1965. Levine had concluded that this had produced a highly efficient industry. Drawing on Levine's experience, Kennedy decided that the airlines and the CAB would be a good starting point.

The Kennedy hearings in late autumn of 1974 and spring of 1975 drew criticism but plenty of publicity. Old CAB hands like Secor Browne could sneer at populist politicians out for a quick-hit issue but the public were fascinated when Kennedy began asking why it cost so much to fly from Boston to Washington when it was so much cheaper to fly from Los Angeles to San Francisco where competition had forced down fares.

One of the most forceful witnesses was Laker himself, invited personally to testify by Kennedy. He was especially angry that the CAB was planning to impose minimum fares now on charters. It was only being done, he argued, to help the IATA carriers who had insisted on getting into charters, which for them were a loss-making operation. It was PanAmania, he said. 'People seem to have lost their senses out of concern over what will happen to Pan American, TWA and British Airways. I submit that it is reasonable to believe that these carriers are taking advantage of the problems which in large measure they have brought upon themselves in an attempt to destroy a segment [charters] of the air travel business in which they don't belong . . . they are high-cost operators trying to provide a service at less than cost.'

Laker's parting shot for Senator Kennedy and his committee was a plea for fewer rules. 'Instead of constricting the market by raising prices, restricting competition and stifling new ideas, we must experiment broadly to increase our productivity in a free unfettered market. No business ever expanded by contraction.'

With a bright, articulate young academic like Levine helping to orchestrate the hearings and define important issues, the airlines complained that the hearings were stacked. But Kennedy gave virtually the whole US aviation establishment a chance to testify, including the CAB. Levine felt it was the paucity of their arguments in favour of regulation that helped convince the public to give competition a run.

Deregulation was tailor-made for Jimmy Carter. He had campaigned on a platform of less government and lower prices. Cutting back the regulatory restraints in air transport was a short cut to both goals. Even though it continued to grumble about Laker's charter violations, the board of the CAB knew what was expected of it after Carter's election as President. All the past obstructions melted away. TWA wanted more hearings before a judge in view of the staleness of the record. No, said the board. It was ripe for a decision. Encouraging low fares was part of its job. Most current air transport legislation proposals included some measures on lowering air fares. The board, having rediscovered the consumer, did not think anyone would seriously question that this service 'would be a boon to the most price-conscious members of the travelling public'.

The board dumped its old allies. It was sceptical of claims that low-fare services would cause massive diversion. Expert economic consultants had solemnly warned the board that 55 per cent of the scheduled carriers' transatlantic traffic would be diverted by travel-group charters. What had actually happened, the board pointed out scathingly, was that only a fraction of one per cent of transatlantic travellers had used this new form of charter in its first full year.

Perhaps his fares were low, the board added. But then Laker was an efficient, low-cost operator. There were too many unknowns to be able to say in advance whether the Skytrain service could operate in a competitive environment. But they did not believe a strictly private-enterprise business like Laker, as opposed to a subsidized public corporation, would become a drain on public funds. If it was not profitable, Laker could raise fares, or get out of the business. The board's only real caveat was an important one – that the British Government should not place any restrictions on American carriers seeking to mount low-fare competition.

On 6 June 1977 the board of the CAB concluded that a foreign air-carrier permit should be issued to Laker Airways. A few days later, President Carter added his final consent. But he made it clear that Laker was not going to have it all his own way. The licence would be for a trial period of one year. Laker would also have to wait for sixty days – he had hoped to start within thirty days of getting permission – to give US airlines time to put their cases for operating similar services to the CAB.

At his Gatwick airport headquarters, Laker raised the Union Jack he had kept furled during the long legal and political battle, popped the champagne corks and finally named the day – Monday 26 September.

Chapter 26

'The heavy sugar'

Laker's five-year battle to get Skytrain flying had earned millions-of-dollars-worth of free advertising and by now publicity was at fever pitch. Lest there was someone left who had not actually heard of Skytrain or its creator, the scheduled airlines took it on themselves to play right into his hands. By plotting together to counter-attack Skytrain in the last few weeks before it started, they convinced many ordinary people that IATA really was a wicked cartel and that Laker was a mortal St Christopher.

Over the years, Laker had been warned frequently that the airlines would try to compete with Skytrain. His off-the-cuff reaction was that by the time IATA had got round to organizing itself, the action would probably be over. More seriously, he felt that the scheduled airlines would be committing financial suicide to take him on at his own terms. They could not compete with his costs. Nor could they offer fares low enough to compete with Skytrain without courting the risk of diverting their own full-fare traffic. The sums seemed simple. Even if half Skytrain's passengers were wooed away from the scheduled and charter airlines, this would represent less than one per cent of the total 1976 north Atlantic passenger market. Was it worth disrupting their existing business to swat such a small pest.

For once Laker had miscalculated. As the final countdown to takeoff day began, he was a very worried man. He told Colegate that he was 'terrified' and almost anyone who would listen that 'they have got together to go for me by the throat'.

The main airlines operating the London–New York run (TWA, Pan Am, British Airways, Air India, Iran Air and El Al), the Infamous Six as Laker dubbed them, had been cleverer than he thought. When survival was at stake, it soon transpired that IATA had a swift, mean bite. They matched Laker's low fares but limited the number of cheap seats on offer, confounding his calculations, and protecting the bulk of their own traffic against self-diversion. But to do it, they had to get together and work out the plan between themselves.

Soon after Carter had approved Skytrain, the airlines hastened to IATA's neat office block, half-way between Geneva's airport and the city centre. There they began thrashing out what to do. The Six were far from unanimous. TWA and Pan Am were all for going after Laker with similar cut-price fares; Pan Am in particular wanted budget fares (book three weeks in advance and get ten days' notice of the flight). Its managers had been trying to sell them to IATA for three years.

IATA fare-fixing meetings are normally held in conditions of great secrecy. On this occasion, the thirty-six airlines involved in what was known as North Atlantic Area Two failed to grasp just how much the atmosphere had changed. Their deliberations, far from being closeted in secret, might as well have been conducted on the apron of Geneva airport.

After such meetings, comprehensive minutes have to be supplied to the US authorities. Laker made use of the Sunshine Act, obtained copies and began handing them around. Though individual airlines were not named, it was possible to pick out the attitudes of different groups of airlines. British Airways and British Caledonian both counselled moderation. The former felt that there should be no action as Skytrain only accounted for one per cent of the market.

The Americans flatly rejected British Airways' arguments that APEX was sufficient defence. If the other airlines did not fall into line with some form of low-fare riposte, they insisted they would force an 'open-rate' situation where there would be no agreement on fares. Even though this bogeyman threat was losing much of its force, it was still sufficient to browbeat the moderates.

Within the British group. there was an element of *schadenfreude*. In the mid-1960s, BCAL had anticipated Laker by applying to the Air Transport Licensing Board for permission to operate transatlantic flights at cheap fares comparable with the Icelandic airline, Loftleidir. So comprehensive had the ATLB's rejection been, that BCAL deemed such plans a non-starter.

British Airways was still battling to get wholehearted acceptance of APEX. Panic, it seemed, was a more powerful force than reasoned argument.

In strict legal terms, there was nothing wrong in the airlines sitting down in the classic smoke-filled room to work out how to counter Laker (although if the US airlines had discussed the elimination of a domestic competitor in such a fashion on their home ground, they would have faced anti-trust action). What 'legalized' the IATA deliberations was that governments had the right to review their fare conclusions.

For many observers, this rare insight into how the airlines could behave was a revelation. It was if Goliath, not simply content with trying to bash David, had brought his chums along to help as well. 'It's like climbing into the ring at a boxing match and finding you have to take on the audience as well,' complained Laker.

The airlines' conduct was blatant to the point of naivete. One airline pointed out that it was not directly affected by Skytrain, but, according to the minutes, 'they did express a willingness to co-operate with the directly involved carriers if they were obliged to take action to compete with Skytrain'.

One carrier – and fifteen others supported this view – wanted some provision for cancelling low-fare plans if Skytrain either failed to go ahead 'or at a subsequent date ceased operation'.

Deeply worried by this collective folly, the BCAL representative rang his London office to say he thought the conference had gone off the rails. What should he do? 'Keep your finger in the dyke for as long as you can. When it bursts, jump clear,' he was told.

The airlines flew away from Geneva with a deal. The Six would offer 2,900 cheap seats weekly each way between London and New York.

Laker angrily accused them of trying to drive him out of business with 'predatory' prices. Pan Am actually told the CAB that stand-by fares 'except as a competitive response to Laker could not be justified on economic grounds'. Complained Laker: 'Their idea of predatory is praying over my dead body.'

He was worried yet still as quick as ever, spotting how he could turn the airlines' behaviour to his own advantage. When the Americans had finally issued the Skytrain permit, it had been with the condition that if the UK Government tried to curb US carrier competition, it would be cancelled. So the CAA, although sympathetic to Laker, as was the US Justice Department, had little room for manoeuvre. What they could do, however, was to accede to Laker's requests that restrictions on Skytrain, particularly the one laying down the use of backwoods Stansted airport, should be lifted giving the scheduled airline counter-measures.

Easing the restrictions was a decisive turning point, opening the way to today's Skytrain-style operation which permits Laker to sell every form of ticket from a full reservation to a cheap stand-by. Some airline executives, particularly John de la Haye at BCAL, were quick enough to forecast at the time that what was emerging was not so much an experiment to help the forgotten man but a fully fledged low-fare scheduled service. There was no doubt Laker was willing to let it happen.

'If they take all the restrictions off, I could operate a transatlantic shuttle, couldn't I?' said Laker. 'I would be where I have wanted to be in the market place for thirty years.'

If the Six had not intervened so dramatically and responded more cautiously, Laker might well have been forced to start Skytrain from an unknown airport with onerous constraints on capacity and booking. The switch to Gatwick in a blaze of publicity virtually guaranteed his success. 'We always assumed America would not permit price fixing or predatory pricing,' he said. He felt the scheduled airlines had only themselves to blame. Just a few days before the first Skytrain flight, he was a happy man. 'I think I am in the heavy sugar. I think I am home and dry.'

Late on the afternoon of Monday, 26 September 1977 Skytrain finally took off for the first time for New York, carrying 272 passengers, paying £59 each. That was the moment when Freddie Laker wrote his name in aviation history.

Bibliography

Books

BERLITZ, CHARLES, with collaboration of J. MANSON VALENTINE, *The Bermuda Triangle* (London 1974).

BLAIN, A.N.J., *Pilots and management: industrial relations in the UK airlines* (London 1972).

BRANCKER, J.W.S., *IATA and what it does* (Leyden 1977).

British air transport in the seventies: Report of the Committee of Inquiry into Civil Air Transport (Edwards Committee), Cmnd. 4018 (London 1969).

BROOKS, PETER W., *The world's airliners* (London 1962).

CAVES, RICHARD E., *Air transport and its regulators: an independent study* (Boston, Mass. 1962).

COLLIER, RICHARD, *Bridge across the sky: the Berlin blockade and airlift 1948–1949* (London 1978).

CORBETT, DAVID, *Politics and the airlines* (London 1965).

CROSLAND, C.A.R., *The future of socialism* (London 1956).

DAVIES, R.E.G., *A history of the world's airlines* (London 1964).

EDDY, PAUL, POTTER, ELAINE, and PAGE, BRUCE (*Sunday Times* insight team), *Destination disaster* (London 1976).

HUMPHREYS, B.K., 'The economics and development of the British airlines since 1945', unpublished PhD thesis, University of Leeds, 1973.

JACKSON, PETER, *The sky tramps* (London 1967).

JONES, DAVID, *The time shrinkers: the development of civil aviation between Britain and Africa* (London 1971).

KNIGHT, GEOFFREY, *Concorde: the inside story* (London 1976).

MERTON JONES, A.C., *British independent airlines since 1946*, 4 vols (Liverpool and Uxbridge 1976–7).

O'CONNOR, WILLIAM E., *An introduction to airline economics* (New York 1978).

PILLAI, K.G.J., *The air net: the case against the world aviation cartel* (New York 1967).

SAWERS, D., and MILLER, R.E., *The technical development of modern aviation* (London 1968).

SCOTT, J.D., *Vickers: a history* (London 1962).

THOMSON, ANDREW, and HUNTER, W.J., *The nationalised transport industries* (London 1973).

WHEATCROFT, STEPHEN, *Air transport policy* (London 1964).

Articles and pamphlets

'An Avro short-haul jet?' *Aeroplane*, 11 March 1960.

BOAC, 'Bonus: a new concept in low-cost scheduled travel', 1969.

'Strategy for the seventies', May 1971.

' "Let's be realistic . . . about charters" ', 1972.

'North Atlantic stalemate: the strategic impasse', 1973.

BAC, 'BAC One Eleven', BAC, June 1962.

'The BAC–107', *Aeroplane*, 9 September 1960.

'Background to the One–Eleven', *Aeroplane*, 18 May 1961.

'BAC One–Eleven', *Flight*, August 1961.

'BAC One–Eleven', *Interavia*, special supplement, 1964.

'The BAC One–Eleven family', *Aircraft Engineer*, March/May 1970.

BUA, British United Airways: application to the Air Transport Licensing Board for scheduled services, parts 1 and 2, 1961.

'BUA', *Aeroplane*, 15 April 1960.

'BUA buys the One–Eleven', *Aeroplane*, 11 May 1961.

'BUA link with Silver City', *Aeroplane*, 25 January 1962.

'British air transport in the seventies: a statement by British United Airways on certain aspects of the Report of the Edwards Committee', October 1969.

'Is there a future for British air transport?' A discussion on the Edwards Report by Keith Legg, P. Martin, D.H.N. Johnson, H. Caplan. J.E.D. Williams, H.C. Brilliant and D.R. Newman, *Aeronautical Journal*, March 1970.

BRISTOW, A.E., 'The independent airlines', *Aeronautical Journal*, August 1970.

CIVIL AERONAUTICS BOARD: Conference for winter season 1974–5, transcript of proceedings.

CIVIL AVIATION AUTHORITY: *Domestic air services: a review of regulatory policy*, 1979.

Financial results UK airlines 1968–74, CAA.

COOPER, M.H., and MAYNARD, A.K., 'The price of air travel', *Hobart Paper 52*, Institute of Economic Affairs, 1971.

DOUGLAS OF KIRTLESIDE, LORD, 'The progression of European air transport 1946–61, with particular reference to BEA', Royal Aeronautical Society, 1970.

ELLISON, A.P., 'The Edwards Report and civil aviation in the 1970s', *Aeronautical Journal*, June 1970.

EMERY, V.S., 'The role of the United States government and United States international air carriers in commercial air transport over the North Atlantic', *Aeronautical Journal*, September 1962.

Future civil aviation policy, Cmnd. 6400, Department of Trade, 1975.

HARTLEY, K., 'The mergers in the UK aircraft industry, 1957–60', *Aeronautical Journal*, December 1965.

HUMPHREYS, B.K., 'Nationalisation and the independent airlines in the United Kingdom, 1945–51', *Journal of Transport History*, September 1976.

'Trooping and the development of the British independent airlines', PhD research paper.

'Hunting's new jet-liner project', *Aeroplane*, 6 June 1958.

IATA: Independent Air Travel Association, Act of Incorporation, Articles of Association, Rules and Regulations.

The state of the air transport industry (annual), IATA.

Trends in international aviation and government policies, IATA, 1979.

Reason in the air: towards a balance of aviation needs, IATA, 1977.

LAKER AIRWAYS:

LAKER, F.A., 'Private enterprise in British air transport', 21st British Commonwealth Lecture, *Aeronautical Journal*, February 1966.

'Skytrain: new Laker bid', *Flight*, July 1972.

'Effect of BOAC capacity restriction on its passenger air traffic', Laker Airways, September 1974.

'Effects of fare increases on North Atlantic passenger traffic', Laker Airways, September 1974.

F.A. LAKER's speeches to the United States Senate Judiciary Committee, November 1974.

HANSARD: House of Commons debate, 29 July 1975, cols. 993–1004. House of Lords debate, 29 July 1975, cols. 908–18.

'Skytrain: a national scandal', Laker Airways, 1975.

'Skytrain: public opinion survey', *Market and Opinion Research International*, October 1975.

Civil aviation policy guidance: Laker Airways Skytrain the balance of payments effects, DoT, 1976.

Foreign air carrier permit application London–New York scheduled service. Docket 25427. CAB, June and October 1977.

COOK, JOHN C., 'Laker, the free enterprise airline', *Airline Quarterly*, 1979.

PAGE, MARTIN, 'Has Laker misjudged his passenger appeal?', *Business Traveller*, September/October 1979.

LEFTLEY, A.C., 'The Carvair story', *Shell Aviation News*, 1966.

SEEKINGS, JOHN, *Guidelines for airlines*, Conservative Political Centre, 1970.

'Segmental seat scheduling', *British Airways*, 1974.

THOMSON, ADAM, Experience on transatlantic routes with competitive farēs. Speech to International Aviation Policy Symposium, Kingston, Jamaica, 1979.

WHEATCROFT, STEPHEN, 'Licensing British air transport', *Aeronautical Journal*, March 1964.

WILLIAMS, J.E.D., 'The role of private enterprise in British air transportation', *Aeronautical Journal*, June 1967.

Wings for peace: Labour's post-war policy for civil flying, Labour Party, 1944.

WYATT, MILES, 'British independent aviation', *Institute of Transport Journal*, May 1963.

Index